D1594436

WITHDRAWN

American Agriculture

THE AMERICAN WAYS SERIES

General Editor: John David Smith
Charles H. Stone Distinguished Professor of American History
University of North Carolina at Charlotte

From the long arcs of America's history, to the short timeframes that convey larger stories, American Ways provides concise, accessible topical histories informed by the latest scholarship and written by scholars who are both leading experts in their fields and polished writers.

Books in the series provide general readers and students with compelling introductions to America's social, cultural, political, and economic history, underscoring questions of class, gender, racial, and sectional diversity and inclusivity. The titles suggest the multiple ways that the past informs the present and shapes the future in often unforeseen ways.

CURRENT TITLES IN THE SERIES

How America Eats: A Social History of U.S. Food and Culture, by Jennifer Jensen Wallach

Popular Justice: A History of Lynching in America, by Manfred Berg

Bounds of Their Habitation: Race and Religion in American History, by Paul Harvey

National Pastime: U.S. History through Baseball, by Martin C. Babicz and Thomas W. Zeiler

This Green and Growing Land: Environmental Activism in American History, by Kevin C. Armitage

Wartime America: The World War II Home Front, Second Edition, by John W. Jeffries

Enemies of the State: The Radical Right in America from FDR to Trump, by D. J. Mulloy

Hard Times: Economic Depressions in America, by Richard Striner

We the People: The 500-Year Battle Over Who Is American, by Ben Railton

Litigation Nation: How Lawsuits Represent Changing Ideas of Self, Business Practices, and Right and Wrong in American History, by Peter Charles Hoffer

American Agriculture: From Farm Families to Agribusiness, by Mark V. Wetherington

AMERICAN AGRICULTURE

From Farm Families to Agribusiness

Mark V. Wetherington

ROWMAN & LITTLEFIELD
Lanham • Boulder • New York • London

Published by Rowman & Littlefield
An imprint of The Rowman & Littlefield Publishing Group, Inc.
4501 Forbes Boulevard, Suite 200, Lanham, Maryland 20706
www.rowman.com

6 Tinworth Street, London SE11 5AL, United Kingdom

British Library Cataloguing in Publication Information Available

Library of Congress Cataloging-in-Publication Data Available
ISBN: 978-1-4422-6927-9 (cloth)
ISBN: 978-1-4422-6928-6 (electronic)

For Glenna Pfeiffer

Indiana barn: a symbol of disappearing small family farm agriculture. Painting by Glenna Pfeiffer, copyright 2019.

Contents

Acknowledgments   ix

Introduction   1

Chapter One: Beginnings   7

Chapter Two: Crop Regions   35

Chapter Three: Market Revolutions   59

Chapter Four: Civil War and Reconstructions   81

Chapter Five: Home on the Range?   103

Chapter Six: Two World Wars and the Great Depression   125

Chapter Seven: Get Big or Get Out   149

Chapter Eight: The Future: What Kind of Agriculture
              Do You Want?   173

Sources   197

Index   215

Acknowledgments

I USED TO WALK AROUND the small hometown where I grew up mostly unaware of farmers. Strange, for without the countryside's farmers the town would have been empty of the grocers, feed and seed, mule and tractor dealers, and bankers and doctors whose jobs depended on providing goods and services to farm families. Today, almost all those buildings are either empty or gone. So are most of the farmers. A buzzword in high government places calls for a plan for the economic redevelopment of rural America and small towns. I think they are two or three generations too late, but I wish them the best of luck.

This book is dedicated to Glenna Pfeiffer. It was with her encouragement and support that I took on the project and I would not have completed it without her. She has been beside me all the way raising questions, pointing out sources, and keeping the faith.

One of our first research stops was the Cummer Museum of Art and Gardens in Jacksonville, Florida, to look at images of plants and American Indian agriculture. There we found the papers of Ninah Holden Cummer, an avid gardener and the museum's benefactor. Her husband's family, Michigan lumber manufacturers, moved south for the final assault on northern Florida's longleaf pine forest. At one time the Cummer Lumber Company was Florida's largest landowner. Unlike so many of their fellow timbermen who followed the cut out and get out philosophy, the Cummers stayed in Florida and left a legacy to the city—the Cummer Art Museum and Gardens.

In Ninah Cummer's papers are words to the effect that trees are plants too. As I researched and thought about this book that sentiment came back to me more than once. In addition to the wild grasses, flowers, and plants she loved, ironically longleaf pines, the source of Cummer's wealth, were rarely, if ever, mentioned in her papers. But trees are the first casualties of agriculture, and after trees the natural grasses beneath them.

A project like this depends on many people—friends, archivists, librarians—and I thank them all: John David Smith, University of North Carolina, Charlotte, and Series Editor, for contacting me about this project; Lynn Norris and Holly Keris, Cummer Museum of Art and Gardens; Patrick Haughey, Savannah College of Art and Design; the Georgia Archives and the National Archives at Atlanta; Martha Lundgren, Bellarmine University W. L. Lyons Brown Library; Jacksonville Historical Society; Coastal Georgia Historical Society; Epworth by the Sea Arthur Moore Methodist Museum's library staff; Brunswick-Glynn County Library, Brunswick, Georgia; Johna Ebling, independent museum and archives consultant; Jon Sisk and the Rowman & Littlefield editorial department. I also thank James J. Holmberg, curator of collections, Filson Historical Society, for his friendship and support, and to the historical society's staff, especially Jennifer Cole and Heather Potter. Last but certainly not least, I thank my teachers.

Introduction

AMERICAN AGRICULTURE IS THE STORY of farming in the
United States from its Amerindian origins to the present. Today, a system that encourages large industrial farms to overproduce subsidized
commodity crops has put small family farms in a difficult situation. This
book traces the history of agriculture in the United States by providing a
narrative overview of significant historical trends explored through specific crop regions and their emergence over time.

American Agriculture takes an interdisciplinary approach and places the
major themes—control, consolidation, and chemical farming—within
the broader context of the nation's history. These themes, or the "three
Cs," carry us through centuries of agriculture from American Indian
farming to "Big Farm" America today. Below are a few words about
the three Cs and their connection to agricultural production, processing,
and distribution. When thinking about control, for example, consider
the control of agricultural resources including capital, land, labor, animals and machines, seeds and fertilizer, pesticides, and daily farm decisions. Consolidation involves bringing together farms and the resources
that make farm production from seed to shelf more stable and longer
lasting. Some farming institutions have exercised enough control and
consolidation to weather the ups and downs of natural disasters, market
fluctuations, and takeover attempts. Agribusiness companies are prime
examples of consolidation and vertical integration. Chemical farming
is possible due to control and consolidation of science, technology, and
engineering resources to produce and manipulate synthetic fertilizers,
seeds, and pesticides through genetic engineering. The central question
is: How did we get where we are today?

Control, consolidation, and chemicals created environments characterized by violence and exploitation. Control of land, for example, required
dispossession of Native peoples and possession of their farmland by

Euro-Americans. By 1840, almost all Indians were west of the Mississippi River. The growth and consolidation of cash crop cultures such as cotton and tobacco created the need for more labor and resulted in the importation of enslaved Africans and eventually led to a sharecropping and tenant farming system that included whites as well. The rise of large-scale industrial farms after the 1970s witnessed the decline of small-scale family farming and so did an expensive NPK (nitrogen, phosphorous, and potassium found in fertilizers) chemical farming system that led to environmental degradation in terms of polluted air and water, deforestation, toxic soils, and violence toward people, particularly those of color and the poor, across time and landscapes. The results have included imbalances of economic, political, and social power, racism, and class conflict.

The following chapters are grouped together to cover hundreds of years of agriculture. Chapters 1 and 2 describe how gender control of agriculture changed and how cash crops encouraged farm consolidation and the growth of slavery. Chapter 3 carries us through a market revolution that transformed the North, giving it an infrastructure of railroads, canals, cities, and factories and a growing population to win the war.

Chapters 4 and 5 treat the pivotal Civil War and Reconstruction eras and their consequences: the victorious North and the Republican Party in economic, political, and social control; the defeated and impoverished South mired in the crop lien system that included freed people and landless white farmers. The postwar expansion of transportation and communications systems brought the remote eastern farmer and livestock landscapes into the national market mainstream and consolidated the North's economic power by 1900.

Chapters 6 and 7 describe the twentieth and early twenty-first centuries when control and consolidation of agriculture led to chemical farming, which benefited from scientific and technological advances—synthetic fertilizers, mechanization, GMOs (genetically modified organisms), and hormones—during both world wars. This was especially true of nitrogen fixation, the NPK model, and the "Green Revolution." Farm consolidation is accompanied by greater specialization in commodity crops such as corn and soybeans on large industrial farms.

Chapter 8 deals with present and future farming issues, many of which are unresolved. "Getting Big" had been the agricultural mantra since the 1970s, but did it pay off for the average US farmer? By the 1980s, the "farm crisis" left thousands of overinvested commodity farmers in debt and bankrupt. NAFTA (North American Free Trade Agreement) was in part a reaction to the crisis, but has it worked for farmers who do not benefit from the trading scheme? One thing is clear. Critics of present-day Big Farm America agree that something is wrong using words and phrases such as "scandalous" and "this ain't normal" to describe the industrial farming world where farmers received a much smaller portion of the dollar in the marketplace than at the beginnings of the post–World War II era.

In 1900, almost 40 percent of the US population still lived on farms. Today, that number is less than 2 percent. Millions of farmers left the land in the twentieth century largely by federal design but not by choice. Between World War II and the 1980s the average farm size increased to 450 acres as small farms worked by tenants, sharecroppers, and independent owners were consolidated into larger holdings. During the 1970s, an emphasis on expanding farm size and increasing commodity crop production was and continues to be subsidized by billions of dollars to plant GMO seeds sprayed with synthetic fertilizers and pesticides. As much as 85 percent of this taxpayer-funded largesse goes to the largest commodity farmers, most of them in the corn and wheat belts of the Midwest. This was no accident. It is the result of a strategy to sweep off less "efficient" farmers who did not have the resources to grow their acreage, mechanization, chemical fertilizers and pesticides, and hybrid seeds and replace them with fewer but larger members of a Big Farm America. The creation of this landscape is the result of federal farm programs, the farm lobby, manufacturers and distributors of farm machinery, chemical fertilizers and pesticides, GMO products, major food producers, processors, distributors, and farm country's representatives at the state and national levels. Despite impressive gains in agricultural outputs, especially in grains such as corn and wheat, the USDA (United States Department of Agriculture) estimated in 2019 that forty million US citizens (about 12 percent) lived in food-insecure households after seventy-five years of farm bill subsidies.

Why do farmers farm? That's a good question given their shrinking presence in American society and in the workforce—less than 3 percent today. It is certainly not the easiest way to make a living or find certainty in what tomorrow will bring. Nature alone can unravel the best-laid farm plan with drought, insect infestation, crop failure, and loss of livestock. It is hard work filled with lots of stress. The suicide rate for farmers is double that of veterans. That stress only increases with mounting debt, mortgage deadlines, and declining crop prices. Many Midwest farmers were hopeful that the years after 2016 would be a good. The region is one of mostly red states and helped put President Trump in the White House. It proved to be a good year for soybeans. That summer, because of the president's trade war tariffs, soybean prices dropped about 18 percent and pork and corn about 15 percent. The cost of farming has not gone down. Rumors of soybean fallout impacting midterm House district elections proved true in the 2018 midterm election.

Kentucky farmer, writer, and environmental activist Wendell Berry believes farmers farm because "they must do it for love." They love to watch plants and animals grow, to work outdoors with their family on land they own, to gain a sense of independence and place, and live "at least part of their lives without a boss." Good farmers, Berry writes, are "stewards of Creation." They conserve soil and water, preserve natural wildlife and scenery. For Berry, "every man is called to be an artist," and small family farms are among the last places to do it. His method of farming harkens back to the pre–World War II traditional agricultural path where farmers worked their own land with their own hands, often with animal power. It was and is today low-input farming. This style of farming has been called "safety-first" farming in that its main goal is to raise enough food to feed the farm family and risk only a small surplus of land and labor on commercial crops. Any surplus is taken to local markets thus keeping the crops' carbon footprint to a minimum.

Since World War II the traditional path has been displaced by commercial or industrial farming with its high inputs of hybrid seeds, pesticides, insecticides, fertilizers, and mechanization. The result is agriculture as industry and big business. The result is an ever-increasing emphasis on efficiency at the cost of human involvement, not only in the past with the removal of millions of Americans from agriculture, but from American Indian farming to the present and into the future. With the growing power and control made possible by technology, including precision farming and robotic driverless tractors that are well into the development stage, is it worth asking how long meaningful human involvement will continue? Especially the spirit of the farmer as artist, invoked by writers such as Wendell Berry as well as others who are drawn to farming out of love of land, nature, and a call to stewardship.

1

Beginnings

THE ORIGINS OF AMERICAN AGRICULTURE

The when and where of agriculture in the United States is difficult to determine. Thousands of years before Europeans made landfall American Indians had solved many of the mysteries of food plant domestication. Scholars agree that there is no one widely accepted answer to this question. Archaeologists T. Douglas Price and Ofer Bar-Yosef write, "there is as yet no single accepted theory for the origins of agriculture— rather, there is a series of ideas and suggestions that do not quite resolve the question."

The Zapotec Indians of southern Mexico domesticated corn more than seven thousand years ago in a region believed to be one of the centers of the "origin of corn." Almost four thousand years ago varieties of small ears of corn were planted in present-day New Mexico. These early farmers also understood the nutritional and medicinal values of many wild plants. However, major questions remain unanswered regarding early agriculture. A wide range of specialists worldwide, including archaeologists, anthropologists, archaeobotanists, botonists, and zooarchaelogists, continue to search for clues to the beginnings of agriculture.

AMERICAN INDIAN AGRICULTURE

Why did hunter-gatherers shift to farming? Was it due to climate change or population pressure? How long did it take Amerindians to give up hunting game and begin to collect berries, nuts, and roots as food sources? There are no conclusive answers to these questions. This hunting and gathering culture developed more than one hundred thousand to two hundred thousand years ago. Based on a study of hunter-gatherers, small groups carried on nomadic lives hunting and gathering, with the men leaving the group to hunt while the women and children gathered small animals, plants, and fruit and nuts. Women created pots and baskets needed to move food from one place to another, but there was little or no planting being done. The social structure was simple and there was virtually no hierarchy. About twenty thousand years before the appearance of agriculture, hand axes and tools were created from stones, animal bones, and antlers. Prior to about seventeen thousand years ago people had made cord and small ropes from natural fibers (grasses, tree bark) for traps and nets. In areas unsuited for agriculture, because of poor soil or marginal rainfall, hunting and gathering continued as a way of life.

Where did agriculture in the United States begin? Did early peoples depend on outside sources that later reached the North American continent, or did they develop their own agricultural resources? Was it some combination of both internal and external origins? Scholars agree that there are as many as eight to ten sites worldwide where plant domestication independently occurred. Five are in the Western Hemisphere and one in the United States. For much of the twentieth century the prevailing idea was that agriculture reached the present-day United States from South America, Mexico, and Asia as a part of a migration of external culture groups. By around 6000 BCE farmers in the highlands of Mexico were cultivating plants in gardens for food and medicine, including maize, peppers, squash, gourds, cotton, and peanuts, among others. In Peru, farmers based their food supply around potatoes, eventually growing up to thirty different crops, but they were slower to discover grains and animals for purposes of domestication.

Throughout the 1990s, the location of the North American region of plant domestication was debated. Based on seeds found in rock shelters in the woodlands of Kentucky and Appalachia, archaeologist and researcher Bruce D. Smith contends that plant domestication developed independently in the eastern region of North America around 5000 cal BP. While this is much later than the emergence of corn in Mexico (9000 cal BP) and domesticated plants in South America (10000 cal BP), some contend that plant domestication at sites in the Western Hemisphere took place at the same time. Altogether, Native peoples domesticated around one hundred plants, though there were no wild grains as we know them. It is important to understand that new discoveries will be made that will answer old questions and that will raise new ones, but the general trend in research and scholarship is to extend the presence of Amerindians and the dawn of agriculture farther into the past than previously accepted.

We know that agriculture did not occur overnight or evenly across time, and that many Indian groups continued to supplement their diets with wild game and plants long after farming became a part of their culture. The dawn of agriculture has been pushed back ten thousand years and perhaps earlier. Before ten thousand years ago almost everyone ate food from the wild; by two thousand years ago many people depended upon farming for some of their food supply. A so-called agricultural revolution had taken place. Climatic warming contributed to the appearance of agriculture at different places around the globe at about the same time. Still, the appearance of agriculture was shaped locally by landscape, climate, and biodiversity as well as by population growth and the decline of wild plants and animals as food sources due to overconsumption. Social structures that had been in place for thousands of years were gradually rearranged around more permanent settlements when domestication of a particular plant and animal took place. Wandering, hunting, and gathering still took place, but time had to be devoted to reshaping the landscape to meet the needs of the new Indian hunter-farmers. Time was also needed to create the tools and granaries needed to plant, harvest, and store crops. Humans and plants became codependent. As scholar Noel Kingsbury observed, "Neolithic people became dependent on plants for their survival, but the plants in turn coevolved and became dependent on people for their survival, assuming genetic identities distinct from their wild ancestors."

Fire was used to manage and control the landscape in order to plant crops. Amerindians cleared the land by starting fires that burned the underbrush and killed smaller trees. Larger trees were girdled with axes. Trader James Adair recorded that a stone ax shaped like a chisel and weighing two to three pounds was fastened to a handle and used to break the bark. The trees, left standing, would soon begin to lose their leaves. As the sun reached the ground, the Indians planted in season using crude hoes to push the soil into small mounds. French explorer Henri Joutel described Mississippi Valley Indians breaking up the ground with "a little pickaxe, which they make by splitting the end of a thick piece of wood, that serves for a handle, and putting another piece of wood, sharp and pointed at the end, into the slit." It took the place of a hoe or spade. Though dead tree trunks and roots remained in the soil even after it lost its fertility, this type of farming allowed for the planting of vegetables such as maize, squash, and beans. In this manner, Adair wrote, "the contented natives got convenient fields in the process of time."

Women were the native agriculturalists. Seeds may not have been the first things they planted. Digging up roots and tubers and carrying them along to eat and then planting what was left over at a new site may have preceded what we know as seed-based agriculture. Yams, for example, were present in northern South America beginning around 6000 BP and were replanted from tuber portions. Early seed planting may have resembled gardening small plots with a few staple crops and more wild plants and herbs. As English writer William Strachey noted in 1610, women "sow their corne ... weed and cleanse the same" and keep their plots "as neat and cleane as we doe our garden beds." Their neat and ordered approach to planting kept unwanted cross-pollination to a minimum.

Women and children were also the major gatherers of wild edible plants, herbs, roots, and nuts. The native shagbark hickory (Carya ovata) found throughout the eastern United States was a popular sweet tasting nut among Indians. William Bartram wrote, "I have seen above an hundred bushels of these nuts belonging to one family." They pounded the nuts and threw the meat into boiling water and produced a "hiccory milk; it is as sweet and rich as fresh cream, and is an ingredient in most of their cookery, especially homony and corn cakes." Amerindians also depended on oak trees for their acorns, which are rich in carbohydrates, as well as wild vegetables and medicinal plants. California Indians ate energy-rich pine nuts and used acorn meal in breads and soup. On southern barrier islands, Indians such as the Guale along Georgia's coast harvested live oak nuts and also made acorn meal. In the present-day states of Georgia and Florida, for example, heart of cabbage palm and saw palmetto, poke, wild onions and radishes, mullin, persimmons, and plums were harvested. Women chose which seeds to save for future planting. Women also chopped and gathered the wood for cooking.

FIGURE 1.1. Indian women managed Native American agriculture.
The Filson Historical Society, Louisville, KY | The History of the Indian Tribes of
North America. Philadelphia, 1842–70. vol. 1

It is not surprising, then, that the earliest European explorers saw immediate signs of agriculture when they arrived. The Atlantic and Gulf coasts were not one long unbroken forest. The tree line was interrupted repeatedly by large and small clearings. Some were planted in Indian crops such as corn, beans, and squash. Others, called "Indian old fields," were abandoned and in varying stages of reclamation by nature. Some of the fallow clearings were managed by the ancient practice of burning the woods in spring to stimulate the growth of herbaceous plants that attracted deer and other game. When Hernando De Soto landed near present-day Tampa in 1539, American Indians had been farming there for several thousand years. Evidence of their commitment to agriculture was found as De Soto and his soldiers crossed varied landscapes and found Indian towns, fields, granaries, and orchards, revealing the degree to which Indian farmers had altered their environments. Extensive fields of beans, corn, and squash—the three sisters of Indian agriculture—stretched several miles wide, along with more than two hundred houses, which were found near present-day Tallahassee. While the extent of these sights may have surprised European explorers during the late sixteenth and early seventeenth centuries, they were common agricultural farming methods of the Amerindians, which were used for thousands of years.

This practice of burn and slash was repeated after several years to create new fertile openings for future crops. The process allowed for new growths of nut-bearing trees, berries, roots, and wild game. The abandoned fields were eventually burned again to encourage the growth of fresh grasses in the spring, becoming in time meadows that attracted deer and other game. The Amerindian impact on forests should not be underestimated, for the woods the Europeans explored had already changed. The clearing of forests had immediate consequences, some not readily apparent. Estimates vary on how much the cleared land heated, but the surface temperature of cleared land could increase ten degrees above the forest temperature or more depending on the latitude. The ground was now subject to direct sunlight as well as unimpeded winds. The trees and native grasses that absorbed moisture were displaced by species favoring dryness and warmth. On the transitional edges where field and forest met and water ran off and accumulated, plants loving cool and moist surroundings thrived. Clearing agricultural land ushered in new microclimates at the surface and at the edge of fields.

Maize was grown at every Indian village. The story of maize, more than other crops, is one of "dramatic change." Among the domesticated plants in North America, once freed of competition with weeds and grasses, it grew robustly and was a central part of the diet. So important was corn that it entered creation myths. The Maya, for instance, believed the human race was made from corn. Today, many scholars agree that what we know as corn is a domesticated teosinte and evolved more than other crops over time due to its open-pollinated seeds, which allows it to regenerate itself. Noel Kingsbury wrote that by the arrival of Columbus Amerindians had already made more changes to corn through their selection of seeds "than humans had to any other plant." The Indians thanked the gods for such a magical crop. As Claire Hope Cummings notes, "By the time Columbus arrived, North America was already a corn-fed continent." In time, East Coast Indians recognized the different varieties of corn by color, size, and maturation. The smaller, early corn was ready to eat about three months after planting while the larger, late corn was ready in about three and a half months.

Estimates of the Indian population along the Atlantic Seaboard vary upward from around 125,000 at the beginning of the seventeenth century. One estimate suggests that approximately half of these Indians lived north of the present-day Pennsylvania-Maryland border and the other half south. Population density was largest in farming communities. Many were located within a day's travel of the sea with southern New England and the Chesapeake Bay regions being the most densely settled.

English naturalist William Bartram described the southeastern Indian agricultural plan and the "produce of their agricultural labours." He observed that Indians settled their agricultural towns on a peninsula with fertile land and good hunting grounds nearby. Corn, potatoes, beans, squash, pumpkins, and melons were planted and fenced to protect the crops "from the invasion of predatory animals." While the fields were planted as "their common plantation," family plots were separated by narrow strips of grass or other borders, such as split hickory or white oak saplings tied to stakes in the ground. Adair described a similar custom: "Every dwelling house has a small field pretty close to it: and, as soon as the spring of the year admits, there they plant a variety of large and small beans, peas, and the smaller sort of Indian corn, which usually ripens in two months, from the time it is planted; though it is called by the English, the six weeks corn."

Noel Kingsbury notes that of two hundred thousand species of plants, only about three hundred have been used in agriculture. The longer a plant has been a part of agriculture, the more it changes over time. Trees are not genetically altered in any great way, so they may be quite ancient. Over thousands of years, the annual replanting molded plants to fit human needs just by their selection for replanting, so there is little doubt that "primitive" people actually had a sophisticated system of plant breeding, and the stories incorporated into their myths.

Adair noted that planting these "out-fields" was a communal project. "Early in the morning on a spring day the entire town is called by conch shell to the public square. They arrived bringing their hoes and axes and plant together all of the family plots as a united community. They plant until finished and harvest in the same way." Indian farmers were called to the fields by whoops and shrill "calls" and told that "he that expects to eat must work . . . as they will not sweat themselves for an healthy idle waster."

Women did the field and garden work until the soil was exhausted and it was time to move to another village site, which took place every dozen or so years. Women practiced hoe cultivation. European artists depicted women using hoe heads made from bones and seashells attached to wooden handles. Family plots of one to two hundred square feet of "commonly square plotts of cleared ground" were planted near their houses. Seeds were planted in small mounds. Despite the commonly held belief that Indians used fish to fertilize the soil, there is no evidence, according to Charles Hudson, "that Southeastern Indians fertilized their fields."

Farming was only part of a larger annual work cycle that included gathering nuts, herbs, roots, and wild plants such as mulberry and sunflower roots by women and children. Samuel de Champlain's 1607 map of Plymouth Harbor included eight Indian houses with adjacent cultivated fields, cleared land, and woodlands. He noted, "Some of the land is cleared and they are constantly clearing more." Women too old to work in the fields kept watch over the ripening crops from raised platforms where they could make noise and drive off predatory animals and birds.

Because corn was planted frequently, the soil became depleted of major nutrients. As a result, the Indians moved to new areas, set up villages, and began the cycle of planting new crops in nutrient-rich soil. According to Charles Hudson, agricultural practices in the Southeast can be referred to as "riverine." By clearing land along rivers and creeks, large amounts of food on relatively small plots of land could be grown. Clay soil was avoided because it was hard to work. Indians favored nutrient-rich floodplain soils, which were often inundated with high water. It was behind this floodplain, on the bluffs, that the Indians located their towns.

By moving from place to place, plants adapted to their new environment and produced new varieties. Farmers recognized and could name these plants, as they differed from those in the surrounding areas. The Hopi separated different strains of corn by color and passed them on from generation to generation. The people who knew the most about plant selection were those who worked with plants daily. They made the decision of what plants to keep and what to toss away.

According to Charles Hudson, two varieties of corn were found on the East Coast at the time of European exploration and settlement: tropical flint corn and eastern flint corn. In time, the more adaptable eastern flint corn seed was carried west and north into the present-day Midwest and Northeast, where it adjusted to the cooler climate and shorter growing season, evolving as a hard northern flint variety.

Once settled in their new farming villages, the men departed on hunting trips for wild game, which along with fish were important sources of protein. The longer the villages remained in one place, the hunting trips grew longer, and nearby game became depleted. Ultimately, the Indian practice of burning the woodlands to encourage the growth of spring grasses that attracted wild game became counterproductive. The fires burned nuts, berries, and grapes and drove off small game and birds. After farming for as few as ten years, fields were depleted of their nutrients and nearby woods were emptied and charred. Women in charge of tending crops and gathering firewood had to walk farther each year. It was time to move again. It is easy to see how the European explorers overestimated the size of the Eastern Woodland Indian population, for example, by basing their estimates on the extent of old fields created by slash and burn agriculture.

Because Indian farming villages were located near creeks and rivers, the fertile soil did not require deep tillage and hoe cultivation was sufficient. There were no animal-drawn plows as we know them, although the Creek Indians in the Southeast, and others, had domesticated horses. The Creeks considered plows little more than "a horse trap." Their houses were scattered, without streets, and interspersed with smaller family plots, surrounded by the larger outfields.

Along the barrier islands of Georgia, a province the Spanish called Guale reached from present-day Savannah to the southern end of Jekyll Island. One Spanish account estimated that there were forty Indian villages in the province. The arrival of both permanent communities and maize occurred on the island about 4,500 BP. The Indians, thought to be linguistically Muskhogean, hunted game and harvested shellfish, as evidenced by the remains of large circular shell mounds. In addition to corn, they planted beans and melons. Each farming chiefdom was led by a mico, or mayor, who was a chief. Only about a generation after Columbus's landfall in 1492, Spanish ships arrived on the Georgia coast looking for Indians to enslave and use as forced agricultural laborers on Caribbean islands.

EURO-AMERICAN AGRICULTURE

On Guale, the Spanish Mission era lasted for more than a century, from 1568 until 1684. The arrival of Spanish missionaries gradually destroyed the social structure of American Indian agriculture. The establishment of the *ecomienda* labor system, where the Spanish Crown rewarded conquerors with a number of natives from an established community whereupon they worked the land, relied on the chief's approval and was led by friars and protected by soldiers. This agricultural system, according to the Spanish, brought natives into the Spanish colonial empire by Christianizing them, teaching them Spanish, and providing them protection from tribal enemies. The hereditary chiefs retained their authority in nonreligious matters and chose unmarried Indian males who were drafted to provide farm and construction labor in exchange for trade goods. The system was rife with abuse and oppression. The movement of farm workers from the coastal islands to "San Agustin," or present-day St. Augustine, and back spread disease and dissention. Some villages were virtually depopulated.

In the 1570s, the Spanish missions in Guale faced resistance when Spanish officers and soldiers were killed by Indians, leading to the exodus of the Jesuits. By the early 1590s, Franciscans had established missions at Indian villages on all the major barrier islands of Guale, but trouble brewed among the native farmers. By keeping the Indians close, the friars hoped to convert them to Catholicism, control them, and use them as agricultural laborers. This practice kept the Amerindians from practicing their traditional customs—feasts, dances, and celebrations. The friars accused Indian elders of witchcraft. Moreover, the Indians claimed the Spanish took away their women, the source of most of the agricultural workforce in Indian society. The Spanish called the chief mico of Guale Don Juan or Don Juanillo. He claimed to have authority over the entire province and ruled from his town, Tolomato. He led a revolt in 1597 that began in Tolomato and spread to other missions, costing many of the Catholic clergy their lives. Spanish retaliation ultimately destroyed the people of Guale.

It appears that the first attempts at European farming, as opposed to depending on Amerindians to give or trade food, took place along the southeastern coast and most likely by Spanish settlers at or near St. Augustine. In 1586, Sir Francis Drake sacked St. Augustine and destroyed much of its agricultural capacity. Before sailing to Roanoke, Virginia, he cut down orchards and hauled off anything usable to assist English settlers there, but most of them had already disappeared when he arrived. The few English survivors in Roanoke were rescued by Drake, but he left behind the Indian and African slaves intended to become farm hands to an unknown fate. Clearly farmers, especially Indian and African slaves, were considered dispensable. As one horticulturalist noted, "growing plants has never been a high-status activity."

Mexico (New Spain) and the Caribbean Islands were the primary focus of the Spanish in the New World. Once it was clear that there would be no quick riches following the expeditions of De Soto and others, the Spanish government cooled toward turning more adventurers loose in North America. However, they did see merit in establishing missions along the Pacific Coast as far north as present-day Santa Barbara as stations for coastal trade and the rescue of shipwrecked sailors.

In 1581, a small group of friars and Spanish soldiers set out from present-day Santa Barbara and reached the southern edge of Pueblo settlements

18   CHAPTER I

in present-day New Mexico, which they claimed for Spain. Subsequent
northward exploration revealed that the Rio Grande River Valley held
agricultural promise. The isolated valley was about two hundred miles
long and, according to modern estimates, it was populated by about forty-
thousand peaceful Indians farming in self-sufficient pueblos surrounded
by irrigated corn fields. Initial attempts to gain a Euro-American agricultural foothold here failed for the same reasons they failed in the Southeast:
the soldiers were not interested in agriculture, the Indians quickly tired
of feeding them from their own granaries, the soldiers took what they
wanted, and the friars' attempts to convert the Indians failed.

In 1598, Juan de Oñate, a Spanish conquistador and governor of the
colony of New Mexico, tried again. He set out with five hundred people, including men, women, children, and eight Franciscan friars. This
expedition established a church as the center of the community at Santo
Domingo, and the friars spread out to other pueblos along the Rio
Grande. Wheat and chilis were introduced by the Spanish and added to
the corn and cucurbits (gourds) planted by the Indians. By the spring of
1599 agriculture among the settlers, which included new families, was
augmented by food levies placed on the pueblos. Again, the Indians tired
of feeding the growing Spanish settlements and the soldiers tired of finding no wealth in precious metals and stones. After a revolt, the settlement
disbanded, and the soldiers returned to the area of present-day Santa
Barbara. A few friars remained, however, and a small core of the original
settlement survived for a century or so.

Although Spanish explorers had traversed the Gulf and Atlantic coasts
since the early 1500s, they were never able to establish a permanent farming community. Indian attacks, disease, and the objectives of the explora-
tions themselves, which were aimed at finding riches—gold, silver, and
gems—and quick profit motives of their investors were all deterrents.
On military expeditions, regardless of whether the French, English, or
Spanish funded them, soldiers were considered the vital leaders and professionals. Farmers were rarely considered worth bringing along and
were deemed second-class citizens. In the eyes of upper-class European
men, this lowly status was only reaffirmed by the fact that Indian women
did field work while the men hunted and went on raids.

With the exception of replacing stone axes with iron ones, there was
little to distinguish between early European methods of land clearing and

the Indian techniques they copied. Because clearing forested land was time-consuming and backbreaking, Euro-Americans first farmed open marshes, meadows, savannas, and Indian old fields. Even after trees were girdled and deadened, massive old growth stumps and roots remained. Early farmers worked the land Indian-style, piling good soil into hills using hoes. Hoe cultivation and hill planting continued for years. It was well suited to smaller tracts of land farmed by family members in places such as New England and North Carolina. One observer from New York recorded that the Indians "make heaps like mole hills . . . which they sow or plant in April with maize."

It took time for the Europeans to realize what it took to be successful farmers in the New World. They need only to have looked at the Amerindian's way of farming. The Amerindians had worked out the seed, soil, and land clearing equation thousands of years prior. Indians knew where the fertile soil was located and built their villages there. They had also learned to clear land, farm it for a few years, and move on to new sites once the soil lost its fertility. Eventually, the Europeans saw the New World as a place to create farming communities for the long term.

THE VIOLENCE OF AGRICULTURE

Many Euro-Americans were initially unable to feed themselves regardless of their origins without reliance on Indian food sources or resupply from Europe. Adventurers and explorers were not interested in farming but in glory. They quickly became dependent on Indians for food. When Indians tired of supplying Europeans with maize from their own granaries the explorers took what they wanted by force. From the Southeast to the Southwest this resulted in violence: sacking Indian towns, abusing and slaughtering native populations, enslavement, and rape. Such was the case at Acoma, one of the eastern pueblos of New Mexico. Tired of abuse and exploitation at the hands of the Spanish, the Indians revolted and killed some of the exploiters in 1598–1599. Spanish soldiers retaliated. They used cannons to reduce the pueblo to rubble. Many Indians were killed and seventy men and about five hundred women and children entered forced servitude for twenty-five years.

Violence against nature also took place. Nature itself changed the landscape. Lightning strikes started forest fires and tornadoes left wide paths of destruction through the woods. Rainfall and floods shifted river channels and coastlines. Insects brought certain species of trees to the edge of extinction. Agricultural needs of humans brought about changes that were even more lasting. Indian old fields near places such as Macon, Georgia, and Tallahassee, Florida, were observed by naturalists such as William Bartram in the 1770s, years after they passed into disuse.

Whenever Euro-Americans and Indians came into contact, the native population decreased dramatically. Between 1769 and 1846, California's Indian population declined by half, from an estimated 300,000 to 150,000 people. California's coastal missions, which used Indian peoples as agricultural slaves, saw about sixty thousand deaths under conditions still widely debated. But the Euro-American's growing need for agricultural land to support export crops such as Indian tobacco in Virginia brought them increasing conflict with the American Indians. Capitalism required rewards for investments. The sooner these rewards arrived, the better it was for English investors, such as the Virginia Company. Early cash crops resulted in a continuous cycle of deforestation, soil depletion, labor exploitation, and land abandonment.

Ultimately, growing these cash crops at the expense of the Native peoples was the direction British policy makers followed. Was King James I satisfied in the exploitation of fish, fur, and timber? What types of projects would appeal to the aristocrats and merchants as profitable investments for their spare cash? Could they always bet on the windfalls gained from piracy and raids on Indian villages? Increasingly, the expectation was that colonial ventures in places such as Virginia would be worthwhile, albeit less spectacular than plundering, if they supplied England with materials the country could not supply for itself in abundance, such as hides, sugar, natural dyes, lumber, medicinal plants and herbs, timber for ship masts, oak for ship hulls, tar and pitch, and citrus fruits. Many of these goods previously had come from or through the Mediterranean. And the people who would harvest this bounty? Landless laborers, debtors, military veterans, minor criminals, men and women of "poor character," children and orphans—in other words, second- and third-class citizens in the English hierarchical social system. By providing useful callings for such folk, God would be pleased, and the investors would make money and some Amerindians might be "saved."

Sir Humphrey Gilbert, English soldier and navigator, won his knighthood by defeating the rebellious Irish, but he dreamed of an Ireland where the Irish and English could live in harmony. He soon turned that dream toward the New World, where Queen Elizabeth gave him a charter that included his right to pay back investors in this New World project with Indian land. Gilbert believed he could establish a lasting English presence along the eastern seaboard, one that could serve as a base of operations for attacks on homeward-bound Spanish treasure fleets.

But there was a problem: the presence of Amerindian farming and fishing communities along the Atlantic Coast from New England to Florida. The populations of many of these settlements had been severely thinned by disease before the early colonists arrived. Gilbert decided to follow the Spanish practice of siding with the "good" Indians, those who did not attack him, in their efforts against the "bad" Indians, the enemies of his new Indian allies. He hoped that his dream of collaboration between the English and Irish could be duplicated in the New World, where English colonists, settlers who would "manure" the soil and raise crops, and their Indian allies would live in a utopian state. It was expected, of course, that the Indian allies would peacefully give up their land to the English and labor alongside them. And if they did not, they could be defeated and enslaved, just as the Spanish had done.

Just how this utopian dream would play out on the mainland was already underway in the Caribbean. In the British West Indies, the English agricultural experiment focused on small islands settled during the 1620s. The English who came to these islands were part of the same wave of immigrants settling the North American colonies along the Eastern Seaboard.

Colonists traveling to the West Indies were expected to pay their own freight and fend for themselves once they landed. Here the problem was not hostile Indians, because most of them had died over a century of disease and warfare since Columbus's 1492 landfall, but the environment—especially the tropical rain forest. Twenty years after Barbados was colonized, its best agricultural land was still covered by dense forest. English indentured servants provided the labor to clear it in exchange for their passage to the islands. It was common in seventeenth-century England for children to become servants in other's households, not only children of the poor, but those of middling farmers and artisans as well. Children were also sent to the West Indies as apprentices. This arrangement was expected to be temporary with several years of bondage during which time the youngsters learned skills. Girls started to work at thirteen and boys at around fifteen. Almost one-third of the emigrants shipped from London to Barbados in 1635 were between the ages of ten and nineteen. After their service ended, the young workers received their freedom. In Barbados, indentured servants were promised their freedom and a few acres of land as well, but land on the island soon ran out.

Barbadian farmers first tried to grow tobacco and cotton, but consumers in England judged the tobacco inferior to Virginia's and their cotton no better. No one was getting rich. Landholders and servants lived self-sufficient lives and waited in fear for the next tropical storm or yellow fever attack. Between 1640 and 1660 the planters switched from white to black labor and from tobacco and cotton to sugarcane. Slave labor had its advantages for planters but unfortunately not for the enslaved Africans. They and their offspring became the permanent property of their masters. Since they were not entitled to freedom, they would not be able to compete with white farmers for the limited amounts of the island's agricultural land.

At Jamestown on the Chesapeake Bay in Virginia, the environment was different from Barbados or even Spanish Florida. This large estuary was about two hundred miles long and fed by numerous rivers creating fertile necks with water fronts that helped the bay's shoreline reach about six thousand miles. Much of this Low Country land was fertile and accessible to boats and ships. It was plentiful and relatively cheap.

After initial attacks by the Indians, the settlers were cautious and later claimed that the land was theirs to "inherite and inhabite" because they had bought the land from the Indians. Disease also took a toll. In January 1608, Jamestown burned, leaving the settlers without shelter during the winter. The settlement was reinforced and resupplied by the London Company the following April, and corn was planted. But throughout the year the struggling colony was unable to achieve food security. In time, the settlers began to clear the immense forests and plant crops. The climate was moist and hot and in the summer the temperature could easily reach 90 degrees Fahrenheit. The long growing season, just over two hundred days between killing frosts, meant the bay region could support diverse crops.

But Virginia's white farmers and planters continued to grow the popular tobacco that drove the West Indian crop out of the marketplace. Wealthy planters snapped up the fertile bottomland, which cost twenty times as much per acre as piney "barren" land where small farmers and poor whites farmed smaller patches. Unlike West Indian islands such as Barbados, white indentured servants had not been replaced by black slaves by 1650 when there were probably no more than five hundred slaves in Virginia. The crop primarily was grown by white labor on plantations and small farms. Thus, more and more fresh young bodies from England were needed to replace those dying in the fields of unhealthy Virginia due to disease-ridden swamps with bad water. In Lancaster County, Virginia, records during the 1660s and 1670s show that only about 11 percent of the white indentured servants were older than nineteen years old, and most of them about sixteen.

There were clear advantages for landlords under this system of white teenage agricultural labor. The start-up cost was the price of transporting the workers from England and food, shelter, and clothing for the duration of their servitude. For tobacco farmers and planters, the longer they could legally keep the youngsters in bondage the better. Therefore, the masters in power changed the laws to meet their labor needs. The length of service for servants arriving in Virginia, without the terms of their servitude specifically stated in an indenture document, was four years if over twenty years old, five years if between twelve and twenty years old, and seven years if under the age of twelve. During the eight years following 1658, the laws were revised by the Virginia Assembly requiring servants nineteen years old or older to work five years and those younger than nineteen years old to labor for their master until they turned twenty-four. Since their age was often about fifteen or sixteen upon arrival, for many that meant eight or nine years of bondage. Under this system tobacco growers did well while the length of servitude was stretched out for servants, delaying their land-ownership, and ensuring that their own crops would not flood the market and drive down prices. Additional years of servitude were added for running away, childbirth out of wedlock, and killing farm animals.

In New England, about three hundred miles north of the Chesapeake Bay, more settlers from England found a different agricultural environment. This one resembled the wood and pasture landscapes of eastern England and included harbors that encouraged fishing and trade. But the vast majority of New England's towns were founded upon agri-culture and animal husbandry. A common pasture or meadow formed the center of many villages. Unlike the Indian-style hoe cultivation found in the Chesapeake Bay region and farther south, New England farmers used "ploughs . . . with good success" based on designs introduced from Holland into eastern England in the late 1500s. Although the soil was often rocky and hilly, farmers were soon growing enough food to feed their families and send a surplus to market. By the 1640s, thousands of bushels of grain were being shipped from Connecticut while West Indian islands consumed large quantities of New England grain, salted fish, and building material. Moreover, New England ships were the workhorses of the carrying trade, shipping wheat, rye, oats, peas, and barley abroad by the 1650s.

AGRICULTURAL REVOLUTION

At the time of European colonization of North America, a gradual agricultural revolution was getting underway in Europe beginning in the sixteenth century and extending into the late eighteenth and early nineteenth centuries. It was a "complex phenomenon" centered in Great Britain, present-day Netherlands and Belgium, and France. Its big con-tribution to agriculture was additional fertility to the soil through cover crops such as turnips, and fodder crops like alfalfa and clover. The tur-nip alone led to more complex patterns of crop rotation, allowed farm animals to be fed over winter, and enclosure, which Noel Kingsbury believes "rationalized" the archaic systems of land ownership. Multi-ple course rotation resulted in an estimated 80 percent increase in food production.

During this period agricultural advances joined those in intellectual, scientific, and commercial sectors of society. A change in attitude by landowners and farmers took place as well. The land-owning elites led this innovation, realizing the need to increase crop production to feed growing urban populations as enclosure moved rural families off the land and into the cities. In northern Europe and the American colonies at this time, richer and better educated estate owners took interest in the productivity of their lands and wrote about them in tracts and newspapers. In Britain, a turning point in agricultural literature took place in about the middle of the seventeenth century. Wealthy men became interested in farming as an escape from politics, law, and government and established farming libraries. Farming began to shed its "low social status" and rural and country life became superior to crowded industrial urban life. With the rise of the developing capitalist economy, wealthy rural elites could become managers and entrepreneurs of a country world of progressive change. Moreover, land-holding peasants who now had to pay rent in cash rather than crops, wanted to enter the market economy too.

Most farmers got their seeds by trading among other growers at county fairs and these gatherings became the place to show, compete, and win awards and thus present the best seed varieties. Mechanization was not a big part of the agricultural revolution at first. Aristocrats were more interested in breeding fine livestock. Farmers paid more attention to raising sheep and cattle breeding.

ORIGINS OF COLONIAL FARMERS

Trends in England's agricultural progress are important in the United States because by the end of the eighteenth century, approximately 60 percent of its white population was English in origin, with almost 12 percent Scotch, Scotch Irish, or Irish, and more than 8 percent German. They attempted to adapt old country farming practices to their new environments. Almost one-fifth were enslaved African Americans, either brought to the colonies from the Caribbean or directly from Africa. Given the preponderance of English colonists, the major settlement patterns followed English agricultural traditions. These traditions included "plantations" meaning literally "a large group of plants under cultivation."

Both Plymouth in Massachusetts and Drayton Hall in South Carolina were seaboard plantations but were very different in their spatial organization and labor sources. Plymouth plantation was a collection of farming villages whose surrounding fields of subsistence crops were planted by white laborers of many families; Drayton Hall was a rice plantation owned by one family whose fields were worked by slave labor housed in "quarters." In New England plantations, some land was held privately by individuals while other tracts were held in common plots. In the South, plantations were usually owned by one person or family.

In some respects, the New England plantation, or village, with its private and commonly held tracts, resembled American Indian practices of small, family-worked plots while major outlying fields were worked in common. Southern plantations tended to be associated with large, cleared fields specializing in a commercial crop—cotton, rice, tobacco— although in both New England and the South these farming communities included outlying and uncleared lands important to both northern and southern colonies.

Southern plantations featured individually owned farms sprawled over many acres. They were sited with good soil and access to waterways for shipping crops such as tobacco. In Virginia and Maryland early colonial tobacco plantations were often 250 to 500 acres and worked by a combination of family, indentured, and eventually slave labor. In South Carolina, rice plantations moved inland, up river valleys and swamplands, and relied upon slave labor to clear cypress, dig canals, and construct rice fields.

Thus, land distribution influenced family and community life for generations, and was often determined by prevailing practices in their old homes in England. Under the open-field village model, farming families lived close together in villages rather than greater distances from each other as in the southern plantation system. In Andover, Massachusetts, where the open-field custom was followed, four- to twenty-acre irregular strips of land were distributed to individual families within the larger open field. Some of these families may have never farmed and there was a shortage of mature children capable of clearing land, turning the soil, and constructing farm buildings. Given the settlers' modest beginnings, few brought servants along with them.

The vast majority of colonial farmers did not own plantations or slaves. In the middle colonies of Pennsylvania and New York and in the southern backcountry the expansion of the farming frontier into the interior depended on farmsteads owned by individual families. This western frontier was a fast westward-moving line in Pennsylvania, Virginia, and North and South Carolina on the eve of the American Revolution.

FARMING SOCIETY

New England winters were long and its coastlines rocky. Though the growing season in this region was shorter than in the South, farmers grew enough to feed their families on subsistence farms, which reflected local farm society. Generally speaking, areas to the west of the coastal zone had better soil and were more likely to become centers of commercial farming activity. Few farmers became rich, but few were poor. Behind these coastal areas of commercial activity that stretched from New England to Georgia was a sparsely settled backcountry—a rural and undeveloped area. The region has been compared to the size of Western Europe. Average rainfall in the backcountry was between forty to fifty inches per year. Overall, it was a good region for small family farms growing diversified crops for subsistence purposes.

The western edge of the backcountry was the Appalachian Mountain chain as set by the British in the Proclamation of 1763. The British believed this demarcation was necessary to keep land-hungry farmers and hunters from yet another round of encroachment on Indian lands. This encroachment thinned the resources of the British government required to police the frontier. After the costly French and Indian War, the British were strapped for cash and loath to spend more money on frontier conflicts.

Due to steep land prices during the 1730s, Pennsylvania farming families began to move southward into the backwoods along the base of the Appalachian Mountains and also, but not always, east of the Appalachian Mountains. More than half of the population of the backcountry came from Ireland, Scotland, and northern England. They were considered disorderly by Pennsylvania officials, who were happy to see them go. Germans, Scotch Irish, Quakers, and the English also brought their own farming heritage to bear. German farmers, for instance, staked out the best limestone deposits in Frederick County, Maryland, and in the northern half of the Shenandoah Valley. Few of them moved much farther south. The Scotch Irish took up lands in the southern Shenandoah Valley and extended the "Irish settlements" to the Cumberland Gap. In southern Virginia, between the North Carolina border and the James River, much of the watershed drained into North Carolina through the Roanoke River basin and had bypassed the early colonial settlement north of the James. Virginians, mostly of English descent, took up these lands in a gradual westward migration that after two decades joined the south-westward migration down the Piedmont from Pennsylvania. By the 1760s, the new Virginia backcountry settlements had been subdivided into eight new counties.

At the beginning of the American Revolution about 250,000 people lived in these remote settlements from Maryland to Georgia. In 1776, about 20 percent of Maryland's population and approximately 25 percent of Virginia's lived in the backcountry, while in North and South Carolina about 40 and 50 percent, respectively, lived in these farming settlements. Georgia's small backcountry had almost 15 percent of its population living there about fifty years after the colony's founding. The timing of settlement in the backcountry varied due to a number of factors. The French and Indian War slowed the flow of settlers into the Great Valleys of Virginia.

Historian Carl Bridenbaugh described this activity as "a movement of humble folk." The Highland Scots and the Scotch Irish seemed to fit this description. They arrived with a few horses, oxen, hogs, and chickens and a wagon or two full of farm implements and household goods. This inventory represented their moveable wealth. Some owned a few slaves but certainly not most. In South Carolina, for example, 79 percent of its white population lived in the backcountry, while in the coastal rice plantation districts enslaved black majorities were common, and by 1740 two-thirds of South Carolina colony's population was black.

At the end of the eighteenth century, the United States was a rural and agricultural society. The largest group was small farmers, also called yeomen. They owned small farms of one hundred to two hundred acres and worked them with family labor or landless white tenants. It is estimated that the yeomanry numbered nearly half of the entire white population and about 40 percent of all people at the time of the American Revolution. These farmers raised enough crops to feed their families, produce their own clothing, pay their taxes, and sell a small surplus of produce at market towns. Nevertheless, an estimated one-third of southern backcountry men were landless and eager to become landowners even if it meant waging war on Indians.

The yeomanry worked the less fertile and more remote land not taken up by large commercial farmers who owned the most fertile property with access to markets, which in the colonial period meant rivers leading to transatlantic trade seaports. In the North, commercial farmers became more diversified growing wheat and other grains, while in the South they concentrated on the proven winners in the transatlantic trade—rice, sugarcane, and tobacco. That trade earned them enough money to purchase the labor of others, either as slaves, indentured servants, or white tenants and sharecroppers.

White indentured servants were eventually displaced by slaves beginning in the late seventeenth century in Virginia and Maryland, much as they had been on West Indian islands such as Barbados. At the bottom of the social ladder were enslaved Africans. At the end of the American Revolution they formed about one-fifth of the population of the new United States. Eighty percent of enslaved Africans worked on southern plantations, usually along the coast, and in some areas, such as South Carolina and Georgia rice country, they formed a majority of the population. The social structure of these farming communities was controlled by violence, abuse, and fear. Unlike black slaves, these servants (20 percent of the white population) had a chance to become small farmers in noncommercial farming areas once their indentures ended. If defined by property, they were poor, but their odds of becoming landowners, especially in frontier areas, was estimated at better than half to three-quarters.

The South Carolina rice country population dominated by planters and their slaves stood in stark contrast to its backcountry characterized by subsistence farmers and livestock herders who followed the migration routes southward. Barbados has been called the "mother" of South Carolina. Before the arrival of planters and slaves from Barbados, as well as from the Bahamas and other islands, South Carolina boasted a white majority. A large area of small farms lay between the coastal rice and indigo plantations and the backcountry region. There were few large plantations in this region. Much of this landscape was covered by long-leaf pine trees and wiregrass, part of the larger southern Coastal Plains pine forest. Because the land was described as "pine barren" with poor soil quality it largely was bypassed by commercial farmers. About 94 percent of the whites owned small tracts of land in the piney woods, most of them around one hundred acres. They farmed even smaller portions of their landholdings in corn, sweet potatoes, and vegetables. The unfarmed sections of their land formed an immense wiregrass open range that stretched into colonial Georgia and North Carolina and supported large herds of cows, hogs, and sheep.

However, the increase of the slave population in South Carolina, which reached heavy majorities in the Low Country by the revolution, expanded commercial rice and indigo plantations up coastal rivers, reducing yeoman access to good soil and rangeland. According to historian Charles Joyner, this expansive slave society "more resembled Caribbean than other mainland societies" with its plantation economy, slave labor system, and European markets.

By the end of the colonial era the quickest way to move up into the landholding middle class was to move west beyond the reach of commercial crops such as wheat, tobacco, and rice. This is precisely what many white freemen did, and it was the dream of many indentured servants. About 80 percent of these farmers, including immigrants and indentured servants, found land in the backcountry east of the present-day Appalachian Mountains. Settling on the frontier involved risks, not the least of which was violent competition for land with American Indian farmers. Wealthy whites in the east bought large tracts of land in hopes that its prices would rise, and their investments would pay off. These men included George Washington.

And because status in the new United States was based on property and land ownership and not, as in Western Europe, on hereditary rank, self-working farmers took pride in their ability to feed, clothe, and shelter their families even when their property in material goods was limited. For such middling farmers, life was comfortable, though not as posh as that of the upper-class planters, but it was not as bad as those of poor whites and slaves.

POLITICS

The political life of American farmers was shaped by the laws and customs governing each of the thirteen colonies. In Virginia, the earliest English colony, voter restrictions were set by the Virginia Company, which appointed the governor and council. The King granted the company an enormous amount of land, which was distributed to farmers from planters to sharecroppers. Even the latter could own the land after seven years. Many of these croppers could vote for members of the House of Burgesses after seven years, and prior to 1670 most white men could vote, but not women and slaves. By the revolutionary era, more back-country land was becoming available and relatively free from Indian attacks. More and more white male Virginians could own land, which was a qualification for voting as imposed by the English government. The one hundred or more acres (sometimes more than two hundred and fifty acres) that settlers received was larger than the fifty acres, the "standard ratio" for rotating tobacco, corn, etc., that had become customary. Small and large farmers depended on the tobacco crop to pay their taxes.

Yet no matter how much tobacco even the elite planters produced, or how much wealth they accumulated, they never felt completely fulfilled, nor entirely sure that they had arrived at the top. The top was defined by their colonial rulers—the lifestyles and manners of the English gentry. Virginians distrusted the King, fearing that if he was not restrained he could enslave them, even as they enslaved Africans who made their new world possible. That is why the planter elite in America saw the small farmers as a good thing—a wide distribution of land holders with votes that could help curb ambitious monarchs, and if necessary form militias against royal armies, ensuring the protection of their life, liberty, and property. Both planters and yeomen farmers produced tobacco, were free men, dealt with Indians on the frontier, and complained about British rule. The yeomanry who shouldered firearms in the organized colonial militia realized they pulled their pants on the same way as planters.

Faced with large slave populations in places like South Carolina and Virginia, whites, regardless of their material wealth, organized militias to control and patrol the black agricultural workforce. Farmers could resist that threat by organizing and arming themselves. They could prevent black slaves from doing the same by making it illegal for them to own firearms and gather without the knowledge of their master.

It was this dilemma that the trustees of the Georgia colony sought to avoid when they created their charter in 1732. They envisioned a "virtuous yeoman's" society that would become "a haven for the 'worthy poor.'" An equal distribution of land and banning slavery, blacks, lawyers, Roman Catholics, and liquor dealers, the trustees believed, would remove the excesses of colonial South Carolina and Virginia. Small farmers would practice diversified agriculture and quickly muster for military duty if the Spanish in Florida attacked. Olive oil, silk, and wine were needed in England and these were expected to be grown on the fifty-acre plots given to the settlers. But the failure to establish any of these crops caused Georgia farmers to look enviously toward South Carolina's coast, where slave-grown rice, sea island cotton, and indigo made many planters affluent through the transatlantic trade since that colony's founding in 1670. The Georgia yeoman's utopia was gone by 1760, when one in three people were enslaved Africans and the power of slave-grown monocultures extended from the Carolinas into Georgia.

Furthermore, the defeat of the best army in the world during the American Revolution instilled confidence in farmers and a sense of optimism for the future. It is important to remember that colonial agriculturalists won the war. American farmers filled out the ranks of the Continental Line (the regular army) and swelled the ranks of the militia when called to join the Continentals. Their leaders, including John Adams, Thomas Jefferson, and George Washington, to name a few, were the products of a farming and planting society who had reached their peak as elite agriculturalists. Their landholdings were sources of income for them and sources of agricultural experimentation as well. They were the colony's version of the wealthy landed gentry in Great Britain who led the agricultural revolution.

As the revolutionary era drew to a close, the agricultural practices of most of the new nation's farmers had changed little since early European settlement. Human labor supplemented by animal power did most of the work. Clearing land still depended on hand power and axes to girdle trees. In some cases, oxen and horses were used to drag crude plows across fields, but much land was still not cleared of large stumps and deep roots. Women and men used hand implements, especially hoes, to prepare the soil for planting and to control the growth of grasses and weeds. There was very little crop rotation and large tracts of land, especially in cash crop–producing areas like Virginia, suffered from soil depletion and abandonment.

By 1790, westward expansion of the farming frontier had reached the Appalachian Mountains and in some places had pushed beyond, especially into the western counties of Virginia, where the tobacco crop's demand for fresh land extended the settlement line into present-day Kentucky as far as the Falls of the Ohio at Louisville. The changes to

American agriculture had already been enormous in other respects. The pictures painted by the brushes of artists and the words of writers to help Europeans understand the agricultural methods of American Indian agriculture no longer fit. Farming villages managed by Indian women growing food crops for home consumption had been replaced by farms and plantations managed mostly by men and dependent to varying degrees on slave labor. All along the backcountry's border crop regions that had reached their limits in the east and exhausted the soil and energy of an older generation were looking west. Planting elites already controlled the richest cash crop land east of the Appalachian Mountains and continued to consolidate their holdings as the frontier line crossed the mountains.

2

Crop Regions

AT THE DAWN OF THE NEW CENTURY "Young America" was poised for an era of unprecedented territorial expansion. It took colonial farmers and planters almost two centuries to reach the Appalachian Mountains. The cost was high. Travelers commented on the wasteful practices of farmers and the worn-out appearance of the countryside. In the Carolinas one traveler wrote that farmers showed "little concern how much the land may be exhausted" and were fixated on "making the largest profit for the present time." In 1800, almost nine hundred thousand people were enslaved Africans, most of them working on plantations. Unsympathetic attitudes toward human and environmental exploitation did not change with an accelerated removal of American Indian farmers. The colonial practice of one cash crop and intensive tillage continued and so did its negative impact on the environment. As Patrick Henry opined after the American Revolution, "he is the greatest Patriot, who stops the most gullies."

This chapter surveys the major expanding crop regions during the Early National period (1790s to 1850s). At that time, crop belts were not formally defined and they sometimes overlapped. No single crop exclusively occupied a region. Climate was the major factor in determining the hazy boundaries of crop regions as were the planting and harvesting practices that farming families had known for generations. As settlers moved west, they normally stayed within latitudinal or isothermal zones similar to those illustrated on the back of modern seed packets. This migration practice allowed farmers to minimize the risk of crop failure with new plants in a new western settlement barring drought and insects. Crop regions expanded spatially over time as westward-moving crop belts faced few natural barriers until reaching the Great Plains at about 105 degrees west longitude.

Regions are also social constructs. Farmers were actors shaping new landscapes with crop cultures. Tobacco, for example, had an architecture all its own with tools, barns, and buildings that branded the region as a distinct agricultural community. Federal and state governments were busy dividing the new territories into new states and counties that became administrative and statistical units. The material culture of crop regions was, and is, represented in hundreds of symbols in novels and songs. Regions become regions "in material and symbolic processes related to nature and landscapes." Agriculture puts its stamp on a landscape like few other human activities.

Despite the enormous costs to dispossessed Native peoples, enslaved African Americans, and the environment, there were virtually no commercial colonial American crops that Western Europeans could not get elsewhere: tobacco and rice from the Mediterranean and the Middle East, sugar from the West Indies, and grain from multiple sources. North America's colonial crops did not take the nation's agricultural frontier much beyond the Appalachian Mountains. But that was about to change.

In 1790, an estimated 250,000 settlers were already west of the Appalachian Mountains, especially in present-day Kentucky. The frontier, defined as an area with more than two people but less than six per square mile, had almost reached the Mississippi River by 1800 in western Kentucky, a bulge created by heavy migration into the Ohio River Valley. But Kentucky was the exception. Elsewhere, the land in most of Georgia, Tennessee, Ohio, and Maine was still in the hands of Indian nations and east of the Appalachian Mountains the good land was taken or already worn out.

During the next fifty years the frontier line crossed the Mississippi River along its entire length. Farmers in the mid-Atlantic states followed the Ohio River below Pittsburgh into Ohio going northwest. In New England farmers moved west into the northern portions of western New York and upper Ohio, Indiana, and Illinois below the Great Lakes. Southerners from Upper South states such as Virginia, Kentucky, and Tennessee crossed the Ohio River and settled along rivers in southern

Ohio, Indiana, and Illinois. In the Southeast, the movement was generally to the southwest, especially along the Piedmont.

As geographer Oliver E. Baker noted almost a century ago, the nation can be divided into eastern and western halves. The eastern half, settled before the American Civil War, is the topic of this chapter. It extended from the seaboard beyond the Mississippi River to approximately the 100th meridian. This half of the nation had enough rainfall to grow crops such as corn, wheat, and tobacco that westward-moving settlers needed and knew how to cultivate. Overall, these tilled crops did well in relatively humid climates using "ordinary farming methods" as Baker put it.

The major crop regions by 1850 were all beneath one thousand feet in elevation. From north to south they were the wheat and dairy belts from New England through New York and western Pennsylvania and into northeastern Ohio and southern Michigan and Wisconsin; the Corn Belt in the lower Midwest covered much of the southern parts of Pennsylvania, Ohio, Indiana, Illinois, and Iowa; the Upper South tobacco and hemp belt in south central Virginia, Kentucky, east Tennessee, and southern Missouri, which joined bluegrass Kentucky and Virginia as a hemp-growing area; and the Deep South's cotton belt, which dominated the region's Piedmont and Mississippi River Valley.

It is easy to imagine farm life in a bucolic setting where neighbors supported one another in largely self-sufficient activities augmented by barter and trade. This, of course, did happen, but crop belts also were centers of capitalistic activity. It is important to remember that middling farmers and planters produced commercial crops for world markets and competed with each other. They priced their crops to recover their costs in labor and land and produce a profit. During the Early National period, most farmers in the North and South were white, but in the South almost four million slaves were captives of a forced labor system that consisted of abuse, fear, and violence. Southern agriculturalists were not the only players in this global system to benefit from slavery. The slave traders, the shipping and insurance industries, and the investors in, and manufacturers of, cotton, hemp, and tobacco products, for example, realized profits that made risking their wealth worthwhile.

INDIAN "REMOVAL"

During the Early National period, the US government subsidized agricultural expansion in several ways: removing Indian nations by treaty or warfare or both; surveying lands and advertising their sale; and distributing the land by lotteries, including rewarding veterans with land warrants. Compared to Europe, where land was limited and expensive, America's western lands were plentiful and cheap. Never had so much land cost so little.

By the end of the 1850s, the nation had forcibly taken possession of its present-day continental territory. In 1802, Georgia was the last of the original colonies to turn over its colonial rights to western lands to the new nation. At no time did Indian dispossession of farm land move quicker than during the presidential administration of Andrew Jackson (1828–1836). Jackson's early experiences with Indians during the War of 1812 and the brutal Creek conflict convinced him that frontier security demanded the Indian nations be removed west of the Mississippi River. The final defeat of the Creek "Red Sticks" by US troops and loyal Creeks and Cherokees at the Battle of Horseshoe Bend on the Tallapoosa River in Alabama in March 1814 revealed much of his intent of instilling fear in them. About 850 Red Sticks were killed at the battle with the body count verified by cutting the tip of each hostile's nose. A scorched earth policy was followed moving through the remaining agrarian Creek villages. Jackson's "hatred" of the Creeks, wrote biographer Robert V. Remini, "had become an obsession."

Even Jackson's loyal Creek allies were eventually dispossessed of their farmlands. They had allowed Shawnee Chief Tecumseh to speak to their people and stir up frontier trouble before and during the War of 1812 with Great Britain. As a condition of peace, Jackson forced all Creeks to surrender twenty-three million acres of land and move west of the Mississippi River. The Jackson-inspired Indian Removal Act of 1830 called for the withdrawal of the southeastern "Five Civilized Tribes"—the Creek, Cherokees, Choctaws, Chickasaws, and Seminoles—west of the Mississippi. The Cherokee Nation resisted. Moreover, some antiremoval Creeks sought refuge with the Cherokee Nation, stating, "We came here to escape the evil of war. . . . But we have been pursued by the White Men and treated harshly, without knowing that we were guilty of any crime." Some government officials believed that the Creek presence in the Cherokee Nation influenced Cherokee reluctance to remove west. The reluctant Cherokees fought removal physically and in the Supreme Court but lost. Cherokee removal began in 1838 when US troops and Georgia militia drove them into stockades and began a forced march later known as the Trail of Tears. About four thousand of the eighteen thousand Cherokee who left on the march died.

Indian nations remaining north of the Ohio River suffered the same fate. When Sac and Fox Indians tried to reclaim their lands occupied by whites in Illinois, the settlers panicked, and the Black Hawk War (1832) followed resulting in the defeat and removal of these Indians. By the end of Jackson's second term almost forty-six thousand Indians had been moved west of the Mississippi River. The United States gained about one hundred million acres of land in exchange for $68 million and thirty-two million acres given to Indians west of the Mississippi River. Indian farm society in the east mirrored that of white society in many ways and consisted of every level of white society from elite planters to middling farmers to poor whites as well as the style of their homes, from log cabins to brick houses. They were dispossessed because their possessions were coveted by whites.

West of the Mississippi, the Louisiana Purchase (1803), Texas annexation (1845), the Mexican-American War (1846–1848), the annexation of the Oregon territory (1846), and the Mexican Cession (1848) added about three million square miles to the new nation. In the Ohio Valley region, a series of conflicts continued for more than twenty years, from the Revolutionary War until the mid-1790s, and led to the removal of Indians west of the Mississippi.

When considering which land surveying system to follow on former Amerindian soils, Congress chose the orderly northern pattern of townships and ranges and rejected the disorderly southern practice of metes and bounds. Although fiscal conservatives wanted western land sold in large blocks and at high prices, by 1820 moderates urged that lands be sold in small tracts at low prices and this method won the day. By 1832, a settler could purchase forty acres of land for about fifty dollars.

Competing for farmland was not limited to Indian-settler contests. It included conflicts along the borderlands of the Upper South and the lower North and Midwest where crop regions met and farmers using slave and free labor competed for fresh western lands. This was especially true when labor-intensive and soil-exhausting crops such as tobacco came into competition with less labor-intensive grain crops such as corn and wheat.

TECHNOLOGICAL CHANGE

The Early National period was one of technological innovation. In 1793 alone, two developments—the perfection of the cotton gin and the introduction of the cradle and scythe for wheat harvesting—helped move the cotton and wheat belts westward to the Mississippi River and beyond. Improvements in plows, reapers, grain drills, grain storage, commercial fertilizers, increased farm production, and improved methods of storing and marketing food were all part of a growing agricultural support sector.

The colonists were reluctant to use iron plow parts. Wood was cheaper and more available. Iron could be brittle and break at critical points such as the mold board, which turned the soil, and the plow point, which sliced through the earth. Fields not cleared of rocks and heavy roots could break iron parts and lead to long delays. There was an unfounded belief that "the iron plow poisoned the soil." It was not until 1797 that Charles Newbold patented the first American cast-iron plow. A New Jersey blacksmith, Newbold was unable to find a market for his invention supposedly because of farmer distrust of iron poisoning the soil.

While much colonial agriculture was based on hill and hoe cultivation, especially tobacco planting, many colonial farmers used plows. Some were brought from Europe while others were made by local farmers and blacksmiths based on known plow designs. The problem with the plow, as evident in ancient Greece, was "soil erosion began to exceed soil production only after the introduction of the plow."

The simplest of these early plows was based on the "ard" or *aratrum*. It was built by joining two pieces of wood driven into a horizontal beam with one end attached to oxen and the opposite guided by the plowman. Underneath, a coulter plowed the ground and an upright handle held by the plowman steered. In Europe, early versions of the ard were mounted on two wheels. During the 1600s and 1700s, this design was improved by adding a mold board and a plow point, all made of wood. Unwieldy, this plow could take three people to work across a field, one to push down and give weight above the plow point, one to steer the plow, and a third to work the team of oxen. In the interior of the North American continent French farmers at Kaskaskia also used wooden plows, called "hog plows" because of their rooting effect, that were similar to those used by colonists along the Atlantic seaboard. The result was often a furrow about three inches deep.

THE WHEAT BELT

Wheat became the North's leading cash crop and was widely grown during the colonial era from Maine to Virginia. South of Virginia and near the Atlantic coast, warmer and moister climates prevented much success in growing this crop on a commercial scale. New England's farmers continued to grow wheat despite problems with "blasting" or mildew, which they incorrectly blamed on salty sea air breezes rather than its relationship to barberry plants as hosts of wheat rust fungus, which grows on the underside of barberry leaves and sends spores that infect wheat. In 1800, New England was still settled mostly along the rocky coastline. Beyond this band of settlement, there was little population in the interior. In the mid-1790s a visitor to York, Maine, wrote that the soil was "rocky and very hard of cultivation" and that as much as two-thirds of it was "incapable of any other cultivation than what spontaneously arises." In New England, north of Massachusetts, many of the common folk living along the coast were fisher-farmers and those living in the interior were timber men and backwoods farmers.

In western New York, the area south of Lake Ontario between Syracuse and Buffalo and the Finger Lakes, especially the Genesee Valley, was a major wheat-growing region. Wheat grew well on the new lands of western New York, Ohio, and Pennsylvania. In 1839 and 1849, New York was ranked third in wheat production only behind Ohio and Pennsylvania; Virginia, Illinois, and Indiana followed. During the 1840s, as wheat fields were cultivated farther west onto rich prairie lands, oak openings, and river valleys, a wheat boom flooded the eastern markets

with grain shipped via the Erie Canal. The consequences were disastrous for farmers in the Northeast and especially in New England, where
farming had been at near subsistence levels until the War of 1812 and
industrialization created urban demand for farm crops. By 1850, commercial wheat growers in New England had virtually disappeared, especially in coastal areas, and many farmers migrated to the Midwest. After
1850, farmers in western New York began growing grain crops to support dairy and livestock industries, but in 1849 it still remained third in
wheat production.

The wheat region's southern boundary extended from Maryland into
western Virginia and Kentucky, where it would be overtaken by tobacco
production. In Virginia's upcountry and Shenandoah Valley wheat
thrived to such an extent that Virginia ranked fourth in the nation producing over ten million bushels in 1839. The rolling countryside of the
Shenandoah Valley and the Shenandoah River's flow into the Potomac
at Harper's Ferry provided seemingly remote wheat farmers with access
to both the nation's capital as well as Chesapeake Bay cities such as
Baltimore.

Slave labor was used to grow many crops including wheat, corn, and
tobacco. When considering the westward expansion of wheat, the crop's
borderland was Maryland, Virginia, and the Ohio Valley. Was slavery
heading north of the Ohio River for tobacco and corn production, which
were much more labor intensive than wheat? During the 1830s, it looked
that way. Wheat production was widespread in the Upper South states
of Kentucky and Tennessee, but a decade later, while east of the Appalachian Mountains wheat growing remained strong in Virginia's Piedmont region and Valley as well as Maryland, and it had fallen behind the
more labor-intensive corn fields in Kentucky and Tennessee. Even in the
Lower Midwest corn production increased rapidly and brought pressure
to use slave labor. The same is true of central Kentucky and central and
western Tennessee. In the Valley of Virginia (Shenandoah and Roanoke
River Valleys) slave labor supported comparatively high levels of wheat
production, especially in the Staunton area. The wheat output differed
from planter to planter, based on crop choices, and from county to county
based on soil conditions.

There was also considerable importation and crossbreeding of
wheat varieties. Presidents Washington, Jefferson, and Madison all

experimented with different wheat varieties, but the most important biological innovation was the importation of Mediterranean wheat in 1819, which was widely planted by the 1850s.

By 1850, the major centers of wheat production were Pennsylvania, Ohio, New York, Virginia, Illinois, and Indiana. Pennsylvania alone produced more than sixteen million bushels. By the late 1850s, with the addition of more Midwestern states, the leaders in wheat production were Illinois, Indiana, Wisconsin, and Ohio, all north of the Ohio River and west of the Appalachian Mountains. On the eve of the Civil War more than half of the nation's wheat crop came from this section of the country. Still, wheat production in Virginia and Kentucky, along with the Mid-South and Piedmont regions, was not unusual, demonstrating that slave labor could be used for wheat growing.

THE CORN BELT

Corn was grown throughout the East. From New England to Florida, it was the premier crop. It grew quickly and provided critical foodstuffs for people and livestock. Because of the problems with growing wheat along the seaboard, corn was the major grain in colonial diets. Although New Englanders preferred white wheat bread because it was associated with the English upper classes, corn bread was associated with England's lower classes and Amerindians, but corn was easier to grow and a less risky option for self-sufficient farmers. Native localized corn varieties developed by Indian women became critical to Euro-Americans in adapting their eastern US seed corn to the new western environments. The varieties of corn seemed endless as they adapted to their own ecological niches.

Corn is a short day plant, meaning that late summer's shorter days stimulate flowering. Migrating farmers understood that their corn seeds adapted to "the daylight conditions of their own latitude." Sensitivity to sunlight could vary from county to county as well as region to region. As farmers moved west from New England and Upper South states such as Virginia and Kentucky, the regional corn types overlapped and flint and dent corn hybridized, creating Corn Belt Dent. In the early nineteenth century, farmers in Pennsylvania and Ohio were experimenting with flint-dent corn from the North and South as it moved west. Farmers who ventured beyond the optimal varieties risked lower yields and declining food security. By the 1850s, such crossbreeding was widespread throughout much of the East.

While migrating farmers carried seed corn from the East that proved reliable, they also encountered local varieties Amerindian populations grew in more arid areas of the West. In some cases, a mix of eastern dent and Indian corn varieties helped move the Corn Belt west, further influencing its variety by the climate of different places, peoples, and its adaptability. It would be with those local Indian varieties that astute white farmers crossbred their corn from the East, gaining greater protection from local plant threats and continuing traditional practices of exchanging seed.

While the Corn Belt is so fixed in our minds as "Midwestern," the first US census agricultural returns in 1839 showed Tennessee, Kentucky, Virginia, and Ohio leading all other states in corn production. Three of these leaders were situated in the Upper South slave states. In that same year, the nation's geographic center of corn growing was near Richmond, Kentucky, farther to the west than wheat at that time. But as the North Central states filled with settlers, Ohio took the lead by 1849, and while Kentucky remained second, Illinois and Indiana replaced Tennessee and Virginia as top corn producers. Within a decade the Corn Belt shifted from the Upper South, across the Ohio River, and into the lower Midwest. As corn moved westward into the prairie states such as Illinois and Iowa, wheat growing there declined. But the term "Corn Belt" would not turn up until the early 1880s.

Corn was fed to cows and hogs and also used in whiskey production, but not all farming cultures considered it worth feeding to their livestock. In the South, many farmers turned their livestock loose on the open range to forage for themselves year-round eating wild grasses, sugarcane, and tree mast consisting of acorns and other nuts and forms of fodder. These farmers saved corn to meet their own dietary demands in the form of corn bread or for trade and barter at local markets. In the Upper Midwest, corn-fed livestock was much more common and wheat bread was more popular. Given longer winters, cattle were sheltered and fed corn during colder months.

As the Corn Belt crossed the Appalachian Mountains and moved from the Upper South into the Lower Midwest during the 1830s and

1840s, southern and Midwestern farm labor traditions came into conflict. While southern farmers, without question, used slave labor to
produce the major commercial crops associated with their region—cotton, rice, sugarcane, and tobacco—they also used slave labor to produce corn. Corn was more labor intensive and was better suited to slave
labor than wheat. Although the Northwest Ordinance of 1787 prohib-
ited slavery there, squatting in advance of Indian removal and government land distribution in the north central states was common. Indiana
senator John Tipton estimated that during the late 1830s "four entire
counties of northwestern Indiana were occupied by squatters." Squatters also moved into the Ohio, Mississippi, and Missouri Valleys, including southerners bringing along enslaved African Americans. Virginian
William Henry Harrison, territorial governor of Indiana, crossed into
Indiana and brought slave labor with him, raising an impressive brick
mansion on the riverbank at Vincennes. These farmers were well aware
that slaves were efficient growers of corn, the major grain in their diet.
On the other hand, farmers whose families migrated into the Midwestern states from New England or the mid-Atlantic states of New York
and Pennsylvania were accustomed to using family and wage labor to
grow both corn and wheat.

Today, the Corn Belt brings to mind the American Midwest, where
cornfields cover much of the agricultural landscapes of Iowa, Illinois,
and Indiana. Here corn became the dominant crop during the pre–Civil
War era. Like cotton, tobacco, and wheat, the center of corn production
moved west not only beyond the Appalachian Mountains, but beyond
the Mississippi River by 1850. The Ohio River Valley, bounded by the
leading corn states, became a center of this early trans-Appalachian corn-
livestock complex.

While the antebellum South was identified as part of the Cotton Belt,
corn was actually the South's leading crop "in terms of weight, value,
and acreage cultivated." As far as labor requirements went in the late
nineteenth century, cotton was most demanding in terms of farm labor
hours, next was corn, followed by wheat. So in the Midwest, shifting
from wheat to corn increased the labor needs of the region. By 1880, cotton required 119 man hours of labor per acre, corn 46, and wheat 20. By
the late 1850s, Illinois, Ohio, Missouri, and Indiana led in corn production, and there was every indication that the Corn Belt would continue to

move west and make Iowa, Kansas, and Nebraska surpass the old Upper South leaders of Kentucky and Tennessee.

TOBACCO

Jamestown's settlers quickly began experimenting with a harsh variety of tobacco grown by Indians. John Rolfe established an experimental tobacco plot five years after the town's founding. Rolfe liked to smoke and hoped that tobacco would become an export crop. The Virginia tobacco was popular in England, and soon the growing of the "weed" was taking place in the streets and settlers neglected their buildings. Eventually, two varieties, Orinoco (harsher) and Sweet Scented (milder), became the basis for much of the tobacco grown in the New World. In 1729, the Chesapeake colonies of Virginia and Maryland exported forty million pounds to England. Unlike cotton, corn, and wheat, tobacco's success depended upon its taste and smell.

The tobacco- and hemp-growing region stretched westward from its colonial base above the Cotton Belt and below the Wheat Belt. By 1800, travelers to Tidewater, Virginia, used words like "abandoned" and "worn out" to describe the formerly productive colonial tobacco lands of the area. The sweet-scented Tidewater tobacco sucked the nutrients from the soil, so farmers moved their fields westward to fresher lands on the Virginia Piedmont. Although tobacco led all exports in value immediately after the American Revolution, prices on the world market fell, due to competition with growers in the East and West Indies and the War of 1812 Embargo Acts. Additionally, soil-depleting tobacco could only be grown—without a loss by American farmers—on fresh, high-producing lands.

During the decades that followed the revolution, tobacco expanded its Upper South range into Kentucky, Tennessee, and North Carolina. These states along with Maryland and Virginia produced approximately 345 million pounds of tobacco by 1859, or about 80 percent of the nation's crop. During the previous ten years, Virginia, Kentucky, and Maryland had almost doubled their production, while North Carolina's gains were even more impressive. The crop also moved north of the Ohio River Valley. After the War of 1812, much of the southern Indiana and Illinois bottomlands were settled by southern farmers. Most of these farmers received land as bounty for military service or bought it directly from the public land offices. Ohio and Missouri each produced about twenty-five million pounds of tobacco and Indiana, Illinois, and Connecticut produced between six and eight million pounds for a total of approximately seventy million pounds. Within the Belt different varieties were grown depending on local climates and grower preferences. As the 1850s drew to a close it was clear that tobacco was not a Deep South crop. There, cotton sucked all the nutrients out of the soil and energy out of its farmers.

Virginia and Maryland's tobacco region was separated by the Potomac River. To the south it spilled over the Virginia borderline into North Carolina. As early as 1820, these three states each had counties with black majorities in tobacco-producing areas. Kentucky and Tennessee's tobacco region was similar in that it also straddled the state line but was not as dependent upon slave labor at this time. There, red Burley tobacco had evolved from Maryland's Broadleaf, but farmers learned to change the taste by adjusting local planting and curing practices. However, the range of tobacco in terms of its expansion was never as broad during this period as cotton or corn.

Growing tobacco was labor intensive, much more so than grain. Tobacco per acre required almost eight times as much labor as corn and almost eighteen times as much labor as wheat. And it took three times as much labor per acre to grow as cotton. Edging its Upper South border into the underbelly of the Lower Midwest, tobacco competed with corn for land and labor. Tobacco growing in the lower Midwest states along the Ohio River depended in part on slave labor. This was especially true in Illinois and Indiana, where slavery existed prior to 1830. Southern farmers were still migrating into the area up until the 1830s.

An adult farmer could produce at most three acres of tobacco using hoe cultivation. White and slave laborers cleared land, built log structures and fences, and prepared the seedbeds. Seedlings were transferred to cleared fields in late April and early May, inspected repeatedly for worms and other pests, and topped in early summer. Harvest in late summer was followed by threading the leaves onto sticks and placing them into barns to cure. The cured leaves were then stripped in late fall and early winter then pressed into bundles for shipping to a tobacco inspection station, where farmers received a receipt for their crop. The appearance of

these stations in frontier county was a sure sign the crop had taken hold
on a commercial scale.

HEMP

Hemp was widely grown from New England to the South during the
colonial era. While some hemp fiber was used for clothing, most of it
was for naval purposes. Hemp grew well in all but the coldest climates
and Maryland and Virginia produced the most. From this Upper South
area hemp production moved to present-day Kentucky on the eve of the
American Revolution, with the first recorded crop at Danville, then a
part of frontier western Virginia. The crop spread to Tennessee, Missouri, and Illinois. Hemp fiber was important for naval rigging and sail
cloth, and was also used to make thread, paper, and cordage. As cotton
production expanded, hemp was in demand for cotton ties and bagging.
Both Presidents Washington and Jefferson grew hemp.

Hemp prices were not as volatile as tobacco's. It also did not wear out
the soil like tobacco and could be planted repeatedly. Seed was sown by

FIGURE 2.1. Braking hemp. The Filson Historical Society, Louisville, KY | Edward and
Josephine Kemp Lantern Slide Collection (012PC27A.007)

hand and after about three months it was cut and tied into bundles to rot in dew and rainfall. It was then dried in a process called retting. Wooden hemp brakes crushed the dried stalks and separated the long fibers from the outer stalk shell. The fibers were then scraped and heckled to split and straighten, and then spun into thread. Hemp processing and braking was labor-intensive and tiring. Hemp did well in Virginia's Piedmont and Shenandoah regions.

COTTON

Of all the crops that moved the frontier westward, none was more important or devastating to the humans that worked it and the environment than cotton. Cotton was the crop that Great Britain's textile industry needed most. In 1794, when Eli Whitney patented his cotton gin, the American South grew very little cotton. By 1850, when raw cotton shipments to Great Britain reached almost 1.5 billion pounds, just over 80 percent of it was grown in the South. As cash crops on the transatlantic trade route, the nation's corn, hemp, tobacco, and wheat value paled compared to cotton.

Native to the Western Hemisphere, European explorers found several varieties of cotton plants in Mexico. One possible route for the migration of cotton into the present-day United States was through Amerindian trading between Mexico and South America to the West Indies and then to the South Atlantic coast. American planters during the colonial period preferred the long staple or black seed cotton variety because it was easier to separate the seed from fiber, and it thrived in salt air environments. French colonists along the present-day Gulf Coast islands in Florida experimented with black seed cotton during the early eighteenth century but were unable to grow the crop with much success on the mainland's interior. This black seed variety spread eastward into the sea islands of Carolina and Georgia during the 1790s.

Green seed cotton was introduced to Georgia by the early 1730s and was first grown on the mainland at the trustee's Savannah garden. It was frequently called Georgia Green Seed, although its origins were probably the island of Guadeloupe and thence carried to English botanical gardens and then to Georgia. It grew well on the mainland, but there was difficulty separating seed from the fiber. Ultimately, many new varieties of cotton seed emerged during the Early National period (1790s–1850s). Mexican cotton, for instance, was easier to pick and resistant to rot, which led to a tremendous increase in the amount that could be picked each day. This variety spread from the lower Mississippi River Valley throughout the Lower South by the 1850s.

Before Whitney's cotton gin, processing picked cotton was labor intensive. Slaves usually ginned by hand no more than one pound per day. The entire process of growing, picking, ginning, cleaning, carding, and spinning made cotton cloth a luxury at the end of the American Revolution. For cotton to be profitable, a solution to separating the short fiber from seeds had to be found.

Prior to the perfection of a mechanical cotton gin, cotton reached Western Europe from the so-called ethnic trade. All members of a family in India, for example, would perform the steps in producing cotton cloth, from planting to picking, from hand ginning to spinning thread and weaving, and cutting and sewing the finished garment. Europe received most of its cotton from communities in the Mediterranean, Middle East, Caribbean, and South America. This "ethnic" cotton was extremely expensive. This same labor-intensive process was followed in colonial America, where yeoman farmers' families grew small amounts of short staple cotton for home consumption creating homespun garments mainly for family use. At the end of the American Revolution, cotton growing on the southern mainland was a small farmer pursuit.

A more efficient way to produce finished cotton cloth also was needed. During the 1700s, thousands of workers in England were already working at different steps in the cotton to cloth process, many of them part-time at home or in workshops before any mechanization took place. The years 1770 to 1790 proved critical in managing and organizing cloth production. Women spinning cotton thread by hand, mostly at home using a single spinning wheel, posed quality control problems. The development of a successful spinning frame in England by Richard Arkwright, patented in 1769, was a critical step but time was needed to work out the kinks. Nevertheless, the weight of cotton spun in England rose from half a million hand-spun pounds in 1765 to sixteen million pounds in 1784. England was set for a major expansion of cotton milling. All it needed was more cotton.

Georgia and South Carolina's sea islands could not produce enough cotton to meet the growing demand in Europe. Cotton production could expand onto the mainland if an efficient method of ginning short fiber cotton was found. Prior to Whitney's gin and the explosion of many other bootleg gins on the market, one method of ginning drove nails though a board in order to catch the seeds as the fiber was hand-pulled through the nails, a time-consuming process. Given the problems of ginning, some observers speculated that slave-produced cotton had reached its peak at the end of the American Revolution and was stuck on the sea islands. Meanwhile, in the New Republic many southerners thought slavery "would fade into economic oblivion."

Whitney's gin, however, freed the spatial restraints of cotton production while increasing the demand for land and labor. The number of enslaved African Americans rose from around 694,000 in 1790 to four million by 1859. And cotton made the South a clearly definable agricultural region with its own identity. This made Whitney, according to Henry Hobhouse, "one of the godfathers of the War Between the States."

Whitney was a handyman who could seemingly fix anything. In 1788, he became a student at Yale University and paid some of his way through college using his mechanical know-how in town. He moved to Savannah, Georgia, after graduation where he became intrigued with the problems of cotton ginning. Whitney soon developed a hand-powered machine that increased the ginning capacity of a single slave from one to fifty pounds a day. Before he could patent his gin, the first model was stolen and soon thereafter reproductions were on the market. The device was simple enough that a village blacksmith could produce it and it spread quickly throughout the South. Because cotton was a crop that required a growing season of about seven months, it did not compete with wheat, tobacco, or hemp. The cotton gin did, however, free cotton from its sea islands confines to spread anywhere in the southern soil and climate. And because there was so much fresh land to the west of the southern Atlantic seaboard, it was more productive for cotton growers to pick up and move their operation to new land than try crop rotation. Land cost about one-fiftieth of what similar quality land cost in Europe. Enslaved African Americans provided most of the labor.

Cotton overtook tobacco, the old colonial mainstay, in crop value in the United States after 1820. Before 1820, most of the cotton was grown

east of the Appalachian Mountains by white farmers. But in an agricultural labor transition that resembled those in sugarcane and tobacco production, cotton increasingly became a crop associated with slave labor.

At the beginning of the 1800s, upland cotton was, with the exception
of the Nashville Basin and southern Louisiana, almost entirely a Piedmont crop stretching from southside Virginia into North Carolina and
more densely into South Carolina and Georgia. Upland cotton's zone was
between the Coastal Plains and the Appalachian foothills and mountains.
As the population moved west along the Piedmont it left the sea islands
to long staple cotton planters and the mainland's tidewater districts to
rice growers. Indigo, once an important Low Country crop, declined due
to competition from growers in Asia and all but disappeared. The low
Coastal Plains between tidewater rice and upland cotton were considered
"pine barrens" and useless for commercial crop production. A tug-of-war
between upland cotton and Low Country rice was won by cotton as more
and more people, and more slaves, shifted to the fresh cotton lands of
the Piedmont. The slave population of Georgia, for example, rose from
29,000 in 1790 to 462,000 in 1860.

By 1810, the value of Georgia's cotton crop was already worth ten
times its rice crop and the steady march of planters and slaves across
the state's Piedmont was just beginning. The cotton frontier advanced
across the state river by river: Savannah to Oconee, Oconee to Ocmulgee,
Ocmulgee to Flint, Flint to Chattahoochee. Most Creek and Cherokee
Indians were killed or removed in the process. Land lotteries disposed of
the Amerindian farm land chunk by chunk and on the cheap. The value
of the slaves needed to clear the land has been valued at between five and
ten times the value of the cleared fields. Planters could care less about soil
depletion and erosion because there was always another river to cross and
more new land opening up.

SUGAR

West Indian sugar plantations were the proving ground for African slave
labor and a major cash crop—sugarcane—in the Western Hemisphere.
The European sweet tooth was so great that tobacco did not overtake
sugar in terms of export value from the New World until after 1800.

Sugar and slaves dominated the Caribbean. The combination of slave labor and a successful cash crop was first demonstrated in the present-day United States by tobacco; sugarcane simply did not take root in America for almost two hundred years. Sugarcane arrived in Louisiana in the mid-eighteenth century with French settlers, but its planting was discontinued shortly before the American Revolution in favor of indigo and rice. Over time, sugarcane was grown in the Deep South, and "ribbon" cane was introduced in 1817. It was grown not only by planters but by yeomen farmers for family consumption and barter usually in the form of brown sugar molasses/cane syrup.

Sugarcane growing and sugar production on a commercial scale in the United States lagged far behind the Caribbean's success story. However, in southeastern Louisiana large and productive sugarcane plantations thrived in the moist climate and sea breezes. Prior to the Civil War almost all the sugarcane in the nation was produced in Louisiana, where as much as one-half of all sugar consumed in the country came from this state. The value of this crop was about $25 million and the planter lifestyles it supported could be seen along Louisiana's sugarcane corridor from St. Francisville to Baton Rouge to New Orleans on both sides of the Mississippi River.

CROP REGIONS AND MIXED FARMING

While the concept of crop regions is useful for purposes of generalization, it is not an entirely accurate description of the agricultural activity in any part of the country. Wheat, corn, tobacco, and cotton were major agricultural products along climatic zones, but many farmers did not participate in their commercial production to any great extent. Rather they practiced "safety first" farming, which is planting food crops and raising livestock first in order to make their households as self-sufficient as possible. In the Deep South, this was called the "hog and hominy" plan, raising hogs for meat and corn for hominy and corn bread. Such farmers strove for self-sufficiency where home consumption was concerned, although it was difficult to be entirely self-sufficient year after year.

Cotton may have been the major commercial crop in the Piedmont South and the Mississippi River Valley by 1850, but there were plenty of small farmers settled among the cotton farms and plantations. Some yeoman farmers grew food crops, including corn and sugarcane, not only to feed themselves, but to trade with neighboring cotton planters who did not produce at levels to meet their own needs. Along the southern Coastal Plains covered mainly by longleaf pines, a so-called Pine Belt of about nine hundred thousand square miles, yeomen farmers produced mainly corn, fodder, sweet potatoes, and raised livestock, especially hogs, cattle, and sheep. They were self-working farm families. Most of them did not own slaves and often worked from twenty-five to fifty acres of cultivated land using white labor. On the northern side of the Cotton Belt a shorter growing season and rougher terrain made cotton planting less feasible as a commercial crop than on the Piedmont. Instead, farmers here grew some wheat, corn, beans, peas, sweet potatoes, and livestock and relied primarily on family labor or landless white tenants. Crop production focused first on household needs. Most of these farmers, as on the Pine Belt, were nonslaveholders or owners of very few slaves. And many of these communities, on the edges, were neither wholly one or the other, entirely commercial or premarket.

THE VIOLENCE OF AGRICULTURE

The tremendous expansion of American agriculture from the Appalachian Mountains to beyond the Mississippi River during the Early National period resulted in American Indian dispossession of hundreds of thousands of square miles and their involuntary removal to reservation lands west of the Mississippi River and Jacksonian Era removals dispossessed most of the rest. Ironically, Indians were primarily agriculturalists who has passed on to Euro-American colonists much of the agricultural know-how that allowed them to survive, grow, and feed themselves up to and through the American Revolution. Twenty years of warfare along the Ohio Valley between the 1770s and the 1790s all but removed the Indian nations to lands west of the confluence of the Mississippi and Missouri Rivers, and Jacksonian Era removals dispossessed most of the rest. Only a few Indian nations remained, notably the eastern band of the Cherokee in the present-day Smoky Mountains and the Seminole Indian nation in southern Florida.

The availability of fresh lands in the west depended on clearing away the natural landscape repeatedly from one frontier to the next. With cotton, Deep South farmers and planters found a worthy replacement for tobacco, one even more dependent upon slave labor than tobacco. And as with tobacco, cotton farmers constantly petitioned for new counties to be laid out to the west once their own land was worn out. Monocultures such as cotton resulted in deep tillage that left the soil exposed to rain and wind for much of the year, causing tremendous topsoil erosion. The process repeated itself year after year. The westward movement of cotton across the region's Piedmont began soon after the cotton gin's relatively easy to design pattern became known. Knock-offs of Whitney's design were readily available. By the 1830s and 1840s, the region's cotton farmers had worn out much of the land. Large gullies were common. Forward-thinking planters looked to new lands farther west, one reporting to his friend that "you and I have been too used to poor land to know what crops people are making in the rich lands of the new counties. I am just getting my eyes open to the golden view."

This "golden view" destroyed the South's Piedmont landscape, and similar thinking did the same in other crop regions where soils were depleted and left as wasteland. Southern topsoil "from Virginia to Alabama lost an average of seven inches" and in some areas lost more than ten. The environmental damage continued as land stripped of woodlands heated up under the southern sun and took a beating from rainfall in excess of fifty inches a year and strong winds. Small streams silted in and became a series of stagnant pools in the summer. Rivers and estuaries silted in as well along the coast. Agricultural lands in the eastern United States lose soil four times as fast as "forested land."

As capitalistic ventures, plantations not only needed a seemingly endless supply of fresh land but also an endless supply of labor. Slavery provided the field hands. During the 1850s, one rule of thumb was ten acres of cotton and ten acres of corn kept "an average hand fully occupied." Hands were rated as full, half, and quarter depending on age and ability to work. Adult men and women were full hands. Almost half of all slave-owning white families owned less than five slaves, and slightly over 11 percent owned more than twenty, but an estimated one-half of the slaves worked on plantations. At least 250,000 slaves were imported into the United States illegally after the 1807 federal law banning the Atlantic slave trade, but slave smuggling increased as the price of slaves rose in the South. During the Early National period, the average price of slaves rose from about $250 to $300 up to $1,800. During the 1830s and 1840s, the average price was often below $1,000 but after 1850 climbed by approximately 40 percent during the decade.

At the beginning of the Early Republic, 90 percent of all slaves were in the east, most of them growing tobacco in Virginia, the Carolinas, and Maryland. Twenty years later these states still had about three-quarters of enslaved African Americans. After the rapid expansion of cotton across the Lower South's Piedmont, some planters and farmers unwilling or unable to move west to richer new lands in Alabama, Mississippi, Louisiana, and East Texas switched to slave breeding and selling, especially in Virginia, Georgia, the Carolinas, Maryland, and Kentucky. Eastern and Upper South slave states fed the domestic slave trade to the Southwest, a key component to the development of the cotton crop region. Hundreds of thousands of slaves were shipped out of these states in a single year.

REFORM

By the 1850s, almost every crop region and section could point to their own agricultural reformers devoted to righting the ills of pre–Civil War agriculture. The worn-out lands and gullies of Revolutionary War–era Virginia had not disappeared; they had only reappeared west in the wake of the wasteful farming practices that considered a forest as an enemy of farming. In the South, James Dunwoody Brownson De Bow's reform-minded journal, *De Bow's Review,* called for agricultural diversification and labor-saving farming devices. These, De Bow believed, would allow southern planters and farmers to break the hold of cotton and turn to new crops that would make the region less dependent on outside food sources such as the Midwest. By becoming better farm managers, southerners could undertake land reclamation in a region where, De Bow wrote, they had been "content to prosecute agriculture with little regard to system, economy, or the dictates of liberal science." Hinton Rowan Helper and Frederick Law Olmsted joined a chorus of critics on the wasteful farming methods of the nation's farmers.

Shortly after the American Revolution, George Washington wrote that the wasteful and destructive practices of the nation's farmers "will drive the Inhabitants of the Atlantic States westward for support" if they did not learn how to improve soil productivity. When Frederick Law Olmsted, a believer in the Jeffersonian ideal that independent farmers were the bedrock of the nation's prosperity and virtue, toured the southern states during the 1850s, he soon changed his mind. Olmsted found the southern plantation system wrecking the landscape and brutally exploiting millions of enslaved African Americans. In this conclusion, Olmsted agreed with Alexis de Tocqueville. On his own tour of America during the 1820s, de Tocqueville commented on the orderly and productive farming practices north of the Ohio River and the ill-kept and wasteful practices of slaveholders south of the river, a difference he attributed mainly to the institution of slavery. But by the end of the Early Republic era, Olmsted concluded that the northern agricultural landscape was not much better than the South's. In his opinion, even the storied New England farming villages had been abandoned or neglected in the hurried westward migrations to the Upper Midwest and were beyond hope. The future of the nation, Olmsted concluded, was not in the countryside but in the city. The control and consolidation of fresh agricultural lands continued as crop regions crossed the mountains and filled the lands between the Appalachians and the Mississippi River.

3

Market Revolutions

As RECENTLY AS THE 1950s and 1960s, many cities in the United States had a large market house. The purpose of these markets was to provide farmers and fishermen with a place to sell their produce to local urban customers. The markets also symbolized a city's commercial prowess. Some of these market houses still survive. Charleston, South Carolina's market dates back to 1788 when Charles Cotesworth Pinckney, a prominent citizen, donated land with the condition that it always be a used as a marketplace. Over the years, and especially during the late twentieth century, vegetables, fish, and meat vendors were displaced by T-shirt and beachtowel hucksters.

Historian John L. Larson wrote that the market revolution was a combination of forces that transformed the nation's landscape from a "loose collection of households and regions" into an "integrated industrial state." At the end of the American Revolution the thirteen colonies had a population of approximately four million people, almost all of them involved in agriculture. By 1860, the nation reached from coast to coast with a population of almost thirty-two million people who had diverse occupations and interests that included factory workers, merchant house proprietors, and shop keepers.

For our purposes, "market revolution" applies to agriculture and describes a combination of developments in science, technology, transportation, communication, and immigration that led to new domestic and international markets for farm products. Historians debate when this occurred but the 1790s or early 1850s is a good starting place. Events that led to greater demand for American crops at home and abroad, such as urbanization or natural disasters including drought, blight, and famine, played a critical role that aided in the rapid change in farming population sizes. During the market revolution the farm population dropped from 90 percent of the population to about 60 percent on the eve of the Civil War.

OVERVIEW

During much of the colonial period farmers and planters relied on waterways for market access. In Virginia and Maryland agricultural produce from farms and plantations was collected along the shorelines of the Chesapeake Bay. Crops were loaded onto sailing ships for coastwise or transatlantic voyages. These crops had to withstand long voyages and unpredictable weather. In New England major seaports such as Boston, and in the Middle Atlantic states, New York and Philadelphia, became important coastal and Atlantic trade centers.

Given the wretched condition of colonial roads, which were often little more than cart paths, colonists depended on waterways for shipment to market, especially for bulky goods such as tobacco. Coastwise trading depended on two-mast schooners and single-mast sloops sailing between Savannah, Georgia, and Charleston, South Carolina, in the South to Williamsburg, Virginia, and Baltimore, Maryland, in the Chesapeake, and to Philadelphia, Pennsylvania, New York, and Boston in the North. In shallow waters such as bays, smaller, shallow draft sailing vessels were used. As settlement moved west toward the Appalachian Mountains, backcountry farmers depended on town merchants to accept their surplus crops in exchange for credit. The merchants became middlemen, shipping the interior crops to coastal trading houses for transshipment to other colonies or across the Atlantic.

Dutch traders in New Amsterdam (New York) originally controlled the northern coastwise trade and based it on the trade model used in Europe. Once the Dutch lost power in North America, New Englanders as well as traders in Philadelphia and New York dominated the seagoing traffic. In time, cargo included lumber, fish, naval stores, rice, indigo, tobacco, rum, and enslaved Africans on a transatlantic scale, and finished goods such as cloth and foodstuffs to the West Indies. Increasingly, southern planters of rice, indigo, and tobacco shipped their crops directly to England and bypassed the New Englanders. Tobacco alone made up about 25 percent of the value of all colonial exports to England.

MARKETS THROUGH WESTERN NEW YORK
TO THE UPPER MISSISSIPPI VALLEY

By 1860, settlement shifted from east of the Appalachian Mountains to the Upper Mississippi River Valley and into eastern Missouri, Iowa, Minnesota, Texas, and Wisconsin. Considering that it took more than 150 years for people to cross the Appalachian Mountains, this was a tremendous story of people on the move. In the Northeast, the beginning of the long migratory path began in rocky New England, where the outmigration of farmers in the post-Revolutionary period was fueled by agricultural depression and sparse agricultural land due to the Appalachian Mountains.

Northern crop regions experienced the often-unforeseen consequence of the earlier market revolutions. Westward moving farmers extended eastern crop regions of corn and wheat causing competition between grain farmers settling on new and more fertile lands in western New York and much of the upper Midwest with those in New England. Many of these western farmers were grain growers whose harvests found markets in the Northeast where local grain prices were lower. As the center of grain growing shifted again across the upper Midwest and onto the tallgrass prairies, farmers in places such as western New York and upper Ohio could not compete and therefore adjusted their operations to become centers of dairy and butter production.

In 1825, the 360-mile-long Erie Canal was completed. It created a system of waterways that linked Buffalo, New York, and Albany, New York, to the Hudson River and New York City. The city quickly prospered more so from the highly settled productive upper Hudson Valley region and less from the western regions of the canal. The city's rapid growth made it the leading commercial hub on the Eastern Seaboard. The western sections of the canal became a major wheat-producing region linked by Lake Erie in 1850 to much of western New York, eastern Ohio, and Indiana. Three major canal networks leaving the lake at Erie, Pennsylvania, and Cleveland and Toledo, Ohio, formed a vast inland waterway system of both natural and manmade components. By 1830, the canal network spawned a string of urban areas between Albany and Buffalo in New York. Troy, Rochester, and Utica, New York, all had populations between eight and ten thousand. On the eve of the Civil

War in 1861, more than four thousand miles of canals fed the nation's navigable rivers and lakes, almost all of it in the North and Midwest. Travel from Chicago across Lake Michigan and Lake Erie to Buffalo moved goods and people along the Erie Canal linking Chicago to New York City. Authorized in 1817 by the State of New York, it paid off as the biggest public works project in the United States to that time.

Once the land south of Lake Erie was filled, newcomers settled in Upper Ohio and Indiana and then onto the tallgrass prairies of northern Illinois and southern Wisconsin. They arrived in remarkable numbers. During the 1850s alone 300,000 settlers from New England and New York arrived in the Upper Mississippi Valley and another 750,000 German immigrants made their way west from northeastern seaports to join them. These groups shared antislavery and pro-homesteader sentiments. They also settled at rising urban centers in the West including St. Louis and Chicago. These changes began during the age of animal power. Nevertheless, the components that created a market revolution were evident. The federal government opened new, cheap land in the West. Farmers from worn-out soils in the East moved there and produced bumper crops on rich, fertile land. Their crops traveled east over the canals and flooded eastern markets putting local farmers there out of business and on the road themselves.

The new upper Midwesterners arrived at a time when a combination of developments expanded and created a change in the direction of trade in the Old Northwest from the South to the Northeast. In part it depended on steam power. The construction of more than ten thousand miles of railroad tracks in the Upper Mississippi Valley during the 1850s, five of which crossed the Mississippi River, set in place the transportation infrastructure needed for the rapid settlement of the eastern tallgrass prairie. The newcomers brought along their agricultural traditions, which included a preference for grain crops such as wheat and corn. In 1850, before the newcomers and railroads transformed the area, about 40 percent of the corn and 10 percent of the wheat crop was sent south down the Mississippi River. By 1860, the South had been largely cut out of the trade, mainly due to railroad construction to Northeast markets, receiving only 20 percent of the corn and only about 2 percent of the wheat.

Between 1820 and 1845 a rapid series of developments also made growing, harvesting, preserving, and shipping agricultural produce easier and more economical. These included the process of canning, more efficient reapers and plows, factory-made farm machinery, and a grain drill that replaced hand broadcasting of seed. They significantly reduced the amount of time needed to produce wheat and corn and increased yields on the more fertile land in the tallgrass prairies. By the close of the 1850s, Indiana, Illinois, and Wisconsin were the leading wheat-growing states.

These developments were critical to meet food demands not only in a Europe beset by famine and crop failure, but in the North's growing urban food market. While the urban population of the United States did not reach 50 percent of the total until 1920 (51.2 percent) the combined urban populations of the Northeast (35.7 percent) and the Midwest (13.9 percent) almost reached that mark by 1860 (49.6 percent). This meant that farmers in the rapidly filling tallgrass prairies and the older grain and dairy regions east of the Mississippi and into eastern Iowa, lower Wisconsin, and Minnesota had growing urban markets to supply and railroads to reach them. This was true not only in the urban Northeast but within the developing urban Midwest. There, urban centers such as Cincinnati, Ohio, and St. Louis, Missouri, each with about 160,000 people, and Chicago with 112,000 people, were major consumers of food and export markets. Cincinnati specialized in pork products; St. Louis in agricultural produce of the Upper Mississippi and Ohio, notably wheat and tobacco; and Chicago in wheat and corn. The movement of people and food was made easier by the combined canal and railroad networks, which joined the steam-powered boat traffic on rivers and lakes.

Food was not an export product of the Lower South. Planters, farmers, and slaves poured into the new states of Alabama and Mississippi after the Creek defeat in 1815. Only about forty thousand people lived in this area on the eve of the War of 1812, but by 1840 there were half a million enslaved African Americans in the area. The domestic slave trade moved plantation labor from the upper and eastern parts of the South to its southwestern states. In fact, the wealthiest people in the South, planters who owned more than twenty slaves, especially in Alabama, Georgia, Mississippi, and Louisiana in the Lower South, often imported foodstuffs from the Midwest because they preferred to use costly slave labor to grow commercial nonfood cash crops such as cotton. Planters represented about 4 or 5 percent of the total white population, which was overwhelmingly noncommercial small farmers and livestock herders, whose markets were local and barter oriented and reached into the urban South in cities including Charleston and Savannah as well as the West Indies. Enough farm produce was grown within urban hinterlands to meet the needs of comparatively small southern cities.

The South constructed very few canals and certainly nothing in comparison with the Erie Canal, which along with the North's rivers and lakes created an effective regional transportation system even before the railroads arrived. The twelve-mile-long Brunswick-Altamaha Canal was planned to move cotton from central Georgia to the coastal port of Brunswick, but by the time of its completion railroad construction made it obsolete. Railroad construction, however, was often intended to link cotton-growing areas to nearby river or tidewater towns, and as a result, the South's railroads were often isolated lines that formed no real regional system. On the other hand, in the North the completion of the Erie Canal network and the Louisville and Portland Canal made it possible for cities in New England, New York, and mid-Atlantic cities such as Philadelphia and Baltimore to become the great markets of farm crops grown in the South and West and large food processing centers.

A major change in the pattern of crop transportation was the shift from a colonial east to west pattern to one that was oriented north to south. Almost all the major commercial crops produced in the nation's interior between 1790 and 1860, with the exception of wheat and corn, would eventually travel southward on waterways to the Gulf of Mexico.

There was no more important natural highway beyond the Appalachian Mountains than the Ohio River. Flowing for approximately nine hundred miles from Pittsburgh, Pennsylvania, to its confluence with the Mississippi River, the Ohio's watershed drained an area the size of France. French traveler Alexis de Tocqueville called it the "Beautiful River par excellence," one that "waters one of the most magnificent valleys in which man has ever lived." Important for westward migrating farmers, de Tocqueville wrote in the style of a western land promoter: "On both banks of the Ohio stretched undulating ground with soil continually offering the cultivator inexhaustible treasures; on both banks the air is equally healthy and the climate temperate; they both form the frontier of a vast state." Rivers entering the Ohio from the North drained much of the Midwest, already becoming the Corn and Wheat Belts.

And rivers entering the Ohio from the South drained the Upper South's hemp, tobacco, wheat, and cotton lands. Real estate speculators realized the agricultural value of this interior heartland. The major difference between the Ohio's northern and southern banks, wrote de Tocqueville, was that the river passed "between freedom and slavery."

From the time the land surveyor, soldier, and militia officer George Rogers Clark of Virginia established a small fort at the Falls of the Ohio in 1778, he, too, recognized that this part of extreme colonial western Virginia was an outlet for farm produce to the Gulf of Mexico. The fort was built on "Corn Island" as soon as its canebrake could be cleared away and planted in corn. Clark's men soon built a sailing ship seventy feet long that could be rowed like a galley. The ship was mounted with cannon to control the falls from excursions by the British and their Indian allies.

A generation before the steamboat era arrived on the Ohio in 1811, farmers turned the interior watersheds into freshwater coastlines lined by small landings, plantations, and farm market towns. All were trading places where corn, tobacco, wheat, hemp, whiskey, and flour were collected and sent downriver. For more than thirty years a seemingly endless menagerie of vessels drifted, rowed, and sailed farm produce down the Ohio and Mississippi Rivers to New Orleans. Interior river towns such as Louisville, Cincinnati, and Pittsburgh, major players in international commerce, boasted custom houses where imports were declared upriver rather than waiting at New Orleans.

During the late eighteenth century and first decade of the nineteenth, much interior shipbuilding took place on the upper Ohio River at places such as Pittsburgh and Marietta, Ohio. Because the Falls of the Ohio at Louisville created major obstacles for these New Orleans–bound watercraft, some shipbuilders moved their yards just below the falls at Shippingport, Kentucky, and New Albany, Indiana, for greater access to the Gulf of Mexico and the world's markets. During the first decade of the 1800s, more than ten thousand tons of coastwise and ocean-going ships were produced in the Ohio River Valley. In 1802, for example, one Pittsburgh shipbuilder launched two schooners, sending one loaded with flour to St. Thomas in the present-day Virgin Islands, and the other filled with Ohio River Valley farm produce to Bordeaux, France. The latter sailing ship then sailed to Philadelphia with French goods, which were in turn sent over land by wagon to Pittsburgh bringing the trade full circle. As one study concluded, this industry showed "how residents of the Ohio valley viewed themselves in relation to the global economic and the larger Atlantic World." All cities in the circle of trade played a role in market revolution.

The interior shipbuilding industry and the trade it carried, however, were severely diminished by the Embargo Act of 1807. The act imposed a complete embargo on foreign trade and was intended to prevent future seizure of American shipping by France and England during the Napoleonic Wars. Symbolically, it was a move to underline the new nation's right to free trade abroad with markets of choice. In reality, the fifteen-month embargo hurt domestic farming and manufacturing more than its intended foreign targets. The embargo, along with the arrival of steamboats, largely put an end to the production of coastal and transatlantic sail shipbuilding along the Ohio River, but not to the trade in farm and plantation produce.

STEAMBOATS

The trip of the steamboat *New Orleans* from Pittsburgh to Louisville in 1811 and soon thereafter onto New Orleans ushered in the steamboat age on the so-called western waters. This tremendous system of interior waterways drained an area approximately half the size of the continental United States. The Ohio, Mississippi, and Missouri were the major rivers, but there were many others feeding them. Steamboat traffic proceeded in fits and starts and did not become commonplace on most rivers until sometime during the 1820s. By 1817, steamboats were found on the St. Louis waterfront and a couple of years later heading up the Missouri River. The completion of the Louisville and Portland Canal in 1830 bypassed the major natural hazard to navigation at the Falls of the Ohio River and had an immediate impact on steamboat and flatboat traffic. The year following its opening, just over eight hundred steamboats, flatboats, keelboats, and rafts passed through its locks carrying cotton, flour, hides, and tobacco.

The movement of the farming frontier into the interior of the nation led to the decline of older eastern cities and the rise of new ones. Prior

FIGURE 3.1. Steamboats and steam technology were important factors during the market revolution. Postcard from the author's collection

to the Civil War, Pittsburgh, Cincinnati, Louisville, and St. Louis all increased their importance as centers of economic activity and agricultural trade. They became what historian Richard C. Wade described as the nation's urban frontier. Steamboats changed these city's waterfronts by demanding wide wharfs and accessible warehouses. Older, coastal trading centers such as Charleston and Savannah in the South and New Haven and Newport in New England declined. Cities that gained in importance during this period were primarily east of the Mississippi River and in the North Central states where corn and wheat were major crops. These urban centers prospered due to the processing and trade of grains and livestock.

It was to this extensive network of rivers that George Keats, brother of English poet John Keats, moved in 1819. He settled at Louisville, Kentucky, and began to invest in the types of economic pursuits that reflected the capitalist activities of the market revolution. Situated at the Falls of the Ohio, the city was a major export point for crops of the Tobacco and Hemp Belts. Keats soon invested in several partnerships involving steamboats and steam-powered flour and sawmills. He advertised his need to purchase wheat for his flour mill and was often prospecting for more

timber to keep his sawmill running in order to keep up with a building boom of the 1830s. Keats also advertised for ten enslaved African
American males between the ages of sixteen and twenty-five, which he
soon leased from a slave labor broker. All the components of the market
revolution were reflected in Keats's activities, including speculating in
timber land, flour manufacturing, steamboat transportation, and hiring
enslaved African Americans.

Later, steamboats reached the Cotton Belt at such places as Macon,
Georgia, not opened to traffic until 1827. In the Lower South, cotton created a demand for steamboats that gradually replaced the use of unpow-
ered barge-like "cotton boxes" steered with sweeps or tied to the side of
riverboats. Steamboats could carry hundreds of bales of cotton. They
supplied the demand for cotton to coastal commission merchants and
insurance companies that handled the transshipment of the expanding
crop abroad. Steamboats also supplied interior plantations and market
towns with trade goods and farm equipment. Like steamboats elsewhere,
southern steamboats were dependent on high water levels. The boats
were less reliable than railroads and the risk of damage to freight was
greater due to boiler explosions, fires, and collisions.

River steamers provided employment for riverbank farmers who supplied fuel at wood landings and for the masters of slaves, who hired slaves
out as deck hands and pilots. Farmers not only sent crops of cotton to
the coast, but also livestock, wool, and other in demand produce. At one
time, Apalachicola, Florida, was the third largest exporter of cotton on
the Gulf Coast. There enslaved workers loaded cotton and lumber onto
the sailing ships leaving the Gulf for England, Havana, New Orleans,
and New York. The Apalachicola River was fed by the Chattahoochee
and Flint Rivers. Their collective watersheds (the ACF Basin) cover
about twenty thousand square miles, a land area the size of Connecticut,
Massachusetts, and Rhode Island combined. It stretches from north of
Atlanta to Columbus, Georgia, and then 350 miles from Columbus to
Apalachicola. The northern portion of the watershed was part of Georgia's Upcountry, while most of the remainder belonged to the Cotton or
Plantation Belts of Georgia, Alabama, and north Florida.

This part of the Cotton Belt was brought into agricultural production about the same time as eastern Iowa's tallgrass prairie with the
same consequences: environmental damage due to deforestation and soil

erosion, violence to American Indians, and overproduction. Well before the Creeks, Cherokees, and Seminoles were removed from the watershed during the 1820s and1830s, hunters, trappers, livestock herders, and squatters invaded this Indian Territory. This was new country, one of the last corners of the Southeast brought into cotton production. It was a raw frontier of log cabins without improved roads, gradually cleared of forest and brought into the world of commercial agriculture. It was only about a generation old when the Civil War began.

Planting and farming families arrived from the lower Piedmont bringing slaves, livestock, and farming implements. After 1828, steamboats began service along the lower valley to places such as present-day Eufaula, Alabama, and Bainbridge, Georgia. Small farmers and herders on good cotton lands were displaced and moved west or east into the open range pine forests. Steamboats were the link to outside markets until railroads reached the lower valley during the 1850s.

Families participating in the cotton economy enjoyed, to varying degrees, some of the benefits that commercial corn and wheat farmers in the Upper Midwest and Erie Canal region. County seat towns with river landings shipped out cotton and brought in hardware, dry goods, and groceries. Farmers bought hoes, rakes, hames, traces, collars, wagons, and building supplies in river towns such as Albany and Eufaula. Farm women had more access to cloth, spun thread, jeans, and shirting as well as needles and pins, both to sew clothing for family and for slaves, thus relieving some of the burden of carding and spinning cotton and wool for domestic clothing production. Of course this depended on the extent of their involvement in the cash crop. Brooms, tubs, buckets, crockery, jeans, sheeting, oysters, sardines, wine, liquor, molasses, coffee, cigars, sugar, smoked and pickled fish, tubs, buckets, and crockery were all shipped upriver on small steamboats before the railroads arrived.

While these developments did free some prosperous plantation and farm women from the drudgery of household cloth production, plain folk and slaves were less fortunate. Homespun remained their cloth of necessity. And overall rural southern women did not have access to off-farm work of the type found in New England mill towns and northern canal boat town villages. For the most part, young women in southern farming regions like the ACF Basin remained within the farm's patriarchal structure with little chance for independence and economic freedom beyond the small numbers of teachers, boarding house owners, and seamstresses.

For the Wheat and Corn Belts, the direction of trade was originally toward St. Louis, which was projected to become the primary Midwestern city, not Chicago, especially during the steamboat era. But once railroads became significant to shipping on the plains, Chicago began to replace St. Louis as the key Midwestern trade center. Railroads linked Chicago to the West and to its trade on the Great Lakes to Buffalo and then through the Erie Canal. Canal boats, steamboats, keelboats, and family boats carried farmers west. Their supplies stacked on the top of rafts looked like a farmyard floating along with animals, plows, wagon wheels, seeds, and pigs. There were also several important highway gaps in the Appalachian Mountains that could be entered from the east: the Genesee Road at Albany, New York, Forbes Road in Pennsylvania linking Philadelphia and Pittsburgh, the National or Cumberland Road from Washington, and the Wilderness Road linking the Virginia Shenandoah Valley settlements to Kentucky and Tennessee. All these overland routes were crowded with moving farm families headed west.

By the mid-1830s, most grain and livestock moved east to cities in New England and New York, not south to St. Louis or New Orleans. Ten years later, Buffalo, New York, was shipping more wheat and wheaten flour than New Orleans. It was in that city that the first grain elevator appeared in 1842. Within a few years a grain elevator district handled the storage and transfer of grain from the West to the East, and floating elevators joined those on shore. Steam-powered grain elevators and large transfer towers began to transform the harbor's skyline. Shortly before the Civil War, Buffalo boasted that it was "the largest grain depot" in the world with more than twenty million bushels of wheat and flour transshipped in 1854. The Midwest was becoming the center of the nation's food and feed production.

An important part of this market revolution was influenced by the immigrants who settled the new lands opening west of Chicago. Much of the land north of Illinois and Iowa was, by climate and soil, ideally suited for hay and forage crops. Settled by Germans especially after the failed Revolutions of 1848, and Eastern European and Scandinavian immigrants, the new lands of lower Michigan, Wisconsin, northeastern Iowa, and Minnesota became the western half of a Dairy and Hay Belt whose eastern half was formed mainly by New England, New York, and Pennsylvania. This area became the center of milk, butter, and cheese production and despite the limited use of refrigerated cars, the colder winter months and block ice extended the season for shipping dairy products.

Cotton, the leading export crop, inspired the construction of the longest railroad in the nation at that time from Charleston, South Carolina, to Bamberg, South Carolina. By 1833, the Charleston and Hamburg railroad was completed for a total of 137 miles and used steam locomotives regularly. Due to its length it was the exception among early southern railroads in that most were much shorter and designed to link cotton-growing areas to coastal ports rather than develop an integrated rail system. Nevertheless, railroads, like canals, began to change the economic and social structures of rural neighborhoods.

By 1835, railroads were becoming increasingly important in other crop regions, especially in the Middle Atlantic states of New York, New Jersey, Pennsylvania, and Maryland. Most of the railroads were designed to move stone, coal, and cotton over relatively short distances. The Granite Railway in Massachusetts was chartered in 1826 and became a common carrier; it was followed shortly by the Mohawk and Hudson line in New York, which used steam locomotives. By comparison, northeastern and Midwestern states developed an extensive railroad system by 1860 with longer lines, so much so that almost every major city was served by one or more railroads. In the Corn Belt, a well-developed network of railroads and canals provided farmers with a convenient way of moving cows, hogs, and grain to eastern markets.

By 1848, the Illinois and Michigan Canal, linking Chicago to the Mississippi River via the Illinois River, was opened. The canal entered the Mississippi about twenty miles due north of St. Louis. And because of these routes, Chicago became a major immigrant city as well and a jumping off point for Swedish immigrants heading to the tallgrass prairie. During the 1850s, an extensive railroad network was constructed in southern Wisconsin and northwestern Illinois serving major portions of the eastern tallgrass prairie. At least five railroads crossed the Mississippi River above St. Louis before 1860. Most of the tracks ultimately converged on Chicago. With its access to Great Lakes shipping to Buffalo, New York, and the Erie Canal, Chicago and New York, not St. Louis and New Orleans, became the great grain trading centers of the nation. The Midwest became the nation's breadbasket.

THE GREAT AMERICAN DESERT

Unlike eastern farmlands that were reclaimed from forestland, there were some, but relatively few, trees on the tall- and shortgrass prairies. Combined, these two ecosystems were enormous, and spatially rivaled the United States east of the Mississippi River and formed landscapes of surprising biodiversity with more than 250 plant species. Largely treeless, the ecosystem of the Great American Desert, as it was coined by people east of the Mississippi River, was destroyed by the 1930s. Also diminished were the tallgrass prairie dogs, whose tunnels both aerated and provided moisture by capturing rainwater and the American bison, who grazed and fertilized the grasses. These grasslands would suffer the same fate as grasslands in the east.

Settlers encountered prairies before they reached the tallgrass prairie of northwestern Indiana and northern Illinois. John Filson, American author, Kentucky historian, and surveyor, created a map of 1784 Kentucky, which was widely circulated in both America and Europe, in his book *The Discovery, Settlement, and Present State of Kentucke*. It was engraved and printed in Philadelphia and translated into both French and German editions. The book was intended to promote the migration of tidewater and European farmers to what was then trans-Appalachian Virginia. The map noted extensive tracts of land north of the Green River, called the "barrens" of Kentucky, which was covered with excellent grasses and herbage. This tallgrass plain was settled between 1790 and 1820 and soon brought into cultivation. About fifteen years later, the tallgrass prairies and oak openings of Ohio were settled by farmers as well.

Settlers moving onto the prairies beyond these early encounters were slowed by the tallgrass ranges of northwestern Indiana and northern Illinois. The major agricultural problem facing farmers on the prairie was the tallgrass. Thick, deep, and wet, tallgrass was difficult to cut and turn with traditional plows. An estimated 60 percent of the "vegetable biomass of the plants" is underground. It was this "underground prairie" that helped make the prairie fire tolerant. Like other grazing ranges, such as the southern longleaf pine forest, fires both natural and man-made reduced invasive plant species and stimulated spring grass growth.

Early settlement of the tallgrass prairie of northwestern Illinois provides another example of how a combination of developments created rapid change in the market. One man who was to play an important part of this New England-to-tallgrass prairie story is John Deere. A bankrupt blacksmith, Deere moved from Vermont and settled at Grand Detour, Illinois, by the mid-1830s. He soon understood that the plows used to turn the rocky and loose soil of New England did not work well on the thicker and wetter soils of the prairie, where farmers had to interrupt their plowing to clean mold boards. His self-cleaning plow was made of steel and first sold in 1838. News of his invention spread by word of mouth around Grand Detour and beyond. Three years later he made seventy-five plows and the busting of the prairie was underway. Deere's plow was joined by other inventions including water-pumping windmills, harrows and mechanical reapers, and new railroad lines, which ultimately converted almost all grassland to farmland.

In Iowa and Minnesota there was a growing demand for new farmland as Illinois, Indiana, and Missouri became more crowded. Lands west of the Mississippi River and north of Missouri were reserved for the Sauk and Fox Indians who were removed from Iowa's tallgrass prairie lands. The first lands were opened to settlers in 1833 following the Black Hawk War. The land rush that followed brought settlers from the Midwest and Upper South. The lucky ones got there first and settled the river bottoms. It wasn't long before Iowa's reputation as "tall corn country" reached even farther eastward, into New York and New England.

Until the 1840s, good public farmland in the West sold at auction with a starting price of $1.25 per acre with a maximum of eighty acres. A farming family could get into the business with about one hundred dollars for land and approximately the same for equipment and supplies. It was little wonder that the settlement line in territories such as Iowa moved daily across the landscape as settlers squatted on land they intended to purchase once a land office was set up, which in Iowa did not happen until 1838. In 1836, there were already ten thousand settlers. To protect their investments, farmers staked out the boundaries of their property and then joined with neighboring farmers to form extralegal claim associations to protect the land they took from Indians from out-side speculators and other land-grabbing newcomers. Two years after the land office opened, just over forty thousand people lived in Iowa and the original purchase from the Black Hawks was settled by farmers.

This tract of land was about forty miles wide and immediately west of the Mississippi River. It was ceded to the United States after defeat-ing the Indians in the four-month-long Black Hawk War, which pit-ted the American Indian farmers against Euro-American farmers, each struggling to control agricultural land. The war broke out in 1832 when Chief Black Hawk crossed from Iowa Territory back into Illinois to reclaim land the Sauk, Meskwaki, and Ho-Chunk peoples believed had been wrongly ceded to the United States in 1804. This large, fertile tract was situated between the Illinois and Mississippi Rivers. Much of it was located along the Rock River and had been farmed by Indians for gen-erations. In 1804, a small group of Indians sold the land without tribal council approval and without a clear understanding of the actual size of the land purchased. When Black Hawk and Indian men, women, and children returned to the river valley to reclaim it, they found their settle-ment occupied by lead miners. They attacked, attempting to reclaim their town. As a result, some of the miners were killed. US officials raised a militia consisting of local settlers who subsequently opened fire on a del-egation of American Indians. In desperation, the Indians fled and after several more skirmishes were blocked from crossing the Mississippi at the Massacre of Bad Axe. More than 150 men, women, and children were killed. In 1832, in a treaty called the Black Hawk Purchase, the Indians sold six million acres of land for $640,000. It opened for settlement in 1833 and was followed by two more purchases. It did not take long for the tallgrass prairie lands to fill up with farming families. By 1840, as much as one-quarter of Iowa's prairie, the center of the tallgrass range, was settled. Ten years later, half had been plowed under, but the more remote tracts located miles from the waterways remained empty.

The fate of the Saux and other tallgrass tribes was similar to the Creeks and other farming nations that stood in the way of white farmer expansion in the West. To most Europeans, the value of land was mea-sured by the amount of labor done to improve it and increase its price. To white settlers, uncultivated land was wasted land. Dark forests and wild lands were signs of sloth and evil. Science and civilization were expected to conquer and subdue nature. Thomas Jefferson saw the sturdy yeoman farmer as the nation's tool to bring natural resources into good use to serve the commonwealth.

AGRICULTURAL EXPORTS

Agricultural products were the nation's major exports prior to the Civil War. By 1820, cotton had replaced tobacco as the nation's most important export crop and accounted for almost 40 percent of the value of all exports. By the late 1830s, with the westward expansion of the Cotton Belt into the Lower South, that percentage grew to slightly more than 60 percent. Little wonder that southern planters boasted about the power of "King Cotton" at home and abroad.

Improvements in internal transportation such as steamboats and the Erie Canal allowed the Grain Belt to play a predominant export role. Wheat and flour were important but were relatively minor crops that made up about 10 percent of all exports, followed by pork. The domination of cotton and food crops is all the more impressive considering that American manufacturing made up only around 10 percent of all exports during the 1820s. The nation's agriculturalists—free and slave—produced three-quarters of the exports by the end of the 1850s. England was the nation's leading export destination. About one-quarter of its imports arrived from the United States alone, while in turn England supplied about 40 percent of American imports. France was an increasingly important export destination as the antebellum period ended.

After a century of stagnation, the population began to grow throughout Western Europe about the mid-eighteenth century. "Growth" became the key word. A higher standard of living, more food, a decline in mortality, and rise in industrial production, especially in England, were all causes for optimism. Many people were moving from low-productivity agriculture to higher-productivity industrial work and services. Still, food production and caloric intake did not keep up with industrial output. Basically, food items were still scarce because the population that had moved off the land could no longer fall back on an even small family landholding. The urban population was growing faster than the rural population and there were fewer farmers to produce key crops such as potatoes. Prior to 1845, potatoes were key. Rich in vitamin C, potatoes grew easily on small patches of infertile soil and were a replacement for grain. If a potato crop failed hunger was sure to follow.

The potato blight had already appeared in the United States in 1843, but it was first noticed in Europe in June 1845 in Belgium. Over the next weeks it spread through the Netherlands, to the coastlines of France and England, and after mid-September to Ireland. There was a "subsistence crisis" that threatened the survival many Europeans.

Just as the North's crop regions expanded westward and canal and railroad systems were growing to make their exports easier, the so-called Hungry Forties in Europe created international agricultural markets for the region's farmers. The Hungry Forties, along with the Irish Potato Famine, hurt not only potato but wheat and rye harvests and led to political unrest. The Irish Potato Famine killed about one million people. England delayed the crisis by repealing the corn laws that had limited the importation of corn into Great Britain to protect its own farmers. The repeal opened the door for corn exports to Great Britain from America and helped relieve what was viewed as a European subsistence crisis during the years 1845 to 1850.

THE FARMER'S PLACE IN SOCIETY

Throughout the Early Republic era farmers as a group helped transform the nation's landscape. They fought in militias and armies that displaced American Indians of their land, defeated the British during the American Revolution and the War of 1812 to win and preserve independence, and defeated the Mexican army during the Mexican-American War. When the market revolution began, farmers represented about 90 percent of the nation's population. Historians' views differ on whether or not the transformation to a more integrated and capitalistic system eroded farmer independence and undermined their political and economic power. What they do agree on is that with each census, the farmer's role as a majority of the population slipped and by 1850 it had dropped from 90 percent to 64 percent.

The American Revolution was hardly over when the Whiskey Rebellion (1791–1794) demonstrated that the farmers' new-found status as winners of the Revolutionary War was not beyond challenge by the central government. The new nation amassed millions of dollars in wartime debt, which Alexander Hamilton, the country's first secretary of the treasury, sought with congressional approval to recover by imposing a tax on distilled liquors. Whiskey was the favorite, especially in the backcountry where corn was a major crop and farmer-distillers sent some of their crop to market in whiskey barrels. These farmers thought the tax was unjust and protested that it was taxation without representation. Many of them were Revolutionary War veterans from western Pennsylvania and present-day Kentucky. They formed an active resistance force and harried and threatened revenue collectors. President George Washington led US militia against the whiskey tax protestors who disbanded without violence. The whiskey tax and its consequences reflected the growing control of the federal government over its citizens' lives.

But farmers as individuals had very little power in the marketplace. A single farmer could dislike the market price offered for his crop and keep it off the market, but acting alone he only hurt himself and his household. Furthermore, to the extent that he had purchased land and farm implements on credit, his ability to follow through was limited by his creditors. Migration, market demand, and the transportation revolution gobbled up fresh land at amazing rates and increased farmer debt. It took about fifty years for the post–Revolutionary War tide of farmers to settle the lands between the Appalachian Mountains to the Mississippi River. By 1850, the settlement line was beyond the Mississippi.

The impact of internal improvements on the market revolution and home manufacturing on farmers' lives should not be underestimated. The market revolution not only changed the speed and direction of trade, it also changed the family social structure. Wherever canals, railroads, and steamboats went the pace of life sped up and consumption of non-farm goods increased. Prior to canals and railroads, farming families in landlocked counties produced many of their own household goods. Clothing, for example, was often produced at home in the form of homespun cloth. Each household had wool cards, spinning wheels, and looms to produce thread and cloth much as the ethnic trade operated on a household level in Europe. As much as two-thirds of the textiles were made in homes during the early nineteenth century. Water-powered mills also ran rural wood and cotton carding operations to support production.

The arrival of the Erie Canal began to change the landscape of western New York during the 1820s and 1830s and the role of cottage industries. Cheap imported cloth arrived on boats at canal towns and soon appeared on the shelves of nearby country stores. These products were manufactured in New England where over a ten-year period ending in 1815 almost one hundred textile mills were established. Farm laborers who lost work in New England by competition with Midwestern grain growers provided much of the workforce. Farm wives and daughters filled most of the factory jobs, but family members of all ages and both sexes felt the impact. Women in New England were entering the wage rather than subsistence economy for the first time and the rural landscape was diversifying. As mill towns expanded, more former farm workers lived in urban areas. By 1850, an estimated 50 to 55 percent of the population of Massachusetts and Rhode Island were living in urban areas such as Lowell, Massachusetts.

Some female mill workers during the 1790s and early 1800s lived at home and walked to nearby mills situated at fall line river towns. Others lived in boarding houses or company housing. Women wage workers became increasingly autonomous and living beyond the confines of their parents' home became more common. Their example led others to become seamstresses, laundresses, and domestics living in the households of others. Studies conducted on New England and the Midwest concluded that these former farm women exercised greater control over their lives and bodies and fertility rates dropped among white women by almost 50 percent during the nineteenth century, most of it before 1880.

Canals and railroads made women's work and their role in consumer society more important than before by externalizing the value of their labor into the market and beyond the control of their fathers. Home manufacturers supplied the family with goods and any surplus could be bartered or traded within the community. But women could not avoid the drudgery of spinning and weaving cloth for the family. Over time, women's roles in the wage labor society increased, especially during and after the market revolution, as members of farm households accessed more work outside the home and the household economy moved from subsistence and barter to a cash economy.

Women in some areas took control of dairy markets in urban areas in the first half of the 1800s. Their incomes allowed them to avoid the traditional jobs they had performed by buying cloth, for example, instead of making it. The same could be said for women who lived along canals, railroads, and steamboat landings where travelers needed food and drink. Gradually, parts of the subsistence household became commercialized and cashbased.

Life in company towns and boarding houses began to give women more freedom and control over their lives. Women working at textile mills found room and food at boarding houses or took a room with a private family. Since these places required a great deal of labor to prepare meals, clean rooms, and do laundry they were also places of employment for women as domestics. For women wage earners, such housing was yet another step into the commercial world. Rather than depending on family to house them, women paid for it out of their earnings. This arrangement, which was common in urban areas, textile mill towns, and in communities where academies required housing for women teachers, was directly at odds with the nineteenth-century ideal of the family home as a shelter from the crude and vulgar commercial and industrial world.

As a result of the market revolution, the farmer's role in American society changed. True, farmers were still producers of crops consumed locally, nationally, and, in the case of cash crops such as cotton, grain, and tobacco, far beyond the nation's borders. Technology had allowed the ever-growing number of farmers to bring new and different landscapes into agricultural production. Forests and grasslands had been cleared and filled with westward moving native-born farmers and millions of new immigrants. During the 1840s, about 1.7 million immigrants arrived in the United States, including hundreds of thousands of Irish seeking refuge from the Potato Famine. Although the vast majority of immigrants did not become farmers, many did become workers on the nation's transportation infrastructure building railroads and working in shipyards and docks in northeastern cities such as Boston and New York. However, immigrants from northwestern Europe, particularly Germans and Scandinavians, had enough money to reach the Upper Midwest, where they found familiar farming landscapes.

During the 1850s, almost three million immigrants from Ireland, Germany, and the Scandinavian countries arrived in the United States. More important for the future of the nation, almost 90 percent of the foreign-born population by 1850 settled in the northeastern and North Central states while only about 11 percent of the foreign-born population lived in the South. Their migration to the interior of the North Central region was made easier by approximately four thousand miles of canals and thousands of miles of railroads that served what would be the nation's economic core region for the rest of the century. By 1860, the population of the United States had increased by about 35 percent, with most immigrants arriving from Western Europe. The food production, industrial, and population center of the nation was the North, a region that benefitted the most from the expansion of food crops and the control and consolidation of the nation's growing transportation and communication systems.

4

Civil War and Reconstructions

At the beginning of the Civil War rural regions of the eastern United States, such as the Appalachian Mountains and the southern Coastal Plains, were often still on the fringes of the market revolution and industrialization. Underserved by railroads as well as rapid means of communication, these stunted regions had a difficult time recovering from the war. In the South, one out of three soldiers did not return from the war, leaving families with farm labor shortages. A new labor system brought millions of both freed African Americans and landless white farmers into semi-free relationships controlled by feudal-like landlords. They allowed their agricultural peons to work their land in exchange for cash or part of their crop. Those who remained on the edges of commercial agriculture and escaped the farm consolidation that followed the new crop lien system knew their days were numbered. When they heard the whistle of a steam locomotive it often belonged to a timber company moving into woodland valleys to carry away the forest and with it the food, shelter, fuel, fodder, and water that supported their households. With the timber gone, the land was plowed under, the grazing range destroyed, and commercial crops planted. Farming families could fall in line and plant cotton or move away.

The Civil War was largely fought by farmers on rural landscapes. One of the earliest civilian casualties was invalid and widow Judith Carter Henry. She died June 1861 in her house rather than leave it as the First Battle of Manassas raged around her small farm. The South's commercial agricultural system based on slavery both caused secession and lost the war. Slavery, which was based on racism and fear, was an extreme liability in times of war, and the Confederate government was loath to arm enslaved African Americans until the war was almost over. The region's major commercial crops—cotton, hemp, tobacco, and sugarcane—were also liabilities. They could not be eaten. Almost four million enslaved African Americans freed up an estimated nine hundred thousand white southerners to fight against the Union Army, nearly 80 percent of the South's military-aged males.

Despite these obvious shortcomings most southerners believed that their agricultural system was a strength. By 1840, cotton exports were of greater value than all other export crops combined. Southerners believed cotton would prove a powerful weapon to defeat any enemy and coerce foreign nations into their corner. They were wrong. The disintegration of the South's wartime agricultural production pulled down its economic, political, social, and military structure. Ultimately, southerners in the lowest of places, its small farming counties and rural neighborhoods, decided where the dwindling food would go: to the homes of its women, children, and old folk and not to Confederate forces unable to protect them from the invading enemy. In the end, the South was overwhelmed by the North's crop regions that had benefitted most from the market revolution in almost every measurable category: food production, transportation systems, industrial might, population growth, immigration, and wealth. The North had 3.5 million men of military age in 1860. Its transportation and communication networks were modern and consolidated and its armies well-armed, clothed, and fed. The wonder is that the South lasted as long as it did.

There were signs a southern defeat could be the result. During the 1850s, as farmers fought a small-scale rehearsal for civil war on the corn fields of "bleeding Kansas" over whether free or enslaved labor prevailed, one southerner, Hinton Rowan Helper, wrote the book *The Impending Crisis of the South* in 1857. His audience was not the planter elite that controlled the South's economy, society, and polity but rather its "nonslaveholders," the white yeomen who made up the overwhelming majority of its farmers who owned no slaves. Helper identified with these plain folk "by interest, by feeling, by position."

Helper used the 1850 US Census returns to compare economic production in almost every important economic category: agriculture, commerce, manufacturing, population size, railroad mileage, and urbanization. Helper concluded that the South lagged far behind the North in making its way through the market revolution. His explanation for this poor showing was explained in one word: slavery. Slaveholders, and especially planters, found this difficult to believe. Slavery made the expansion of the Cotton Belt from the Atlantic to East Texas possible. Slave labor was necessary to clear the forests for large plantation. Planter inputs in labor, land, and supplies were costly but the rewards could be great, at least until the soil wore out and they moved on to repeat this environmentally destructive process again. But in the planters' eyes this was necessary to meet the demand for cotton during the Industrial Revolution, first in England and then in New England.

Cotton made planters so much money that they were loath to put their slaves to work growing any other crop. Some were so "carried away" by cotton they imported food from the Midwest that they could have easily grown themselves. As a result, Midwestern corn and hog farmers sold planters food for enslaved African Americans and made money by doing so. British and northeastern textile manufacturers bought cotton and made money producing cloth. Southerners left out of this trade were the plain folk Hinton Rowan Helper identified with by interest, feeling, and social status. These plain folk grew their own food and made most of their own clothing and occasionally sold a small crop surplus to local planters and they accounted for 75 to 80 percent of southern families.

At the opposite end of the Cotton Belt's western frontier was Charleston, South Carolina. Today, charming, historic, and romantic, it was the nation's major slave importing center, the so-called "Ellis Island" of American slavery. Ship after ship brought human cargoes across the Atlantic in their cramped and filthy hulls. The enslaved Africans who survived the voyage faced a violent lifetime of abuse, brutality, oppression, and racism. They were auctioned from slave marts like the one at Chalmers Street, which is today the Old Slave Mart Museum. Theirs were lives of stolen opportunities.

The major goal of the war from the southern point of view was to preserve and expand slavery, which Confederate Vice President Alexander Stephens called the "cornerstone" of the Confederacy. In the North, preserving the Union was the initial goal but President Lincoln's 1863 Emancipation Proclamation added the destruction of slavery as a precondition for ending the war and unconditional surrender as its term. The North's victory, with its Republican Party free soil and free labor ideology, meant that the Midwestern white farming traditions would continue for the foreseeable future, and that farmers there would see little competition from black farmers. Moreover, racism in some Midwestern communities increased during the Civil War as civilians on the home front, who supported a war to restore the Union, disagreed with the Lincoln administration's decision to add emancipation as a war goal. Northern free persons of color faced racial slurs and loss of life and property. The great wheat and corn boon of the shortgrass prairies would not benefit blacks very much. One agricultural consequence of the Civil War was the creation of one of the largest white majority regions in the United States in the rural Midwest and North Central states.

The Upper South was transformed into a collection of battlefields where both Union and Confederate armies fought and fed themselves. The Confederacy lost important food crop areas early in the war. Early military defeats in the Upper South took away some of its most important grain-producing areas leaving a cotton-heavy region behind their lines. The government's tax in-kind program and its impressment of crops were only two of the food shortage issues faced in Richmond. At home, livestock rustling was widespread. Many planters refused government directives to curtail cotton planting in favor of grain production. Patriots who did grow corn and sold it to poor folk at reduced government rates sometimes found their buyers had only turned around and sold it on the black market at a higher price. The region's small farmers produced enough grain and livestock to feed their families when they farmed at full manpower levels, but when the Confederate army thinned the ranks of producers to serve on the front lines it was only a matter of time before the agricultural system collapsed. The North's belief that their agricultural world was more productive and better able to feed both its army and the home front in the long run proved a more powerful ally than "King Cotton" was to the South.

The consequences of farm implement improvements in the North, especially mechanical reapers, grain drills, and mowing machines, meant the Midwest needed less agricultural labor to grow grain, which had allowed numerically more northern and Midwestern men to enter the army without diminishing food supplies.

Various estimates put the number of men who died during the war between 620,000 and 750,000 soldiers or more, with as many as 40,000 of those deaths being African American soldiers. As many as six out of ten were farmers and more in the South, where a higher percentage of military-aged males (75 to 80 percent) served in the war than in the North (about 50 percent). Almost seven out of ten of those who came home to the South had been farmers, compared to about one-half of all Union soldiers. As many as fifty thousand civilians, including women, children, and older men left at home to tend farms, died as a result of the war. Unfortunately, it was their misfortune, and that of four million newly freed people, to enter a postwar era of agricultural depression that lasted for the remainder of the nineteenth century in both the United States and the Western world. Nowhere was it a good time to be a small-scale agricultural producer. The expanding postwar railroad system gave the North greater control over the economy and consolidated capitalism's grip on the nation with its ups and downs in the marketplace. Crop regions of the North largely escaped occupation by troops and the destruction that came with them. The Corn, Wheat, and Dairy Belts were poised to continue expansion on the plains and in the Upper Midwest.

In the South, the home was reconstructed by the war. There were empty chairs at the kitchen table of many homes where soldiers did not return. Roads, bridges, and public buildings were gone or in disrepair. Fences and fields were greatly neglected, and farm implements were broken, worn out, or missing. A devastating outbreak of hog cholera killed much of a favored source of meat in the region. With so many men in the army, farm women had held the home front together. They formed soldier's aid societies, knitted socks, and sewed together homespun uniforms. They petitioned the governor to keep blacksmiths and millers at home when they were threatened by conscription. Women looked to put their family and home back together.

At the end of the war, approximately four million enslaved African Americans were freed. The South's roads were filled with freed blacks searching for family members separated by the domestic slave trade and the expansion of the Cotton Belt. Food was in short supply. Poor black slaves and poor whites received some rations as temporary aid from the Freedmen's Bureau (1865–1872) in the form foodstuffs. The Thirteenth,

Fourteenth, and Fifteenth Amendments to the US Constitution legally
freed blacks and extended them the right to vote as well as citizenship.
In order to prevent black farm workers from receiving the full rights of
citizenship, southern states passed harsh laws called Black Codes, which
effectively returned freed people to an enslaved-like status. They had
no rights in the courts and their freedom of movement was restricted by
labor contracts. These contracts were the result of black farmer resistance
to the continuation of plantation labor routines that used gang labor and
sent all field workers out together. Plantations and large farms were
divided into plots farmed by individuals and families. The contracts
were enforced by state laws and were good for one year. White landlords
furnished farm laborers with land and housing in exchange for a share of
their cotton crop.

RECONSTRUCTIONS

Following the Civil War sweeping social, economic, and environmental changes followed that were not confined to the American South and
did not end in 1877. Reconstruction carried with it an enormous amount
environmental destruction nationwide as the Industrial Revolution and
exploitation of natural resources in all regions of the nation continued
with no federal government intervention. Between 1865 and 1920, entire
landscapes were reordered to fit the needs of industry and agriculture.
These changes were apparent to travelers along the ever-growing number of railroad lines in the South and West where farming towns, granaries, and crop processing mills rose along their tracks. With the themes of
consolidation and control in mind, this chapter examines two areas of the
South, the Coastal Plains and southern Appalachia, together forming the
less developed parts of thirteen states, and the Great Plains.

Both the Appalachian and Coastal Plains formed major cattle grazing
ranges that were still viable after the Civil War. The Appalachian region
stretched from New York to northern Georgia and Alabama while the
Coastal Plains extended from the Carolinas to eastern Texas. Taken
together, these regions formed large pockets of grasslands within the
Cotton, Dairy, Tobacco, and Hemp Belts, and sent cattle, hogs, sheep,
wool, and hides to urban and coastal markets. As late as 1880, these

important eastern ranges had not been transformed by rural industrialization or commercial crop monocultures, but like the shortgrass prairies of the Great Plains, were beginning to feel the pressure.

THE CROP LIEN SYSTEM

From a labor standpoint, in 1860 the South was much more a farming region with about 80 percent of its workforce in agriculture as compared to the North's 40 percent. But large areas of the South clearly did not belong to any crop region, including the southern Coastal Plains and the Appalachian Mountains. Both were remote, sparsely populated, and largely covered by forests, but the Coastal Plains were gently rolling to flat while the Appalachians were rugged and mountainous. Once railroad construction penetrated both regions and began to break down their isolation, the self-sufficient farming and livestock herding economies declined. Deforestation in both areas destroyed open range resources and access to the keys to subsistence households—food, fodder, fuel, and clean water. Consolidation of smaller "safety first" farms, first as timber company holdings and next as larger agricultural units, took away control of farming operations from yeomen hands and placed them in the hands of corporate officers and neoplantation managers.

On the Coastal Plains the crop lien system, where the landlords and merchants provided farmland and provisions to landless farmers in exchange for a lien on their cotton crop, began taking control during the late nineteenth century as timber cutting increased and cleared land was turned to agricultural purposes. Railroads made it possible to ship commercial fertilizers such as Peruvian guano into the region. Fertilized loams became the new cotton lands of the Deep South. After 1865, cotton production increased as the crop expanded into both the Upcountry and the Coastal Plains. Both railroads and timber companies advertised these agricultural advantages widely in newspapers and pamphlets. Down on their luck Piedmont cotton farmers left behind their worn-out red clay lands and headed for the piney woods. They were joined by cotton planters ready to start over again in the new counties of the Coastal Plains as well as neoplanters who entered the cotton world for the first time. In both cases the planters needed farm laborers. Their preferred choice was

African Americans who had an extremely low rate of land ownership, which the planters were determined to keep that way.

The Coastal Plains was and still is a predominantly white, sparsely settled region. But the migration of both white and black newcomers determined to expand the Cotton Belt after the 1880s was a lethal combination. Kept up by fear, poverty, racism, and violence a postwar agricultural dystopia arose in pine lands that had been overwhelmingly white and self-sufficient before the Civil War. These areas became centers of rural segregation enforced by violence and lynching and were maintained by white economic, political, and social control.

About four miles east of Eastman, Georgia, Gum Swamp divided the rural farming lands of Dodge and Laurens Counties. Before the Civil War, this section was mostly covered with pine trees and wiregrass, a poor farming area of yeomen farmers and livestock herders much like those found on the southern Coastal Plains stretching from the Carolinas to East Texas. This was not a part of the prewar cotton South.

In 1878, a traveler wrote about this part of Georgia as if it had not been reconstructed at all as far as agriculture was concerned. After crossing

FIGURE 4.1. Farm families were often on the move during the agriculturally depressed late nineteenth century. The Filson Historical Society, Louisville, KY | Edward and Josephine Kemp Lantern Slide Collection (012PC27A.082)

Gum Swamp and riding east he saw fewer farms and farmhouses. The swamp, with its hardwood wetlands, formed a boundary between East-man, already becoming a cotton market town, and the more distant pine forest he encountered with few farms, fewer houses, and mere huts. This area was still a part of the vast open range formed by the longleaf pine forest. The tiny windowless log hut he inspected from the safety of this horse had a quilt for a door. This area and others like it became over the next thirty years a part of the New South's expanding cotton empire and one of the most lynch-prone neighborhoods in the South.

The changing agricultural landscape meant people's attitudes changed toward cash crops, free black farm labor, and declining forest resources as deforestation pushed back the tree line. Traditional thoughts about the main purpose of farm toil being to feed their families first and sell or trade any surplus farm produce second had to be adjusted to the realities of the crop lien system.

By comparison, the crop lien system was firmly entrenched in the Old South's cotton-producing areas on the Piedmont and Upcountry regions of the Carolinas, Georgia, Alabama, Mississippi, and East Texas. In counties in these areas upward of one-third of the farms were worked by sharecroppers. The Coastal Plains of the South Atlantic and Gulf Coast states were still covered in longleaf pine forests and largely free of share-cropping areas. Over the next thirty years the landscape changed dra-matically. This was the beginning of the end of the open range system in the Coastal Plains South.

Most of these newcomers, white or black, farmer or farm laborer, were born after the Civil War. The few white farming families who lived along Gum Swamp before the Civil War were joined by black house-holds, sometimes in groups of two or three who found work on a land-lord's cotton farm. As the lumber and naval stores industries declined, their workers moved into the cotton and crop lien system. White farm-ing families, consisting of a husband and wife in their thirties and forties often with three to seven children, were wary of black newcomers even if they were newcomers themselves. There were multiple cases of lynch-ings in the Gum Swamp neighborhood between 1900 and 1915, most resulting from alleged black male threats to white women. None of these cases ever made it to court or beyond the banks of Gum Swamp before the accused were lynched. Gum Swamp became the boundary line of a newly settled area that imposed its white supremacy on all its inhabitants. But the desire to control farm tenants and sharecroppers did not stop with African American men.

In 1912, tenant farmer Ella Dean-Doston was murdered in Laurens County, Georgia, along with her adult son. Both were shot at their home by a neighboring tenant farmer named Steve Tompkins, whose large family lived a short distance away. Both Dean-Dotson and Tompkins were landless tenant farmers; Steve Tompkins employed the Dean-Doston family to work on his farm. Ellen was about forty years old, twice widowed, and four of her five children were farm workers. Ellen decided to tenant farm elsewhere and Tompkins denied. In order to stop her, he broke into her house and started shooting. The landless widow had little protection although her son tried to defend them. Neighbors in the community gossiped that the widow and her neighbor were lovers and that her attempted move to another location was an effort to end the relationship. Others argued that the widow's son was engaged to Tompkins's daughter, which Tompkins objected. Tompkins escaped a sentence of hanging due to a technicality that the grand jury presenting the indictment and the murder trial jury both consisted of the same white men.

Along the county line between Dodge and Laurens, no one seemed safe in the struggle over farmland and labor. In August 1919, another violent outbreak near Cadwell, Georgia, resulted in the murder of a black lay preacher named Eli Cooper by a mob of white men. His body was left in a black church at A. P. Pettway's plantation and both body and church were burned. The white community at Cadwell contacted the governor and offered a reward of $500 for information leading to the conviction of those responsible. Local newspapers reported that Cooper's offense was an attempt to incite blacks to rise up against white oppression in the area along the Dodge and Laurens border. By voicing his objection to years of injustice, Cooper was accused of "incendiarism."

According to the *Atlanta Constitution,* his murder was one of a number of violent acts against the local black community. The mayor and city council at Eastman, Georgia, passed a resolution condemning "the burning of negro churches, school houses, and lodges, and in the greater crime of the murder" as did citizens in Laurens County to assist law enforcement officials in "bringing the guilty culprits to justice." No one was ever convicted of the murder of Eli Cooper. The extent of the violence and arson aimed at the African American community suggests that the collective white vigilante action used to intimidate blacks was intended to enforce rural segregation by burning black cultural institutions, killing their leaders, and forcing blacks to leave the area.

The intimidation of farm laborers was a hallmark of the South's crop lien system, itself a creature of control and consolidation. In 1902, Pat Hill of Roanoke, Alabama, testified at a peonage hearing that he was seeking work for one dollar a day and learned that he must pay two dollars a week out of his wages for board. He and other farm workers decided to leave the farm. Hill testified that he was picked up and arrested for leaving the service of his landlord. He stated he was worked like a "convict" and whipped twice. The story was common among farm workers. A combination of businessmen, sheriffs and policemen, and county court judges created a system to keep a steady flow of cheap convict-like labor heading to cotton farms and other places of business needing labor. Ellen Dean-Dotson no doubt felt trapped with no way to escape. The roads that led from such places became the scenes of abuse, capture, violence, and murder as the struggle for survival continued.

For one of the first times in American history, free white farmers, too, as opposed to enslaved African Americans and white indentured servants, had crop choices dictated to them by a contract fixing acres, cotton production, crop sharing, and tenant labor responsibilities. The stripping away of choice reduced their sense of freedom and food security as woodlands and range disappeared or were banned from trespassing. If one refused or broke the contract, dismissal from the landlord's estate was almost certain. These developments made them all the more dependent on landlords and furnishing merchants who distributed Midwestern meal, flour, and hog meat on credit. Rather than feeding themselves from garden crops, they were reduced to eating from cans.

By 1910, Georgia's agricultural ladder, as well as the South as a whole—with landless wage workers of both races and genders at the bottom, tenants in the middle, and farm owners at the top—was filled with such people. However, the ladder was fixed by race. About 41 percent of white farmers owned their land and almost 27 percent were cash or share tenants. About one-third of white farmers were at the bottom of the ladder where they worked as sharecroppers and wage workers. On the other hand, almost two-thirds (64.5 percent) of African

American farmers were sharecroppers and wage workers with wage hands accounting for about 50 percent of all black farmers. Only about 7 percent of all African American farmers in Georgia were landowners. Clearly, the labor system kept most of the state's black farm workers in a state of uncertainty and poverty as wage workers and croppers. White farmers were unquestionably better off as a whole as landowners than blacks (41 percent compared to 7 percent) and fewer farmers at the bottom of the agricultural ladder (32.5 percent of white farmers compared to 64.5 percent blacks), but there was plenty of abuse and desperation to go around.

APPALACHIA

According to historian Ronald Eller, time and geography set the Appalachian South apart from the rest of the "American experience." The same could be said for the Coastal Plains South, but once the forest was gone and its open ranges were overrun with cotton farms, the Wiregrass region lost its physical identity and disappeared. During the post–Civil War era both regions came to be seen as backward and isolated, possessing a sense of "otherness" that Eller used to describe the mountains. In 1880, the crop lien system still had a minimal impact in the Mountain South, where the traditional social structure persisted: farmers owned their land, commercial agriculture was minimal, family labor was the norm, and there was little interest or demand in technology or capital. In such rural areas, some livestock, food crops, and help from kin and friends made it possible to get by in the isolated valleys. Eller says there was no "overt" class consciousness. There were courthouse and merchant elites, but they did not have the power they did in the Lower South. More social power remained with the "yeoman farmer" class and the mountain elite, like the Coastal Plains elites, who were in a position to act as intermediaries between the local yeomanry and outside commercial and industrial types.

Most sawn lumber was localized in Appalachia in 1890. By 1900, 75 percent of the forest still stood. About 10 percent of the forest remained in virgin condition despite some of the largest trees being cut. The timbermen arrived by the 1880s as the northern forests neared depletion. For local farmers this meant the loss of timberland and hog mast for livestock but also marked their entry into nonfarming such as working in the sawmills. During early logging, between 1880 and 1890, selective cutting of big trees took place, followed by the timber boom of 1890 to 1920. Some companies such as the Stearns Coal and Lumber Company combined their coal and timber operations.

Before the 1880s, both farming regions had small family farms as the core of their economies. These farms were often nearly self-sufficient in supplying most of the family's food, shelter, and clothing from local resources. They were largely noncommercial and did not produce cotton, hemp, tobacco, or sugarcane on a large scale. In the mountains most farm families worked less than fifty acres of farmland. Corn was the major food crop. Much like Appalachian farmers, Coastal Plains yeomen raised subsistence food crops of corn, sweet potatoes, and peas on small farms and raised cows and sheep on open range beneath the pines, while hogs fed on the mast-rich hardwood bottomland. The thinly populated nature of the Coastal Plains made it easy to acquire land. In Montgomery County, Georgia, only about 7 percent of the heads of farming households were landless tenant farmers or farm laborers.

For both the Coastal Plains and mountain regions, the years after 1880 became transformative decades for farm families. Their societies and cultures were reconstructed but in different ways. The Mountain South farms, which had been the major resource for family subsistence and income, declined both in terms of farm size and income. Railroad construction opened the mountains to mining and deforestation, creating new industrial landscapes controlled by corporations from the Adirondacks to the Smoky Mountains. Agricultural workers were drawn to non-farm occupations in sawmills and coal mines. At the same time, timber and mining companies defined their boundary lines in legal terms and declared their land by postings with trespassers liable to arrest and prosecution. Small farms soon became dependent on company stores and mill towns for consumed goods and services. By the early twentieth century these families, according to Eller, "had become socially integrated within the new industrial system and economically dependent upon it as well." The new society featured a more rigid social structure especially in company towns.

Railroad construction during the 1870s and 1880s also opened up the Lower South's longleaf pine forest to deforestation on a massive scale. The region shared fully in the nation's postwar railroad boom. Without Appalachia's coal and other mineral resources, however, there were few immediate industrial pursuits in the pine forests to follow up the timber harvest and provide jobs for displaced farm families. During the 1880s, however, it became clear that with railroad construction and commercial fertilizers, including phosphates, cotton production could expand from the Cotton Belt onto the Coastal Plains as long as the sandy loam was cleared of pine trees. Here, a new cotton kingdom of sharecropping and tenant farming rose, and once independent farmers became trapped in the crop lien system.

The rise of commercial agriculture on the southern Coastal Plains also put in place a more rigid social structure. Landless sharecroppers and tenants were at the bottom and landlords, town professionals, lumber company owners, and furnishing merchants were at the top. Cotton displaced the more diversified and self-sufficient agriculture of the prewar years. Cotton soon became the only crop that farmers could borrow against for land, food, and fertilizer. By the late 1880s, Coastal Plains counties outpaced the older cotton-growing areas in fertilizer consumption. Indeed, fertilizer agents often refused to extend farmers credit to grow food crops in favor of cotton. The amount of cultivated land increased tremendously but farm size diminished to tenant-sized plots as "cotton madness" followed closely behind deforestation when commercial farmers turned under natural grasses and planted the cash crop. The destruction of the open range in the southern highlands and lowland Coastal Plains destroyed two of the largest grazing ranges east of the Mississippi River by 1920.

There were deeper meanings to the demise of the open ranges than landscape change. The social backgrounds of the coal and timber kings (1870–1920) were different from those of local farmers and herders. About 75 percent of those in the mountains were born outside the region. In the longleaf pine forest, there were plenty of small southern operators, but many of the largest timber landowners were from the North. William E. Dodge and his family were from New York. His firm, also partly owned by the Meigs family, controlled much of the pine timber business in southern Georgia. Dodge-Meigs also cut over much of the northern white Pine Belt and were heavily involved in Adirondack Mountain range deforestation. Georgia lumbermen Nelson and Henry Tift both had Connecticut roots, although unlike Dodge and Meigs they resided in the South. Henry Tift owned eighty thousand acres of pineland, and when his interests were added to those of Henry Sears of Sears-Roebuck fame, the two had a total of about two hundred thousand acres. The Cummer family of Michigan moved into the north Florida Pine Belt and operated extensively there until the forests were exhausted.

Members of such northern commercial and industrial families were well educated and well connected. Their influence extended to the governor's office and state legislators and to the best lawyers and judges available. Also important were their ties to the local county seat town professionals who acted as intermediaries between the country people and outsiders. They knew that they were different and appeared as such to farmers because, as Amos Tift wrote, "he wore store bought clothes to church" and they did not. One visitor to a mill town wrote a note telling his kin that they would recognize him from the town folk because he would be dressed looking like a stranger.

When land disputes arose, rural farmers and livestock herders rarely won in the courtroom. In the federal case of *Dodge v. Williams*, the Georgia Land and Lumber Company filed action against nearly two hundred families claiming their lands and seeking their dispossession. About 15 percent of the defendants named in the case were women, not including those who were involved in charges brought against their husbands and fathers. The end of the open range had a direct impact on women and their roles within households. Women were responsible for spinning wool into thread and for producing homespun cloth, which was traded in local stores and expanded the household economy. As late as the 1890s, wool was still an important export item from the South Georgia port of Brunswick, east of the sheep ranges located in the pine forest. A woman's ability to earn money was diminished by farmer and herder dispossession. Corporate control of land diminished self-sufficient farming and posted land-denied farming households access to creeks and woods with their fish and game. When added to the crop lien system, the loss of forest access made local food sourcing more difficult. Increasingly, food in cans and in sacks bought on credit from furnishing merchants or at company stores became common along with Midwestern pork, which replaced the livestock on the vanishing open range.

The long agricultural depression that followed the Civil War set in motion migrations of farming families over short and long distances. Cotton Belt farmers left the eroded red clay lands of the southern Piedmont region and moved onto the cutover Coastal Plains and expanded the Belt into areas that were never commercial cotton growing areas. It was no coincidence that the appearance of cotton mills along the southern Pine Belt arrived after the big lumber mills began to shut down due to timber depletion. In 1900, aware that the forest was disappearing, Henry Tift set up his own cotton mill at Tifton, Georgia. Mountain farmers left their fields and worked in lumber mills, and once the trees were gone found work in coal mines. Without forests and range or agricultural land, farmers' options were limited, and many moved to the region's growing cities on the edges of the mountains at places such as Lexington, Kentucky, and Knoxville, Tennessee.

THE GREAT PLAINS

The grazing lands of the Appalachia and Coastal Plains South were not the only nor most extensive rangelands to begin disappearing from the landscape during the late nineteenth century. That distinction belonged to the Great Plains. Taken together, from east to west, the tallgrass, mixed-grass, and shortgrass prairies formed plains that rivaled the size of the nation's total landmass east of the Mississippi River. They stretched from western Illinois and Michigan to the Rocky Mountains and from the US-Canadian border to northern Texas and eastern New Mexico. This enormous range was characterized by extremes in climate and weather. The moister tallgrass prairie supported waist-high grasses while the richer mixed-grass prairie formed a transitional zone between the tallgrass and ankle-high shortgrass lands. Hundreds of plant species grew on the Great Plains, including some trees along rivers and creeks that covered at most about 10 percent of the land area. The grasslands overwhelmed all other features and the senses of newcomers. The prairies supported the important animal food sources for Native peoples and later Euro-Americans that included bison, elk, deer, rabbits, pronghorn, and prairie dogs.

Eastern farmers were encouraged by Civil War– and Reconstruction-era congressional acts to migrate to the Great Plains, especially those in the North and Midwest. These included the Homestead Act of 1862, which offered 160 acres of free land to anyone, man or woman, who was a citizen (or soon-to-be) unless they had taken up arms against the United States. This meant that Confederate veterans did not qualify as homesteaders and veterans who lost farms due to deforestation became trapped as tenants or sharecroppers unless they could purchase privately owned land in the West. By 1900, about six hundred thousand claims were filed for eighty million acres, including African Americans who became citizens during Reconstruction. Homesteaders complained that 160 acres was not enough land to farm in the semiarid western grass-lands, and under the Timber Culture Act of 1873 farmers could file for another 160 acres if one-quarter of the land was planted with trees within four years. The Morrill Act of 1862 provided land grants to western states to establish agricultural colleges. Eastern states were also allowed to select land totaling 140 million acres to raise money for their agricul-tural colleges. None of the land went to farmers. Between 1862 and 1900, another one hundred million acres was controlled by speculators.

This region, much like the eastern mountains and forests, had seen little railroad development compared to the North. About 181 million acres were granted to railroad construction projects. And railroads were responsible for bringing many thousands of people to the Great Plains, booming Nebraska's population, for example, from about 123,000 in 1870 to just over one million in 1890. During the first decade of the twen-tieth century Congress passed the Kinkaid Act (1904) and the Enlarged Homestead Act (1909) to encourage grants to homesteaders on marginal semiarid lands of the plains especially near the corners of Colorado, Kan-sas, New Mexico, and Texas.

Moreover, crop regions again shifted into new areas and destabilized older eastern sections of the same crop region. Farmers now settled semiarid areas of the plains in Kansas, Nebraska, and the Dakotas, moving first into river bottoms where water and timber were available and creating small agricultural settlements. At the same time, railroads were establishing a pattern that often resulted in small urban areas boasting as many settlers as farm country, many of them merchants and professionals selling goods and services to rural folk. Between 1870 and 1890, farmers had crossed the semiarid regions of the plains and founded Fargo and Bismarck in North Dakota and Pierre in South Dakota. Both the Great Northern and Union Pacific railroads attracted settlers in the Dakotas and beyond during the 1880s in Montana where Bozeman and Billings were laid out on the Northern Pacific. To the south, the Union Pacific and the Kansas Pacific reached Denver, Colorado, and Cheyenne, Wyoming. Wherever a new railroad line went, the scenes of the "Dakota Boom" and its associated homesteading, rapid population growth, and new towns were repeated—especially after Bonzana farmer Oliver Dalrymple, land speculator and owner of a one-hundred-square-mile wheat farm, demonstrated how grain could be profitably grown.

But all was not well. The New West was hit hard by severe winters during the 1880s as well as drought during the late nineteenth century, which only exacerbated the settlers' unfamiliarity with a challenging climate on the sod house frontier. This was also a period of nationwide agricultural unrest, much of it the result of foreign competition in grain and cotton markets once dominated by American farmers in the Midwest and South. Now farmers were more dependent on creditors, merchants, and railroads for services and were less self-sufficient in food and clothing. Crop prices were unpredictable except in that they always seemed certain to fall.

These conditions made farming households during the "Gilded Age" uncertain about the future. They blamed banks, railroads, grain elevators, and warehouse companies for gouging them at every turn and lowering their income while raising their costs. Their creditors told them overproduction of farm crops flooded the marketplace and drove down prices. Farmer protests were greatest in the northern Prairie and Plains regions. Decade after decade new farmer organizations appeared—the Grange, the Greenback Party, the Farmers Alliance, and the Populists. These efforts also met with some success in the South, but southern white farmers were unwilling to join hands with black farmers and stop the segregation and violence that enforced white social control. The post-Civil War years did see the passage of Granger Laws, the regulation of interstate commerce by Congress (1887), and the Sherman Anti-Trust

Act (1890) aimed at breaking up monopolies. States established agencies for the inspection of fertilizer to ensure farmers were not buying worthless bags of dirt instead of the rich imported guano they sought to fertilize their fields.

Before the arrival of automobiles, railroads had a virtual monopoly on quick and reliable transportation. With each passing decade, railroads took over a greater share of public passenger and freight transportation from steamboats, which relied on unpredictable riverways. Railroads soon replaced cast-iron rails with more durable and reliable steel rails, engine parts, and wheels, which made them even more reliable. The Central Pacific Railroad, chartered by the State of California in 1861, was built from Sacramento to the Nevada Border. The railroad was completed in 1869 and ran east-west through the center of the mixed-grass and shortgrass prairies. The North still led all regions in railroad mileage in 1870, but the South experienced a postwar boom in railroad construction as well. Great Plains states accounted from one-third to about one-half of the nation's annual railroad construction between the end of the Civil War and 1900. Transcontinental lines such as the Union Pacific were funded in part through federal land grants to the railroad corporation. Union Pacific Railroad, chartered by Congress in 1862, followed the Platte River and ran from Omaha to Nevada's western border.

Once a landscape of shortgrass prairie grazed by bison, the Corners region became the center of an ecological crisis known as the Dust Bowl. On average, this region received less rainfall than the tallgrass prairie to the east. It was similar in some ways to the southern Coastal Plains and the Appalachian region in that once its grasses were plowed under there was little to prevent severe erosion due to rain and wind. The shortgrass prairie land along rivers and streams was settled first, but farmers gambled they could extend winter wheat planting into marginal lands with limited rainfall. They invested in expensive farm equipment and in fertilizers during the 1920s when rainfall was plentiful. In normal times they could expect a good yield but there had been droughts during the 1890s and others followed during the 1930s. In 1934, winds blew enormous dust clouds over Chicago and dropped millions of pounds of dust on the city.

As the post-Civil War era began, the North had by far the most efficient and extensive transportation system in the nation. This network was a key part of the market revolution. By 1890, the railroad map of the South resembled the density of the North's in 1860 as remote areas were integrated into the nation's railroad system. This development was key to economic growth in the mountains and Coastal Plains South, where bad roads and trails were barriers to moving farm produce to market and getting commercial fertilizers onto the fields. It was also key to their consolidation within the larger national economy. In the southern bottomlands of the Lower Mississippi River Valley a railroad boom between 1880 and 1900 increased mileage from seventy to more than seven hundred miles. Desperate state governments sold hundreds of thousands of acres of fertile tax-forfeited land to railroads such as the Georgia Pacific. Because of barriers imposed by dense forests and swamps, construction costs were high, but the railroads benefitted from growing lumber and cotton shipments as farmland was brought into production. The familiar pattern of sharecropping and tenant farming was repeated here. By 1880, 60 percent of the population was black. Attracted to the region by chances of a new start, they were joined in the bottomlands by landless whites from the hill country.

At the beginning of the new century, many of the more remote areas of the eastern United States were brought into the national transportation network and farmers had extended crop regions into new areas. Cotton farmers in the South extended their region farther into both the Upcountry and the Coastal Plains as well as into the Lower Mississippi Valley bottomlands. The cost was high. Input costs in land, labor, and fertilizer were not met by output profits, especially during the 1890s. By 1920, about one-half of all southern farmers were tenants. On the Great Plains grain farmers pushed the cultivation of wheat to the limits of cultivation in the winter Wheat Belt. These areas had been both lowland and highland open ranges and important hearths for the origins of the nation's livestock industry. But consolidation of farmland into fewer hands and the rise of tenancy and sharecropping meant that fewer and bigger farmers controlled what they grew and at what price it sold.

The Civil War alone killed about 435,000 farmers nationwide and left many others disabled. Their widows and orphans lived in dire isolation with little support beyond their communities. This single nation-changing event moved farmers off the agricultural landscape more than any other. The destruction of eastern rangelands meant those remaining in the east were unable to become as self-sufficient as they had been before the war. By 1900, about 38 percent of the US workforce lived on farms, but 35 percent of the nation's farms were worked by tenants. Most farmers were still full-time operators but there was little hope that the country's 768,000 nonwhite tenants and croppers would own their own land in a society where farmland ownership was increasingly becoming a white man's privilege. In the West, however, slightly less than one in five farmers were tenants, and the social baggage of being an itinerant could be escaped. There they could leave behind the problems of crop over-production, tight money, tenancy, and two major political parties who ignored their needs.

The Civil War and the long agricultural depression of the late nine-teenth century led to the failure of many farms, particularly in the South. Railroad construction expanded the range of cotton growing into new areas such as the Coastal Plains region where landlords benefited from poor tenant and sharecropper labor under their control. In the West, wars of dispossession were waged on American Indian nations through the remainder of the century. As historian Eric Foner wrote in 2019, "Reconstruction can also be understood as a historical process without a fixed end point." The consequences of these reconstructions are still being lived out today.

5

Home on the Range?

FARMERS DURING THE LATE EIGHTEENTH and early nineteenth centuries were usually not the first people to settle a new region. Livestock herders claimed that distinction as they pushed beyond settled farming communities in search of fresh grasslands for their cattle. From the South Atlantic Seaboard, cowmen moved their livestock from the flatlands of the coastal Carolinas and Florida into the Coastal Plains of Georgia and Alabama and westward all the way to Texas. Spanish ranchers from northern Mexico brought a cattle culture from the Old World to the New World and into the grassy plains region of southern Texas. And in the Ohio Valley region, eastern cattle moved into the new lands of the Northwest Territory and into the Trans-Mississippi West. As the cattle frontier moved west, the bison withdrew even more from the east. Ultimately on the Great Plains, Spanish explorers brought horses to the Americas during the Spanish conquest starting with the second voyage of Columbus in 1493, and to the continent in 1519.

OPEN RANGE

Contrary to what you may have seen in movies, the open range system of livestock herding, where cattle roam freely, unrestricted by fences, regardless of ownership, did not begin in the American West after the Civil War under the watchful eyes of Hollywood-like cowboy figures. This form of livestock herding took place as early as the human domestication of animals and was practiced worldwide. Indians, and later Euro-Americans and African Americans, established the use of the open range and its abundant sources of natural grass and fodder. The open range cowboy culture, associated with present-day Texas cow drives and the High Plains of the American West, was a combination of Amerindians and colonial English and Spanish practices carried over vast plains to create the iconic images associated with cowboys, cattle drives, and cattle towns.

According to early European explorers, dogs were the only animals domesticated by the Amerindians. The site of early documented direct importation of livestock points mainly to Virginia and New England, but it's likely that the earliest introduction of European livestock and animal husbandry was accomplished not by English colonists in Virginia or New England, but by the Spanish on the barrier islands of the South Atlantic Seaboard and the Gulf of Mexico. The establishment of these settlements followed earlier expeditions by Spanish explorers such as De Soto and were northward extensions of the colonial empires that followed Columbus's landfall in the Caribbean. De Soto and others brought along livestock on their expeditions. De Soto alone brought more than five hundred horses and pigs. Some were lost and became feral or domesticated by Indians.

Within thirty or forty years of Columbus's arrival, the Spanish were hunting for Indian slaves along the barrier islands of the southeastern United States to replace those decimated by hard labor, disease, and violence in the mines and plantations of Spain's Caribbean empire. These expeditions discovered a long-established pattern of Indian settlement on southeastern barrier islands along the Georgia and Florida coastlines. There Timucuan and Guale Indians lived on corn, melons, beans, and shellfish and hunted deer and other game. The arrival of the Spanish missions on the islands between present-day St. Augustine, Florida, and Port Royal, South Carolina, brought with them livestock, including cattle, hogs, sheep, and horses. These animals routinely followed the expansion of the Spanish encomienda system, which demanded tribute from conquered indigenous peoples, including assigning laborers to specific landlords, wherever it went into the New World, including the American Southeast and Southwest. The system reshaped native culture by controlling Indian labor and behavior by making them responsible for livestock as well as crops. The domestication of livestock among the native agricultural populations at missions on present-day Sea Islands by Jesuits in 1568 and later on other barrier islands had further advantages. Cattle were confined on narrow strips of land between the Atlantic Ocean and saltwater marshes. There they could be managed in an environment where predators—wolves and panthers—could be kept in check by hunting and trapping. In this way livestock was integrated into the mission agricultural system of growing crops such as olives and oranges and raising livestock for export to St. Augustine, the Caribbean, and to the larger Spanish world.

On the mainland, sheep, for example, were much more vulnerable to attack by natural predators than cows and hogs who escaped and became feral and were better able to fend for themselves. Indians domesticated some runaways. By the close of the colonial period evidence of American Indian animal husbandry was common. European travelers recorded Indian ownership and use of livestock, especially cattle and horses. Native peoples used both the open savannas and woods-ranching practices.

American naturalist William Bartram recorded American Indian use of open savannas, such as Payne's prairie south of present-day Gainesville, Florida, during the 1780s. Indian cattle grazed on the savannas and wiregrass ranges of the Coastal Plains South. Travel corridors left deep traces noticeable for "ages" according to Bartram. In northern Florida Bartram described an unusual sight: "a troop of horse under the controul and care of a single black dog, which seemed to differ in no respect from a wolf of Florida. . . . He was very careful and industrious to keep them together." Colonial-era cattle changed in appearance over time due to interbreeding and became more manageable. Livestock served many purposes: draft animals, food, materials (hide, horns, hair), and fertilizer and they differed by herding instincts and ability to defend themselves.

Compared to Europeans, Americans put more emphasis on sheep for wool production than for meat. Sheep, like cattle and goats, are ruminants; they graze on slopes where other animals are reluctant to go. Sheep raised for wool were found in sparsely populated areas with broken terrain beyond the reach of commercial crop production. Sheep raised for commercial meat were found closer to urban areas and coastal trading centers.

The Spanish explorers who introduced horses and hogs to America left behind ruins as well as the Indian culture they destroyed. The old high road from the St. Johns River to present-day Pensacola was by Bartram's time "almost obliterated" but there were still "to be seen plain marks or vestiges of the old Spanish plantations and dwellings; as fence posts and wooden pillars of their houses, ditches, and even corn ridges." Gone, too, were the large Indian agricultural settlements near present-day Tallahassee encountered by Hernando De Soto. After noting that this area would be good to produce almost "all the fruits of the earth including corn, rice, indigo, sugar cane, cotton, to name a few," Bartram added, "I suppose no part of the earth affords such endless range and exuberant pasture for cattle, deer, sheep." Canebrakes, the "foilage of which is always green," provided "hearty food for horses and cattle."

WOODS RANCHING

Indian men found new roles as the first cowboys. During the late eighteenth century, it was not uncommon for William Bartram to encounter male Indians "being again engaged in their business" of ranging the forests and plains in search of livestock. This type of American Indian woods ranching was widely practiced in the southern pine woods with its year-round supply of wiregrass fodder. European adventurers recognized that livestock could walk along with them through the forests of North America and were an important source of food and transportation. De Soto brought hogs on his expedition and some of these were left behind on the range where they proliferated and were domesticated by Indians as a part of their agricultural complex that depended heavily on corn cultivation.

Historical geographer Ralph H. Brown estimated that by 1650 there were about fifty thousand "native cattle" in the British colonies, or about one animal for every two people. The cattle were products of interbreeding on the range involving many European varieties brought over since the beginning of exploration of the New World. There were strictly no cattle native to the present-day United States. The Indian cattle that naturalist William Bartram and the trader James Adair saw in the eighteenth century may have evolved from animals left behind during the Spanish expedition of the Southeast or survived after the English capture and destruction of St. Augustine. These cattle were small, maybe reaching upward of 350 pounds. The Seminole chief Ahaya Secoffee, called Cowkeeper by Euro-Americans because of the large size of his herds, had moved from Georgia into Florida to find better grazing ranges away from English settlers. Spanish and English travelers and traders recorded similar activities in Indian South Carolina and Indian Florida while Euro-American settlements still hugged the coastlines.

Between 1607 and 1611, the first farm animals were brought into the British colony of Virginia. By 1620, there were possibly five hundred. The importation of animals from the West Indies and Europe, restrictions on killing cattle, and the natural increase of their population resulted in about thirty thousand head by the late 1630s. The Massachusetts Bay Company was largely responsible for cattle importation to Boston, although transatlantic voyages took a heavy toll on animals crossing the Atlantic. Some cattle arrived in the Old Northwest from French outposts along the St. Lawrence River Valley. Livestock arrived at the Massachusetts Bay Colony on "nearly every ship" during the 1620s and early 1630s.

Cattle grazed the woods and meadows and looked half-starved. They overgrazed spring growth before the grasses could flower and seed. Most were rough and tall natural grasses. They were plentiful and "very ranke" according to Captain John Smith, and "although they be good and sweet in Summer, they will deceive your cattell in Winter." Hay growing had not developed in England by the time the colonists departed so the cattle brought over were on their own and diminished in quality until after the American Revolution. The chief advantage of cattle in the seventeenth-century South was its ability to survive in the wild and on poor grasses.

One of the earlier free-range centers in the east was the colony of South Carolina. Founded in 1670, the colony became the site of early cattle raising due to its year-round mild climate and wiregrass ranges. Livestock brought into the colony from the West Indies became the foundation of an important industry. For half a century after its establishment, the colony became an important source of salt, meat, and hides exported to Barbados and other British West Indian islands in exchange for slaves to work the colony's expanding rice production. According to historian Peter H. Wood, it was the cattle trade that generated, in part, the capital to establish the rice industry. Farmers in the pine woods turned their cattle loose and rounded them up at branding time in the spring. The Low Country cow culture became the basis for many of the markers of the western cattle industry at its juncture with Spanish open-range herding in northern Mexico. Cow hunters and cowboys were hired by livestock owners to round up their property and bring them to cow pens. These cowboys were both white and black and ranged the higher pine wood-lands behind the tidewater rice belt.

In New England, Brown credits the Narragansett Bay area as home of the first colonial stockmen, one of the first regions "to assume pre-eminence" in this capacity. The factors that led the Narragansett area to become a "grazing country" included a range along the western shore of the bay and inland some fifteen miles almost to the border of Connecti-cut. This was "a lowland of gentle relief" and included nearby islands. This area was open and clear of woods due to Indian occupation and their own use of it for agriculture, fishing, and livestock. The pastures were upland and not wet and thus not subject to the cattle "rot" found in Florida.

Colonists grew grain and herded livestock there. The Narragansett Bay area had one of the largest slave populations in the North and some very large estates. Brown estimated that there were as many as three thou-sand slaves by 1750 along with a handful of Indians. This area became known for its livestock, including horses and sheep, which were sold in other colonies such as South Carolina and in the Caribbean islands. Hides supplied local tanneries with leather for shoes, boots, and other products. By 1800, there were several million head in the new nation.

THE SOUTHERN RANGE

The southern Coastal Plains extended from southeastern Virginia to East Texas and stretched from the fall line to the Low Country. Much of this vast tract was covered by longleaf pine trees and wiregrass, a natural and valuable forage plant for cattle and sheep for most of the year. Over time the livestock herding cultures of Indians and Euro-Americans moved inland. The value of the Coastal Plains range attracted southern small farmers and livestock herders into the Carolinas and Georgia during the colonial and Early National period, a migration stream that would eventually reach Texas where it met an even earlier stream of livestock herding from Mexico. Entire communities of herders in South Carolina's Low Country, for example, migrated to southern Georgia and northern

Florida as rice production in South Carolina's Low Country expanded. Arriving in the 1810s and 1820s, they found little competition from commercial farmers who specialized in cotton growing on the Black Belt and barrier islands.

West of the Carolina rangelands were forests where population density was low and livestock herding was a major economic pursuit. In the early nineteenth century, it was in this remote region, away from the commercial agricultural worlds of cotton, rice, and sugarcane, that southern livestock expanded westward. The wiregrass range in its entirety covered 92 million acres of forest landscape suitable for woods ranching, most of it still uncleared when the Civil War ended. In addition to the Lower South's grazing lands, the Mountain South supported a similar herding culture, which included marking and branding cattle and turning it loose for most of the year to forage and fend for themselves. This culture moved westward along the Coastal Plains and across Kentucky and Tennessee occupying lands bypassed by commercial farmers raising cotton, hemp, and tobacco. By the 1820s, Carolina herders were moving into the recently ceded Lower Creek lands in southern Georgia and Alabama while in the Upper South they had reached Missouri's "Little Dixie."

Corn was the major food crop of forest ranchers and they used most of it to feed their families. Some choice hogs and cows were penned and fed corn to fatten them up for the family table, but most, including sheep, ranged the woods until springtime grazing on grasses and foraging. In the spring they were rounded up and driven to cow pens, where they were marked and branded. Some livestock was driven to coastal markets such as Savannah and Charleston, where they were consumed locally or exported to the West Indies.

In the Midwest, the southern tradition of open-range herding and grazing met the corn-fed livestock culture of the Upper Midwest. Southern range hogs fed on mast—acorns, nuts, and roots. Called rooters and razorbacks, these hogs were thin and rarely fed corn in the South where crops, not livestock, were fenced to protect them from foraging free-range animals. In northern pork markets corn-fed hog meat was preferred over mast-fed southern hogs because northern tastes found open-range hog meat too dark and soft. Deforestation had a direct impact on mast, forage, and fodder as well as a decline in wood for fencing.

The differences in attitudes toward livestock reached back to the Old World. In Great Britain, for instance, mixed farming characterized many lowland farming communities in southern and eastern England. Farmers set aside more land for crops—corn and wheat— and less for grazing cattle. In the uplands of northern and western England and in Scotland, Wales, and Ireland, stock raising was more important than farming to household wealth and the open-range system prevailed. Farmers there considered the open-range one great commons and opposed the enclosure of farming land by fencing as an "intolerable grievance." New England Puritans continued the mixed farming and enclosure traditions with orderly stone fences piled along the edges of fields as farms expanded over time. Southern farmers continued the open-range custom, a practice that was upheld in southern courts by challenges to the custom, especially by livestock-killing railroads.

THE WEST

For much of the first half of the 1800s, the reports of military expeditions and other explorers, using their eastern references to describe an unfamiliar landscape, described the Great Plains as a vast internal desert. Early expeditions to supply frontier outposts and trading stations, however, indicated that large numbers of draft animals needed to haul supplies had little problem feeding themselves on native grasses well before railroad surveys and construction began to dispel the prevailing "desert view." Large herds of buffalo suggested that there were good grasses for grazing, especially the "bunch and buffalo grasses" that provided "excellent grazing during the entire year without human aid." The region's rivers and streams provided adequate water. Before 1800, bison ranged as far east as the western borders of some the new American states. Within twenty years the bison herds were well west of the Mississippi River. Between 1850 and 1870, the great western bison were divided into southern and northern herds by railroad construction and their decimation by railroad excursion hunting parties.

POST–CIVIL WAR

Following the Civil War much of the nation's open-range tradition vanished, particularly east of the Mississippi River. On the southern Coastal
Plains and in the Mississippi River Valley deforestation and cotton production, which turned under wiregrass in a preview of the destruction of
the Great Plains grasslands, destroyed most of the productive range by
1900 and earlier in the Carolinas and Georgia. While open-range laws
remained on the books in some southern states well into the twentieth
century, the expansion of commercial agriculture such as cotton and later
tobacco broke up the longleaf pine ecosystem. Deforestation led to higher
surface temperatures and drier topsoil, which eroded under subtropical rainfalls, and silted in creeks and streams where livestock watered.
Dried-up watering holes were frequently discussed in rural newspapers
during the 1880s and 1890s as deforestation led to rising surface temperatures and drought conditions in watering places seldom seen dry.

The decline of range, fodder, and forage increased with greater deforestation. By 1910, many ranges were gone due to timber cutting and commercial farming. Lumber mills shut down, throwing men out of work
and their wives and children often ended up at cotton mills. Women
whose husbands were injured or killed while employed by lumber companies had little or no recourse in legal action against corporate lawyers.

At the end of the Civil War enslaved African Americans were eman-
cipated and the Union persevered. The nation was divided by what was
called the Great Plains, which stretched from the Mississippi River to the
Rocky Mountains. California and the West Coast were separated from
the eastern states by the unsettled, semi-arid plains inhabited mostly by
Indians and bison.

The US government believed that this large open range, most of it
public land, should be settled by farmers who would create permanent
communities and increase the tax base. In 1862, President Lincoln signed
the Homestead Act, which offered 160 acres to anyone who would settle
the land for five years. Although much of the land passed into the hands
of agricultural colleges and speculators, farmers began to move west. It
soon became clear, however, that without some type of effective fencing
on the treeless plains, the strategy of agricultural settlements would fail.
In 1866, A. T. Kelly of Peoria, Illinois, patented the first all-metal barb in

the nation and ten years later Joseph F. Glidden's version of the wire sold three million pounds, providing effective fencing on the plains.

During the 1870s and earlier ranchers had their eyes on the western grasslands. Many belonged to a free-range cattle-raising culture whose origins were southern and Spanish. Well before southerners began to migrate to present-day Texas, Spanish missions brought cattle into the ranges along the Gulf Coastal Plains and moved up the Rio Grande River to present-day Taos and Santa Fe. Thousands of cows roamed year-round on the grasslands and were rounded up by Mexican cowboys and branded. The Texas story was an extension of the same mission expansion in present-day California, Arizona, and New Mexico. Free rangers believed that all livestock had access to vital grasslands and water regardless of who owned the land. Before the Civil War and before the arrival of railroads, there were few markets for cattle and the herds grew to large numbers.

One of the early leaders in the Texas cattle industry was Richard King. Unlike many southerners who farmed and raised cows on the side, King did nothing but ranch and speculate in land to increase his ranges. By 1885, he owned four ranches and 825,000 acres of grazing land in the Grassy Plains area of Texas between the Nueces and Rio Grande Rivers. King did not believe in the prevailing southern open-range custom and patterned his ranches after Spanish cattle operations that included a fort, mission, and hacienda surrounded by private land. It has been estimated that King's ranches sent one hundred thousand head of livestock to northern markets between 1869 and 1884. The cattle that mixed and bred in southern Texas combined smaller scrub cattle and brahmin traits of survival in humid, subtropical ranges and heat and parasite tolerance.

The growth of the cattle industry on the plains north of Texas during the postwar years was astonishing. In 1860, about 130,000 cattle were in Kansas and Nebraska. By 1880, their numbers had grown in those two states to about 2.6 million. The ranchers who moved west after the Civil War and established cattle ranches, such as the JA Ranch owned by Charles Goodnight in the Texas Panhandle in 1876, moved Texas cows north over trails to railroads in Kansas in order to reach Chicago and eastern markets. The railroads that came to cow country spawned cattle towns where buyers waited for the herds to fill cow pens. Early feed lots fattened up beef on cotton seed oil mill by-products. Over time, the rangy Texas longhorns

FIGURE 5.1. Beef became an important source of meat as urbanization increased. The Filson Historical Society, Louisville, KY I Red Star by Wilhelm Eilerts (2013.35.1)

were improved by interbreeding with larger Angus and Hereford stock that could withstand the cold northern plains. Wherever railroads and miners went in the West cattle ranches sprang up to feed the workcamps well before the farmers arrived to create permanent communities.

The ranchers soon clashed with the profence and anti-free-range farmers who brought the wire fence with them. Land and water rights became central concerns in the West, especially where public lands were concerned, and still are today. But the disastrous winter of 1886–1887, a harsh season across the continent, largely ended the open-range conflict. Overgrazing and a drought in the summer of 1886 resulted in range fires and dried-up water holes, not only in the Great Plains region but throughout the nation. Future US president Theodore Roosevelt, who owned interests in a cattle ranch, wrote a friend that the winter freeze was "a perfect smashup all through the cattle country of the northwest. The losses are crippling."

The origins of the cattle industry in California began with Spanish missions and colonies in the San Diego area during the 1770s. One of the state's unique natural features along the coast is its Mediterranean climate with cooler temperatures, longer growing seasons, and plentiful grasslands. Wheat and fruit orchards were significant products, but the climate also encouraged forage and fodder resources like those in the Southeast, which were managed by American Indians using fire. Spanish missions raised crops in their gardens using Indian labor while their cows and sheep were tended by Indians as well. Eventually, ranchos, individually managed ranches similar to those along the Mexico-Texas borderlands, were granted by the Mexican government and their owners were required to maintain at least 150 head of cattle. After the Mexican Congress passed an act secularizing the California missions in 1833, many were abandoned, and their ranges granted to the ranchos. The cattle were valued for their hides and tallow, not meat, but that soon changed.

California was admitted to the Union as a free state in 1850 with a population of about 93,000. The Gold Rush in 1848 and the arrival of Mormon colonies created a greater demand for beef, although the price dropped after the Gold Rush ended. During the 1840s, California had enough cattle to supply some of Oregon's needs. Similar to California, Oregon enjoyed with a long growing season, relatively mild winters, and grasslands that supported livestock as well as many of the crops that settlers arriving from the east over the Oregon Trail had grown, particularly in the Willamette Valley. The valley's extensive prairies were good range for cattle. Prior to his death in 1841, Ewing Young had amassed a herd of about six hundred cattle. By 1880, California's cattle range was full.

MODERN ERA

Many farmers continued to keep livestock long after open ranges in the eastern United States disappeared as monocultures expanded their hold on the nation's farmland. A horse or mule was a necessity to provide work power in the fields before tractors became commonplace. A milk cow was important as a source of milk and cream even in towns, where small garden plots, chicken houses, and smoke houses made them look more like a collection of farms than a small urban area. These outbuildings included hog pens, which became especially noticeable in summer heat. Chickens provided eggs and meat. On the farm or in town the continuity of farm life reached into the early post–World War II years. Cows were kept primarily for milk and the cream and butter that could be made. Beef cows were not very common before the age of refrigeration. Groups of farmers called "meat companies" scheduled each participating family's beef slaughter with planned and sustained distribution in mind. One small-farm wife in Washington State made just over $300 selling poultry and eggs in 1943 while her husband's cattle auction sales brought in about $1,300.

By 2012, cattle and calf production were a $76 billion industry. Most of these animals were grain fed and moved through slaughterhouses and processing centers owned by four major meatpacking corporations. Their operations had similar antecedents in the western cattle industry where feed lots were needed to fatten beef cattle after the long drives up from Texas to railheads in states like Kansas. Before the invention of refrigerated cars, cattle were shipped by railroad to Chicago and other eastern cities for slaughter, processing, and distribution to growing urban centers in the East. Today, it takes from two to three years to move beef from farm to fork. Some cattlemen resist grass as a main feed source, considering it inefficient because cattle must be moved often to fresh grass. Most cattle spend from about 90 to 140 days in feed lots.

Today, the center of feed lots with one thousand or more cows remains east of the Rocky Mountains on the semiarid plains. Nebraska, Texas, Kansas, Iowa, and Colorado are the leading cattle on feed lot states. By 2017, Kansas, Nebraska, and Texas alone accounted for about 65 percent of cattle on feed in feed lots of one thousand or more capacity. They are primarily situated in the middle of the country especially in the shortgrass central Great Plains, the former range of the American bison and states with plentiful grain supplies. Cities traditionally important to the beef industry such as Fort Worth, Texas, and Oklahoma City, Oklahoma, continue to play a role, but the real power is held by the "Big Four" meatpackers: Tyson Foods (Springdale, Arkansas), Cargill Meat Solutions (Wichita, Kansas), JBS (Greeley, Colorado), and National Beef Packing Company (Kansas City, Missouri). In 2020, these four

meatpackers controlled about 80 percent of the thirty-five million beef
cows slaughtered in the United States.

The "Big Four's" ability to control the beef industry is of concern to the
actual cattle ranchers and farmers who grow beef. Over a thirty-year period
between 1980 and 2010 their numbers dropped from 1.6 million to about
950,000, a loss of 650,000 ranchers and farmers. The years following the
"Get Big" 1970s, the disastrous 1980s, and NAFTA have not been good for
cattle ranchers. They fear that their fate will be the same as poultry growers
and hog farmers who are controlled by contract agreements with the packing houses that leave little of the independence of action their cattle country
heritage would suggest. Many of the smaller beef ranchers have already
been cut out of the business by large meatpackers who want to maintain
their share of the US beef market and control the number of cows moving
through the slaughterhouses and processing plants. The United States is
the world's largest producer of beef. Most of it is "fed cattle," meaning they
are grown only for slaughter. Once a calf has been fed for 400 days, half off
its mother and half eating grain or grass, it is sold to a feed lot. There it is
fed for another 120 days to reach the ideal industry weight and must then
be sold within two weeks to a meat packer. To continue to feed cattle after
this period means they will gain weight and have excess fat.

The Packers and Stockyards Act (PSA) of 1921 was passed by Congress to ensure that there was "effective competition and integrity" in
markets for livestock, meat, and poultry. There was concern at the time
that the "Big Four" meatpacking companies were attempting to prevent
fair competition and influence prices. In 2005, Alabama cattleman Henry
Lee Pickett filed a lawsuit against Iowa Beef Processors, Inc. (IPB), now
Tyson Fresh Meats, Inc., at the time the largest meat packer in the nation.
Pickett and others representing cattle producers who sold feed cattle to
meat packing plants on cash markets filed a class action lawsuit. They
charged that IPB violated the PSA by using unfair and anticompetitive
marketing agreements to lower cash prices for beef over an eight-year
period. The lawsuit came to represent a class of cattle producers who
sold to IPB during the mid to late nineties. The jury agreed with the
plaintiffs that the meat packer had engaged in anticompetitive practices,
but when the case went to US District Court, Judge Lyle Strom entered
judgment in IPB's favor due to "technicalities." The National Farmers
Union believes that the USDA failed to enforce antitrust laws.

Ranchers and farmers are afraid "their way of life is being trampled" by big government while facing rising costs for feed and fuel and lower prices for their beef. After a rancher-led occupation of a public wildlife refuge and the resulting standoff in Harney County, Oregon, ended in the killing of rancher Robert LaVoy Finicum in 2016 by law enforcement officers, some ranching families have become fearful of the future of grazing rights on public lands, which they believe should be managed at the local level. A "don't tread on me" mentality is alive and well reflected by "LaVoy" bumper stickers.

According to the USDA, cattle and calf production reached 94.8 million in 2019, up from 93.3 million in 2017 with fewer operations with less than fifty head of cattle. These small operations of fifty or fewer cattle accounted for almost 70 percent of all cattle producers but only about 11 percent of the total number of cattle and calves. Clearly, consolidation in the industry followed NAFTA and imports of Canadian and Mexican beef, some US cattle ranchers say, have caused a $32 billion trade deficit in beef products.

Outhouses and septic tanks have the potential to pollute groundwater and drinking wells. Chicken houses and meat processing buildings do as well. In the small town that I grew up in, the slaughterhouse was next to the stockyard. It was a small cinder block building that backed up to a stream where livestock body parts and offal could be seen floating away. People fished in the same stream and miles downriver some folks were baptized and went swimming. The Federal Water Pollution Control Act of 1948 might just as well not exist. The fact that these processing plants were small and locally owned may have caused some people to look the other way.

The rise of Concentrated Animal Feeding Operations (CAFO) changed the equation. It is part of a cattle processing system that is unlike small-town food processors in terms of size and potential pollution. The greatest concentration of large feed lots are along a line from eastern Texas to Oklahoma and into Kansas, Nebraska, and Iowa. In 1967, the Kansas legislature passed a bill to control drainage from CAFOs that were the source of polluted water containing disease-bearing microorganisms, feces, nitrogen, and phosphorus. Before 1963, an estimated 75 percent or more of the cattle in Kansas was fed on small farm feed lots around the state. By the late 1960s, just over one-half of the state's cattle were confined in about one hundred commercial lots. Some people were slow to acknowledge that feed lot runoff polluted groundwater just as farm pesticide and fertilizers do. The 1972 Clean Water Act called for the implementation of pollution controls and established wastewater standards, but "EPA" remains a dirty acronym among some farmers and ranchers who see its efforts as another "burden" placed on their shoulders by an overreaching government bureaucracy.

Chickens, turkeys, ducks, and geese were also kept by farmers and town folk. Women were often in charge of this operation with children helping as egg gatherers and feeders. Eggs were an important source of food at home as well as for sale or barter to stores in both the country and town. Some people increased the size of their flocks for commercial purposes to bring in additional home income not only for eggs and meat but for feathers. Eggs found ready markets in town. Chickens and eggs were also favorite items for trade and sale to rolling stores, small stores that operate from trucks, and peddlers, who also sold chicken feed on their routes through the countryside. Their trucks were usually operated from farming towns and became more important during wartime when gasoline rationing cut down farm to town travel. For many farm families, chicken raising was seasonal and local. Some women bought chicks in the spring and raised them to kill and cook during the summer July 4 celebrations and family reunions.

One study of the growth of poultry contract farming in Georgia concluded that the fall in farm income during the 1920s sent farmers deeper into debt with the state losing about fifty-five thousand farms during that decade alone. The 1930s were no better, with the Agricultural Adjustment Act (AAA) plowing up seven hundred thousand acres of cotton in the state. As farmers searched for a way to land a new crop tenants and sharecroppers were moved off the land.

With the decline in cotton growing during the 1930s, southern farmers began to look for other sources of income. Poultry production during the 1940s and 1950s began to expand using the same crop lien system that had supported cotton growing. Merchants extended credit to farmers to purchase chicks, seed, and put up chicken houses. Women and children were no longer central to growing chickens, now called broilers, that were grown year-round and increasingly indoors. By the 1950s, poultry raising, once a secondary source of income to help tide farmers over in bad cotton crop years, had displaced cotton entirely on many farms. Credit was furnished to poultry growers by town bankers, merchants, hatcheries, and national corporations. Just as cotton farmers could not choose their crop, poultry farmers could not divert their attention from broiler production contracts that left little room for diversification.

In time, the process of year-round broiler production expanded wherever cotton growing had dominated. Many poultry growers held onto their land under the contract farming system but were demanded by buyers to invest in large chicken houses and feeding machinery that ensured their product would conform to buyer expectations. Companies such as Tyson and Perdue demanded that farmers buy expensive chicken houses and equipment, thus shifting the costs to chicken growers. Today, this year-round business can be found nationwide but the centers of production are largely east of the Mississippi River. In 2019, Georgia, Alabama, Arkansas, North Carolina, and Mississippi led the nation in broiler production. The value of poultry and eggs sold as a percent of total agricultural products is especially high in the former Confederate states, particularly in areas where cotton was formerly grown. In 2019, the states of Iowa, Ohio, Indiana, and Pennsylvania led egg production.

Milk was in great demand during World War II for US armed forces and its allies. After the war, small dairy farmers often could not afford to meet costly sanitation requirements, so consolidation followed. Despite a slump in demand during the Great Depression, the nation's growing urban population increased the demand for milk during the early twentieth century. However, the US Public Health Service reported in 1924 that too much of a city's population could depend on a few milk processing plants thus potentially increasing the spread of milk-borne epidemics such as typhoid and scarlet fever. Because milk stood second only to water as a disease spreader, demands for statewide milk sanitation programs increased the calls for costly improvements in milk processing, packaging, fermentation, water quality, storage, and milking barn equipment.

In 2012, milk and dairy farms produced about $35 billion in value of sales ranking behind beef, poultry, sheep, and goats. California was the major milk-producing state in 2018 and has been since the 1990s, followed by Wisconsin and Idaho. Those three states, plus New York, Pennsylvania, Texas, and Michigan all produced over ten billion pounds of milk. Comparatively little milk is produced in the South, while the old

Dairy Belt, stretching from New York and Pennsylvania westward to Michigan and Wisconsin, is still very much in evidence. In 2018, Wisconsin, New York, and Pennsylvania accounted for 55 percent of the milk produced in the nation while California produces slightly over 19 percent of dairy production, giving the Dairy Belt a solid presence in the nation's east and west.

Hog meat was a key food in many rural areas, especially in the South and the lower Midwest where southerners migrated. As mentioned above, hogs in these areas were turned loose to fend for themselves and fed on mast, especially acorns. Hogs were earmarked in order to identify them by owner. Small hog holdings were penned up in lots made of boards or wire fencing, especially in towns where it was not uncommon to see pigs wandering in streets and in and out of stores during the early twentieth century. These hogs were used to feeding on kitchen scraps and whatever waste they could find between being "slopped" when penned. In the 1950s and 1960s, hog farms began to grow, sometimes housing hogs by the hundreds.

As of 2020, Iowa, Minnesota, North Carolina, Illinois, and Indiana led the inventory of hogs and pigs in the United States. Iowa was the largest hog-producing state in the nation turning out close to 40 percent of all hogs and pigs early in 2020. Since 2000, North Carolina has increased hog production to the point of becoming third in the country. Most hog operations (almost three-quarters of the total) have fewer than one hundred head, but they account for less than 1 percent of hogs produced.

On large factory farms, which began with poultry operations during the 1950s and hogs in the 1970s and 1980s, animal waste and air and water pollution are environmental problems. Animal feces and urine are collected in pools. Some farmers use the waste for fertilizer and spread it over their fields. The stench from these large pools, called pig manure lagoons by pork companies, is inescapable to local residents who claim it devalues their property. In 2015, five hundred residents in eastern North Carolina, many black or Hispanic, filed legal action against major pork producer Murphy Brown, the hog growing division of giant Smithfield Foods. Since the 1990s, the rise of hog farms in the state increased dramatically in counties such as Duplin, and the industry claims that revenues are near $8 billion per year and employ forty-six thousand people.

The central theme of livestock production is the same as grain production: the consolidation of smaller landholdings into fewer but larger corporate operations. As historian Paul K. Conkin wrote, "large-scale farming departs widely from most images of the traditional family farm." The owners of large factory-like operations such as chicken and hog farmers or beef producers under contract to meat buyers have little control over the day-to-day operations geared to the production goals and timetables of huge corporations such as the "Big Four." The emergence of factory farm operations shook up the rankings of farming states in livestock production. Due largely to the efficiencies of factory farming, as of 2020 North Carolina was only behind Iowa and Minnesota in hog production and California leads the old Dairy Belt states in milk production. Gone are the days when, as Conkin wrote: "Cows had names. Chickens flocked around the wife who scattered the cracked corn."

Hired hands have always been an important part of the livestock industry. From the days of colonial cow hunters to the post–Civil War emergence of the classic western cowboy, hired labor in addition to family members was often needed to manage livestock. In 2019, hands hired directly by US farms and ranches numbered 629,000. Most work in crop agriculture, but a significant proportion work with livestock such as cattle, poultry, and hogs. The USDA described them as one of the most economically disadvantaged groups in the nation although most of them work on the largest operations with sales of more than $500,000 million per year, which would include factory farms and feed lots. Their largest concentrations are in California and Texas and in the Midwest, where about half are Hispanic. These descriptions do not reflect the images of traditional family farms.

Today, most of the nation's leading livestock states are west of the Mississippi River and east of the Rocky Mountains where the eastern migration trails ended. Most of these states occupy landscapes once covered with tallgrass prairies inhabited by Plains Indians and grazed by their primary food source—bison. The modern sheep industry is centered mostly in the West and Central sections of the country. In 2020, Texas, California, Colorado, and Wyoming account for 39 percent of all sheep and lamb in the nation. In the West, sheep raisers manage larger flocks than those in the central and eastern United States where flocks are small and fenced. Sheep raising has been on the decline since the late 1980s and early 1990s. In 1990, there were 11.4 million head, but by 2020 there were about 5.2 million head of sheep and lamb.

Today, about seven in ten American Indian farms specialize in livestock that include beef, sheep, and goats. Just over one-half specialize in those three animals alone, compared to only 6 percent for vegetable growers. Fifty-seven percent of those farms are made up of less than fifty acres. The largest concentration of these livestock raisers is at the Four Corners region of Arizona, New Mexico, and Utah with Apache County, Arizona leading. In 2012, they represented just under 2 percent of American farmers. Goats are easier to manage than cows, can live on marginal lands, browse in small areas, and produce good milk and fleece depending on the breed. Sheep, like goats, are relatively inexpensive and provide meat and wool. Although Texas currently leads the nation in sheep production, the states of California, Colorado, and Wyoming account for about one-quarter of the nation's sheep in 2020.

There are consequences to range herding. Domestic livestock herding is allowed on about 160 million acres controlled by the Bureau of Land Management (BLM) and the US Forest Service. Over the last century, the federal government has made this semiarid land available to citizens at low cost, but it is marginal farmland at best. Thomas Fleischner wrote that livestock grazing is the "most widespread land management practice" in the western United States. He observed that more than 70 percent of the West is grazed including wildlife refuges and national parks. Because the best cattle grazing land is situated along waterways, these areas are overgrazed, their stream banks collapse, their biodiversity declines, and the expansion of less desirable shrubland replaces trees and increases silting. Stream temperatures can rise or fall by about twelve degrees, which can change the food supply and lead to the decline of natural species of fishes.

Alternatives to factory farms and feed lots have always been with us in the example of traditional agriculture. Small farmers raised a mix of livestock, feeding them on grasslands in the case of beef and letting chickens range free to eat what they could find. The practices of organic farming were accessible through J. I. Rodale's (an early advocate of organic and sustainable farming in the United States) publications and efforts to encourage a new generation to live in more natural ways. During the Carter administration some of the first efforts were made to use federal initiatives to encourage sustainable and organic livestock. Robert Bergland, President Carter's secretary of agriculture, directed the USDA to examine and report on these alternative movements. The report concluded that organic methods were more sustainable than industrial farming. Bergland created an organic farming resources coordinator position, but when the Reagan administration took office, Earl Butz, his secretary of agriculture, called the organic movement a "cult" and abolished it. Largely because of the lobbying power of the agribusiness establishment, organic livestock has had a hard time gaining traction in the farm bill process, which has steadfastly sent billions in subsidy dollars to the wealthiest farms and ranches.

FRACKING THE RANGE

Today, the combination of the three Cs—consolidation, control, and chemicals—threatens western grazing lands on a scale unimagined twenty years ago. Hydraulic fracturing (fracking) involves well drilling and the high-pressure injection of fluids, including water and chemicals, into subterranean rock formations to fracture them in order to release natural gas and petroleum, resulting in environmental degradation. The process called "hydrafrac" was the result of experiments during the late 1940s with successful commercial application in 1950. It was licensed to Halliburton, a multinational corporation specializing in oil field services at home and in the Middle East. Prior to becoming US vice president from 2001 to 2009, Dick Cheney was US secretary of defense from 1989 to 1993 during Operation Desert Storm and CEO of Halliburton until July 25, 2000. At that time presidential candidate George W. Bush chose Cheney as his running mate in July 2000.

In 2004, the EPA issued a report on fracking, although it does not regulate control of the practice under the Safe Drinking Water Act of 1974, as a part of an Energy Task Force initiative led by former vice president Dick Cheney, chairman of the task force. The purpose of the task force was to prepare the nation for an inevitable future energy crisis and to make the United States less dependent on foreign sources of energy such as petroleum. The EPA report, reportedly reviewed by Halliburton staff, concluded that the nation's shale gas resources would play a "key role" by becoming an "important economic, energy security, and environmental benefit." The report recognized that circumstances such as low water supply and spills and leaks of hydraulic fluids could allow chemicals to seep into the groundwater, but "data gaps" made it difficult to completely assess fracking's impact on drinking water locally or nationally.

In 2000, there were about two thousand fracking wells in the United States responsible for less than 7 percent of the nation's natural gas production. By 2015 that percentage was at 67 percent. Nonhydraulic fractured wells produced the remaining 33 percent in 2015. Fracking transformed the rural landscape of the West, much of its grasslands, and some of that under private ownership or the BLM. During the years since fracking became widespread, it has polluted groundwater and air, reduced farmland, and leaked chemicals from both live and closed wells. The *Denver Post* reported in 2017 there were about sixty thousand active and more than twenty thousand abandoned oil and gas wells in Colorado alone. There was usually little or no monitoring of plugged and closed wells. The resulting competition for water and land by both fracking operations and farmers and ranchers is intense.

6

Two World Wars and the Great Depression

DURING THE EARLY DECADES of the twentieth century, the nation's farmers hoped for a brighter future. After thirty years of agricultural depression during the late nineteenth century they doubted it could be any worse than what had passed since the end of the Civil War. By the 1890s, wheat and corn brought less in the market than it cost to grow. Cotton dropped from fifteen cents a pound to five or six cents by the late 1890s. It was a mystery how urban workers could not afford bread due to its high price tag, yet western farmers burned grain rather than sell it too low. One farmer said, "There is a screw loose."

The forty years between 1914 and 1954 brought American farmers unprecedented challenges both at home and abroad. Despite the impressive record of agricultural output (each farmer produced enough to feed five families in corn and wheat), many farming families faced barriers to self-sufficiency as the era began. Woods ranching was all but gone. The nation's eastern woodlands, the source of food, fuel, fodder, and water for small farmers since the colonial period, had been devastated by deforestation. Expanding commercial agriculture in the wake of the timber harvest in crops of corn, cotton, and wheat destroyed native grasslands in the Midwest and Southeast. Sharecropping and tenant farming reached new heights both in terms of numbers of landless farmers and in terms of farming practices such as deep cultivation, which sucked nutrients out of the soil and left it vulnerable to erosion. According to southern author Harry Crews, whose parents sharecropped sixty acres in southern Georgia during the Great Depression, they were "tired people savaged by long years of scratching in soil already worn out before they were born."

During the Great Depression there were more than eight million American farmers, black and white, living as landless farm laborers.

FIGURE 6.1. Prior to 1945 many farms depended on animal power. The Filson Historical Society, Louisville, KY | (ARG-20)

In 1931, when North Carolina ecologist B. W. Wells described the consequences of pine belt deforestation as "one of the major social crimes of American history" his assessment described the destruction of all American grasslands used for range. Such lands had helped American farmers remain self-sufficient for generations. Without the critical forest resources that Indian physicist and environmentalist Vandana Shiva described as food, fodder, fuel, and water, the nation's farmers, especially the millions mired in sharecropping and tenant farming, fell to the lowest levels of society, a rural caste plagued by poor diets, disease, and hunger. The disappearance of the range left such families with "no cows or hogs and no smokehouse" and dependent on fatback, grits, and biscuits.

The half century between 1914 and 1954 saw major parts of an agricultural infrastructure emerge that would end farmer isolation, bring them into the modern era, see science and technology make farming more productive, and find government more involved in their daily lives.

Farming as farmers knew it at the beginning of the twentieth century would no longer exist as most of them remembered it by the 1960s. And for the millions who left rural America during those decades, the end of that life could not come fast enough. These sweeping changes would set up American agriculture for the scientific and industrial farming we know today. By 1950, the 31 percent of the nation's workforce represented by farms in 1910 had dropped to just over 12 percent.

Compared to the bad years of the late nineteenth century, the early years of the twentieth century were good ones for farmers overall. The agricultural population remained stable due to migration to urban areas, which offset natural increase. When war began in Europe in August 1914 the demand for food increased. Still, wheat was the only part of the crop economy where both an increase in output and acreage took place. US farmers saw their first billion-bushel wheat harvest in 1915 and a boom in wheat production followed. Wheat acreage rose to seventy-four million acres by 1919 compared to forty-seven million acres during the immediate prewar years. Wartime demand for wheat encouraged farmers to buy more acreage, equipment, and expand production. They plowed under more Great Plains grasslands where considerable diversity in land use still existed. Corn production remained stable and all other grains combined represented about a 12 percent increase. Hogs led the way by increasing production 23 percent. Cotton production during the war years never reached 1914 production levels. Most of the nation's farmers saw only modest levels of increased acreage. The big winners were in the Midwest and on the Great Plains, where wheat and pork production increased to meet demand.

It appeared that the increased demand for agricultural products might carry over into peacetime, but in 1920 farm prices declined steeply as the postwar economy adjusted to declining demand in Europe. Farmers everywhere were hard hit, but especially in the Midwest, where wheat farmers had expanded their acreage by buying land at the top of the market and incurring fixed costs such as mortgage payments and interest on loans. After the stock market crash of October 1929 gross farm income dropped from about $14 billion to around $6.5 billion by 1932. Although farm expenses declined as well, net farm income in 1932 was only a little over $1.8 billion, less than one-third of the 1929 level. Farm closures became common.

For Americans, the war itself was fairly short, over in nineteen months, but social changes lasted longer. The Selective Service Act of

1917 authorized the federal government to raise a national army. All males between the ages of eighteen and thirty were required by law to register for conscription. By 1918, the age span was widened from eighteen to forty-five. Young men left the farm and entered an international conflict in stages: from home to basic training in tent and barrack cities; to major East Coast ports for transatlantic troop ship voyages to France; and then by railroad, trucks, wagons, and on foot to the front lines. This process alone carried them from isolated farms to cities and dropped them into an international war. It is doubtful that their stateside training prepared the three million men who were inducted into the military from the twenty-four million who registered for the draft under the Selective Service Act for what they witnessed, especially in the trenches. The slaughter of modern warfare left many wounded and traumatized. We can only speculate about the psychological damage that joined the loss of limbs as well as those wounded by chemical warfare who never regained full capacity of their lungs. They returned to the farm now exposed to a larger world that moved faster and seemed incompatible with the world they had left at home.

Home was different too. Women were mobilized for war as well. By the end of 1918 about three million women replaced the men who had worked in the food, textile, war industries, logging camps, steel mills. About thirteen thousand women joined the navy as stateside clerical workers called "yeomanettes" and freed up men to join the fleet. On the farm, women and girls took on larger roles in farm management, referred to by the press as "farmerettes." The number of women military nurses rose from about four hundred to more than twenty-one thousand by the end of the war. Ten thousand of these women served in hospitals; they joined another eight thousand Red Cross nurses, many of who had served in France and Belgium before US entry into the war.

The role of the federal government also expanded beyond the Selective Service Act of 1917. The US Food and Fuel Control Act, passed in August 1917, encouraged the production and conservation of vital war materials. Also known as the Lever Food Act, it began to set the prices of essential food products. At the beginning of the war in Europe in 1914, Britain was importing 60 percent of its total food supply from foreign countries, including 80 percent of its wheat and two-thirds of its bacon. Wheat farmers believed that the government set wheat prices low and complained to Congress, but legislative relief was vetoed by President Wilson, which cost Democrats votes in the Wheat Belt during the 1918 election.

Wilson appointed Herbert Hoover to head the Food Administration. Hoover had the power to fix prices, control exports, and establish guidelines for home consumption. The public relations campaign called for school children to become farmers and enroll in the School Garden Army. Meatless Tuesdays and sweetless Saturdays encouraged citizens to regulate their home consumption, while hotels and restaurants were called on to cut back on wheat bread and instead serve "victory bread" made from at least 20 percent of grains other than wheat. By the end of the war about 25 percent of food production had been diverted to the war effort.

White men and women were not the only people to leave the farm during and after the war. About three million African Americans joined the countryside exodus. Black soldiers who served overseas in segregated and largely noncombat units found it difficult to return to a home front world of segregation enforced by white authority and violence. This was an agricultural world that did not benefit from the higher wartime agricultural prices, especially in the South where cotton was the major crop. And this world did not change during or after the war. Blacks lived and worked at the bottom of the agricultural ladder. Nate Shaw of eastern Alabama was one of them. He was hired out by his father to a white farmer as a plow hand at the age of nine and hauled logs to earn extra money. He eventually saved enough to get married and moved into a house on a white man's farm.

Nate's house was typical of the pine log and rough board and batten shacks that went up across the landscape during the early twentieth century. It was "just a old common-built house," Shaw recalled, with a single fireplace. "Whenever a white man built a house for a colored man he just ran it up right quick like a box." The windows were without glass or screens. "Didn't put you behind no painted wood and glass, just build a house for you to move in then go to work." Such houses were drafty and filled easily with dust and dirt blown through the cracks. Some families wallpapered the inside walls with newspapers and magazines to keep out the wind and grit. The early twentieth century was a time of increasing rural segregation, especially in the South, and the houses that Shaw described were "built for colored folks."

It is partly for these reasons that as many as half a million black southerners left the region for jobs in the North or in urban areas of the South. The years just before and during World War I were considered prosperous for the nation's farmers as a whole, but farmers in the South suffered despite cotton reaching forty cents per pound by 1920. A major problem was a natural pest called the boll weevil. The insect entered the United States from Mexico during the early 1890s and ate its way across the Cotton Belt from Texas to North Carolina "just a-lookin for a home" as Mississippi blues singer Lead Belly sang in the song "The Boll Weevil." The boll weevil had reached eastern Alabama by 1909, where sharecropper Nate Shaw believed that white landlords blamed blacks for the insect problem, telling them that "if you don't destroy them boll weevils, we'll quit furnishin you" with seed, fertilizer, land, and credit. The weevil attacked the cotton boll before it opened, dropping it to the ground to rot. As Shaw recalled, "Couldn't nobody pay on his debts when the weevil et up his crop." Children walked the rows of cotton collecting the weevils in exchange for pennies. According to Georgia farmer Milton Hopkins, "Others had their younguns mop the cotton squares . . . with lead arsenate." Farmers attempted to offset the impending weevil crisis by increasing cotton planting before the weevil reached their area. Some shifted away from cotton to other crops or, as was the case with African American farmers, migrated out of the region. The damage to the Cotton Belt was severe. Some farmers had planted hundreds of acres in cotton and only a handful in corn, leaving their families even more dependent on furnishing merchants for much of their food.

During 1920, farmers hoped that the wartime gains in farm acreage and high prices for not only foodstuffs but for cotton would increase. As a part of the World War I effort, the federal government built a hydroelectric dam in northern Alabama and used the electricity it made to make synthetic nitrates for producing ammunition. After the war, the Muscle Shoals plant, a part of the Tennessee Valley Authority, was converted to fertilizer testing and manufacture to supply farmers with nitrate fertilizer. Despite these efforts, the 1920s were disappointing for farmers. Once wartime demands dropped, prices fell as well. President Harding believed that farmers should help themselves and refused to offer federal support for a depressed farm economy. When the Great Depression gripped the country during the 1930s, farmers could rightly claim that they had already been in a depression since 1920.

Part of the problem was the federal government's historical land distribution policies. Since the beginning of the formation of the United States, the distribution of western land favored speculators, including national leaders such as George Washington. Politicians in the East favored high land prices while those in the West supported lower prices that would attract immigrants and build the local economy. Land and timber companies were determined to keep squatters off their lands regardless of region and routinely posted signs on their properties warning away hunters, trappers, and farm families who depended on the woodlands for food, fuel, and grazing for livestock. Civil War– and Reconstruction-era land grants such as the Homestead Act of 1862 benefitted speculators and monopolies such as timber and industrial farming companies by providing large land grants. In Alabama and Florida, for example, lumber companies acquired thousands of acres of land between the 1890s and 1920 that could have benefitted small farmers and livestock owners. Local county elites seized control of the richest agricultural land and increasingly populated the countryside with black sharecroppers and tenant farmers, running out poor white squatters and yeomen farmers. Taking a broad view of the agricultural landscape between 1920 and 1954, the cumulative impact of government and big agribusiness and natural disasters was to sweep millions of farm people off the land regardless of region.

One in three Americans still lived on farms in 1920 but their access to good farming land was unequal. Millions of farmers were landless with little legal recourse to protect themselves from eviction for debts incurred under the crop lien system. Debt became cumulative as the price of seed and fertilizer was carried over from year to year even as the price of cotton dropped to five cents a pound. As one farmer recalled, when "cotton fell to a nickel a pound" in 1914, "A man couldn't pay nothin' much on his old debts and nothing at all on his new ones." African Americans were among the first to leave the land. From 1916 and into the depressed farming years of the 1920s and 1930s, up until 1970, millions left the South and headed north in what's called the Great Migration. Some settled in the Upper South cities such as Louisville, Kentucky, and St. Louis, Missouri, some ventured further north to Chicago, Illinois, and Detroit, Michigan.

As these migrations continued, once prosperous small farming towns declined and social centers of farming society began to dry up. Grocery stores, doctors' offices, schools and churches, and movie houses closed as rural people left the land. Those left in the countryside often lived in tenant shacks along dirt roads leading out of town. They made up the majority of who was left to make up the farm population. The vanishing continued as land consolidation due to foreclosures continued to favor the wealthy few who could consolidate thousands of acres of small farms into growing agricultural operations specializing in commodity crops worked less by farm hands and more by machines. It would take time before the hollowing out of rural America would hit the point of no return, but by the 1950s it was on its way. There were no longer many small farmers in the countryside to come to town to trade for supplies, and the big industrial farms bought their hybrid seeds, chemical fertilizers, and pesticides from wholesalers. Eventually, the country schools would shut down, too, as school consolidation sent most students to the county seat town to attend school.

FARM RELIEF

Farmers realized what was happening and reacted by forming their own organizations, such as farmers' cooperatives, and fielded their own political candidates in local, state, and national elections. From the Grange and Farmers Alliances of the 1870s and 1880s to the Southern Sharecroppers Union of the 1930s, farmers, regardless of race, understood that their labor and sweat created wealth enjoyed by others—landlords, furnishing merchants, fertilizer dealers—who took their rent, crop shares, and hope. The world around the farmers was rapidly changing. During the twentieth century their numbers would dwindle from more than 30 percent to less than 2 percent of the nation's population. They were never able to mount an effective opposition to the growing power of industrial farms and their allies.

The problems that distressed American farmers peaked during the Great Depression. The farm programs that emerged in the 1930s to address agricultural overproduction, crop price supports, and crop insurance are still with us in some form today. For much of the early twentieth century the agricultural sector seemed to be heading in the right direction compared to the depressed late nineteenth century. Increased demand for farm products during World War I pushed up crop prices and farm income only to see them fall sharply after mid-1920. Part of the farm problem was self-inflicted. Buying land in the Midwest at $500 an acre to cash in on the demand for wheat and other foodstuffs in wartime Europe more than doubled farmers' long-term debt during the late 1910s. That debt reached almost $11 billion by 1923. Drought and falling farm prices created a sense of emergency among farmers and a sense of urgency among their representatives on the local, state, and national levels. Although some people thought crops such as tobacco were depression-proof, prices opened in 1931 in some tobacco markets at half of the 1930 price. By 1932, the net income from agriculture was less than one-third of the 1929 level.

The farmers who invested in new land and new machinery to meet wartime demands were a relatively small number of all farmers, but they were vocal and called on their representatives in the state houses and halls of Congress to do something about it. During the 1920s, the call for "Equality for Agriculture" was a popular slogan in farming states. Its proponents argued that agriculture deserved its fair share of the nation's income and if the ratio of farmer income and expenses was kept equal to that between 1910 and 1914, prewar purchasing power would be restored. Rather than take low prices at auctions, farmers interrupted them with shouts and threats. Congress was ready to listen. The McNary-Haugen bills taken up by Congress between 1924 and 1928 proposed that a fair value for farm products could be realized at home by establishing a protective tariff to protect American farmers from imports. It also called for establishing a federally chartered corporation to buy enough commodity surpluses to drive prices to a fair value level and sell them abroad. Farmers paid an equalization fee, or tax, to support the price-support plan's operation. This plan was passed twice by Congress and vetoed twice by President Calvin Coolidge. Despite its failure, the effort demonstrated that farm relief could find support in Congress. In 1929, Congress passed the Agricultural Marketing Act, which became the first pledging federal support to stabilize farm prices, but this effort was overwhelmed by the rapidly falling farm prices of the early Depression years. Meanwhile, farmers continued to grow commodities to make up for falling prices.

Up to this point, federal subsidies to support agriculture had not amounted to much. The Morrill Act of 1862 established landgrant colleges, the Hatch Act of 1887 supported research for agriculture, and the Smith Lever Act of 1914 supported some educational programs. None of these aimed at having direct impact on prices and production levels, which should have been set by the free market. In 1916, Congress passed the Federal Farm Loan Act to support farmer cooperatives with loans. Today, it is known as the Farm Credit System. In 1929, Congress passed the Agricultural Marketing Act. The act created the Federal Farm Board, whose goal was to increase commodity prices by placing surplus farm products into storage.

In April 1932, President Franklin Roosevelt delivered one of the first radio speeches of his four terms in office from Albany, New York. Later called "The Forgotten Man" speech, he declared that about half of the nation's population "earn their living by farming or in small towns whose existence immediately depends on farms." However, they were getting less for their crops than it took to produce them. They had lost their purchasing power. These fifty to sixty million people should get a "new deal" that would lift them from "the bottom of the economic pyramid."

The free market approach was about to change. Depression-era legislation established the precedent that the federal government should help support the livelihood of farmers, first as an emergency measure and eventually as a long-term solution to the farm problem. The principle of the free market was set aside as the nation's agricultural sector plummeted during the early 1930s.

The Agricultural Adjustment Act (AAA), signed into law in May 1933 and part of the Farm Relief Bill, had at its center voluntary crop acreage reductions by farmers to control overproduction in some key crops. An allotment system was created for cotton, wheat, and hogs and a year later for corn and tobacco. With the exception of plowing under cotton and killing hogs during the first year of the AAA, its most controversial yet long-lasting legacy was the voluntary allotment system. Farmers agreed by contract to roll back crop acreage in exchange for parity prices. Farmers who joined the system created local associations and elected county-level committee members to self-regulate planting and quota levels. Each farmer's crop quota in acreage and past production became his established base for that particular crop. The base was permanent and could be handed down from generation to generation and passed along to a new owner if the land was sold.

The local committees were formed by a handful of farmers that were, according to one man who participated in surveying tobacco acreage, "usually made up of the more successful or prominent farmers." Although it might seem apparent today, he continued, "this base acreage became the foundation of an enduring aristocracy." To expand farming operations during and after the depression, successful farmers had to acquire land "with an established base," the one that had been set by the rural elite.

Small farmers who grew crops of corn and wheat often opted out of the allotment system. Their land did not become vested with any AAA-established base to pass on to their children or sell to another farmer. And of course, landless sharecroppers and tenant farmers did not participate in the allotment system. As a result, New Deal programs such as the allotment system did nothing to help the nation's poorest farmers, regardless of crop traditions and region, survive the Depression or prepare for the future as agriculturalists. Furthermore, the landless poor often did not receive allotment payments for reducing their crop acreage below parity levels although the AAA called for them to receive a share. Croppers and tenants, especially if they were black, saw their share of the crop plowed under to meet allotment quotas of their landlord. The largest farmers of commodity crops covered by the AAA received that money and often used it to buy more land with an established base and invest in mechanization. They understood that the days of the sharecroppers and tenant farmers as they had existed since Reconstruction were numbered. The landless, tired of hard work and debt, joined the Great Migration and "emigrated in every direction."

THE DUST BOWL

During the 1930s, the Dust Bowl brought on severe and damaging dust storms to the dry southern Great Plains. Drought and poor agricultural practices caused the event. The drought of the "dirty thirties" was considered severe in twenty-seven states, but the hardest hit were Kansas,

Oklahoma, New Mexico, Colorado, and Texas, which had been deep plowed and planted in wheat since settlement during the 1890s. The drought brought human misery to almost all households. Even the better, tighter, well-constructed houses couldn't keep the dust out, and the poorly built tenant shacks with wooden windows and no screens snowed with sand particles, which invaded food, clothing, and bedding. People, crops, and livestock perished. In 1935, Congress declared soil erosion a "national menace" after passing, the year before, legislation that assisted farmers on the brink of bankruptcy taking 140 million acres of federal land out of the public domain to begin conservation efforts. The Drought Relief Service bought cattle in emergency areas in order to aid farmers, though about 50 percent of them were unfit for the beef market. The Soil Conservation Service, moved from the Department of the Interior to the Department of Agriculture, concluded that an estimated 850 million tons of topsoil had blown away.

The drought made it clear that crop overproduction not only depressed prices but also destroyed the soil's ability to heal itself and hold its own. Industrialized wheat farming had destroyed the grassland's topsoil just as surely as deforestation had destroyed eastern ranges and laid them open to decades of commercial farming. Modern agricultural practices were not sustainable. The millions of microorganisms in the soil that maintained its structure and broke down dead plants and animals had disappeared, many of them destroyed by chemical fertilizers. Sir Albert Howard, one of the early leaders of organic farming, believed these microorganisms were the key to healthy soil and healthy plants. He feared that "in years to come, chemical manures will be considered as one of the greatest follies of the industrial epoch."

The Dust Bowl was a teaching moment too big to ignore. The drift of dust from the Great Plains darkened the skies of eastern cities including New York and Washington, DC. In 1936, the Soil Conservation and Domestic Act was passed. Under its mandate the secretary of agriculture made payments to farmers under contract to reduce crops such as cotton and tobacco and take the acreage out of production and begin soil conversation steps. A new AAA act was passed in 1938 after the first AAA was declared unconstitutional by the US Supreme Court because it sought to regulate farm production by collecting the processing tax. The new act used the old acreage allotment system ostensibly to boost the soil conservation effort rather than impose new taxes. The 1938 AAA increased the power of the Commodity Credit Corporation (CCC), created in 1933, to support the prices of corn, wheat, and cotton against the vagaries of the market. The CCC had made loans to farmers and used their crops as security and if prices fell they took title to the crop, stored it, and canceled the farmer's debt. If prices rose, farmers could sell and repay the loan. After 1938, the CCC took in large amounts of these three crops and after war broke out in Europe sold most of the surplus at a profit. Such surpluses were also used to support popular food relief programs, including school lunches and food stamps.

With some tweaking, the New Deal programs along with World War II helped pull agriculture and the nation's economy out of the ditch. Some of these programs survived and today form recognizable components of the farm bill, including programs for crop insurance, conservation, disaster aid, marketing loans, and research. Repeated runs to reform these programs have met with little success, thus leaving the taxpayers with enormous bills, an estimated $428 billion from 2019 to 2023. With each passing decade the proportion of farmers in the labor force dropped from about 30 percent in 1910 to just below 3 percent in 1990, and yet the farm lobby in Washington, with the support of urban legislators who support the bill in part because of nutrition programs, continue to pass farm bills calling for hundreds of billions in taxes. While the farm lobby claims that these subsidies help stop hunger around the world and support small farmers who truly need aid, most of the crop subsidies go to the wealthiest farmers. Economist Vincent Smith estimated that 15 percent of the largest farm businesses receive 85 percent of farm subsidies. Some of their names are on the Forbes 400 list of the wealthiest Americans.

Despite the gains in soil conservation and efforts to stop soil erosion, the amount of harvested farm acreage of 350 million acres in 1920 was about the same by 1954. While it is true that New Deal legislation passed during the mid-1930s temporarily reduced acreage, the declining use of horses and mules and their replacement by tractors eventually freed up land that had been used to grow fodder for draft animals. It would not be until the 1960s that the acreage would drop slightly below three hundred million.

TRACTORS

The period of 1914 to 1954 was still the age of animal power on the nation's farms. In 1930, an estimated twenty-five million horses and mules were used to plant and harvest crops. Early tractors pulled other machines such as combines and threshers. During the late nineteenth century, most of them were heavy and powered by steam. By the beginning of World War I, there were fewer than one hundred thousand tractors in the United States, some of them fueled by kerosene and a few still by steam. In 1920, the West led all regions in tractor use with 7 percent of all farms using them, followed by the North at 6 percent. The South, still mired in cotton production and the crop lien system, had only 1 percent of all farms using tractors.

After the conversion from kerosene to gasoline, from hand cranks to electric starters, and from pulling existing animal-drawn plows to custom-made tractor plows, the number of tractors rose to three hundred thousand by the early 1920s. Henry Ford's mass-produced assembly line introduced the Fordson tractor in 1917. It sold for $750. Competition with other tractor companies such as International Harvester drove down prices to around $400 but Ford temporarily dropped out of the tractor wars on the eve of the Great Depression.

With level lands and a drier climate, Midwestern Corn and Wheat Belt farmers led the way using the expensive, heavy, and powerful tractors that pulled multiple plows across the Great Plains. Some of the earliest "prairie busters" were steam powered. Some regions in the eastern US lagged behind the Midwest because its soil received more rainfall and was hilly. During the mid-1920s, International Harvester introduced its Farmall, so called because it could be used to break the land and cultivate row crops with a variety of attachments. The tractor had reached maturity by 1930 with just over one million in use. The North now led all farm regions with 24 percent of farms using tractors, followed by the West with 19 percent, and the South still last with only 4 percent.

Still, almost seven million farms were without tractors. They were expensive, costing as much as a good team of horses or mules, were likely to break down, and required gasoline rather than home-grown fodder for power. Owners were reluctant to let farmhands operate the expensive equipment, some tending to use them only when they themselves could operate them. In the South, sharecropper and tenant farmer labor allowed the world of horse and mule plowing to continue into the 1950s and 1960s. Some farm workers preferred to work with animals rather than machines. One Alabama tenant farmer said, "I weren't in the knowledge of handlin a tractor and keepin the breakdowns off it. . . . I knowed as much about mule farmin as ary a man in this country. But when they brought in tractors, that lost me." The South was one of the last areas of the nation to make the transition to tractors.

The significance of the tractor's impact on rural America's economy and society should not be underestimated. Today, tractors are so commonplace, including down-sized yard tractors common in suburbia, that we tend to overlook them. But farmer John Froelich's idea to upgrade his clunky steam-powered thresher by adding a gasoline tank and engine was a game changer. The machine threshed more than one thousand bushels of grain a day and moved safely at speeds up to three miles an hour using about twenty-six gallons of gasoline. Froelich soon opened the Waterloo tractor factory with several partners in 1895, an operation that would eventually be absorbed by John Deere.

Sears Roebuck & Company's mail order catalog entered the tractor field first by selling farm implements made by the David Bradley Company in Bradley, Illinois. Bradley, a farmer and machinist, relocated from New York state to Chicago during the mid-1830s and like other easterners, such as Vermont-born John Deere, saw an opportunity when confronted by the farming challenges of the shortgrass plains. During the Depression, Sears sold tractor kits with appropriate Depression-era names such as the "Economy" and "Thrifty" models with Ford and Chevrolet automobile engines and steel wheels. By the 1920s, Sears offered a "guaranteed" tractor-ready plow for about eighty dollars as well as tractor disc harrow for $66.50. Largely because of the Sears connection and its mail order catalog business, the David Bradley brand became a household name, turning out cob crushers and feed grinders in addition to plows and harrows. The introduction of the David Bradley walk-behind garden tractor in 1946 led to such popularity that the David Bradley Company became the largest manufacturers of such machines in the world. Tractor and associated implement factories employed thousands of workers to meet the growing demand.

According to some economic historians, the tractor helped increase food production that allowed rich and poor, at home and abroad, access to lower-priced food. This transition also marked the beginning of the end for animal power on the nation's farms. Also, crop acreage needed to feed working animals such as horses and mules could now be planted in commodity crops and increase farm income. Since tractors could perform all the steps in farming formerly done by humans, including plowing, planting, cultivating, fertilizing, and harvesting, fewer farmers were needed. The great migrations from rural to urban areas coincided not only with the Depression but also with the rise of the tractor. Within twenty years, tractors replaced animal power on all but the most remote and hilly terrains and by the 1960s horses and mules plowing crops became a rare sight. Tractor production reached its peak in 1951 when 564,000 of them rolled off the assembly lines.

THE BIG FARM PLAN

Gradually, the agricultural landscape was being rearranged by outmigration, tractors, and by all-weather roads. Before the Depression of the 1930s most rural roads were in terrible condition. One county's roads were described as being in "fearful" shape and the prosperity of the countryside as "clogged." In inclement weather, poor roads made travel difficult or impossible. Heavy spring rains levied a hypothetical mud tax on farmers, eating up valuable time and wearing out teams and wagons. One Kentuckian said of rural travel, "I could go by mud roads or dust roads or the railroad." Many states created highway commissions and even designated roads that were surfaced as part of the federal highway system. On the eve of the Depression, Kentucky, for example, had designated almost four thousand miles of surfaced roads as links in the federal system, but once off those highways travel went downhill quickly. Prior to the arrival of good roads, farming families stayed close to home or took the nearest train. Independent-minded farmers still saw neighborhood roads, which they had been called upon to keep in good shape by county government, as a truly local issue rather than part of any larger system. This was particularly true of "settlement" roads. Normally not much more than five miles long, these private lanes crossed farms and linked them to public county roads, which led to county seat towns and markets. They were considered a local resource dependent upon local farmers for upkeep and not part of a larger road system.

There was no federal road construction funding for rural areas until 1916 and the passage of the Federal Aid Road Act. In 1921, the Federal Highway Act created the Bureau of Public Roads, which fell under the supervision of the secretary of agriculture. However, it was not until 1925 that Congress passed the Federal Aid Highway Act. Before that act named highways (Lincoln and Lee, for example) and state numbering systems were under the oversight of private highway clubs. This led to confusion among interstate travelers. The 1925 act set standards for roads receiving federal funds and placed their management under state highway departments. Gradually, roads that had been little better than dirt wagon trails became standard-sized two-lane highways. The miles of surfaced roads increased to almost 522,000 by 1926.

The state of roads in rural areas was connected to the extent to which farmland had been improved. In the Midwest, 74 percent of the land was improved compared to about 50 percent in the South by 1920. Upper South states such as Kentucky fell somewhere in between. It would take Depression-era road projects funded by federal and state governments to convince farmers that paved roadways were part of a worthwhile and "technological" system dependent on cooperation and engineering know-how. The USDA closely watched and measured the distance between farms and "all weather roads." By the end of the 1930s, New Deal road projects had expanded the road system to such an extent that 90 percent of the population lived within ten miles of a Federal Aid Road.

Increasingly, electric power lines followed the new highways into farming country. Still, only about 10 percent of the nation's farms had electric power during the early 1930s. The New Deal's Tennessee Valley Authority (TVA) made cheaper electric power more available in Tennessee, Alabama, and Kentucky. The TVA example led Congress to create the Rural Electrification Administration, which helped establish rural electric cooperatives throughout the nation. About half of the country's farms had electricity by 1941 and by the mid-1950s electric lines had reached most farms. The TVA was also a major player in using electric power to produce synthetic nitrates used in munitions and in nitrate-based fertilizers. The Muscle Shoals fertilizer research center in northern Alabama became a center for experimentation and education in the use of new nitrate-based fertilizers that would dominate the postwar years. Farmers whose lands were condemned to make way for lakes to power the generators joined the millions already on their way off the land. Kentucky Dam, the largest in that state, would take about three hundred thousand acres of fields, forests, and farming communities out of agricultural production and move about 3,500 people out of the lake's footprint.

New highways, rural electrification, federal crop production controls, and chemical fertilizers would all become important parts of the postwar transformation of the nation's agricultural landscape, but fewer and fewer of the literally millions of white and black landless farmers would remain in the countryside to enjoy them. One African American farmer of a small farm hoped to get credit to buy fertilizer and said the dealer "turned me down just like I was a dog." Farmers at the lowest end of the economic ladder could not afford to purchase the new, electrified, and labor-saving washing machines, not to mention a tractor.

Rural families believed farm life was superior morally and culturally to city life. Cities were corrupt and sinful. As one South Carolina woman recalled, "We thank God for our life on the farm. We learned to cope with situations when we were young—circumstances help to make you stronger." So long as local roads were good enough to reach local markets and local churches, the centers of social life, farm families were not inclined to speed up their ties to cities and erode household self-sufficiency. Living on the land reinforced their faith that rain would fall, and harvests would be bountiful because they worked hard, led simple and virtuous lives, and kept the faith.

Despite the economic challenges of the Depression era, farming families' greater participation in consumer culture was reflected in their growing attachment to home radios. By the 1930s, the price of radio sets had dropped, and manufacturers advertised battery powered home radios for rural areas without electricity. By 1930, about 27 percent of rural families owned radios. The 1923 Sears, Roebuck catalog offered a Westinghouse for sixty-five dollars that was the "ideal radio for campers, tourists, and persons situated in the rural districts." The catalog offered a more complete list of radios in its radio catalog sent postpaid on request.

Radios helped shape a national mass culture, in part because sponsors wanted their radio advertisements to appeal to the widest possible audience regardless of region. Regions became less important as listeners heard calls for unity during President Franklin Roosevelt's "fireside chats" and World War II calls for sacrifice for the national good. Name brand automobiles, cosmetics, fertilizers, and farm equipment developed rural followings over the radio. The same mail order catalogs that sold radios and farm implements also offered rural customers a department store on pages that touted the superiority of mass-produced "luxurious parlor sets" and comfortable bed sofas and "guaranteed work shirts" that undermined the traditional home manufacture of furniture and clothing. Vernacular designs in almost everything domestic were replaced by a new urban aesthetic that increasingly made rural America appear to be a backwoods landscape.

Among farmers there were distinctions shaped by race and class, despite commonly shared experiences with land, crops, animals, and their sense of independence. Farmers who did not own land were frequently forced to move to another place due to exploitation by unscrupulous landlords. In the South, the Cotton Belt was home to one-third of the nation's farm population, or about two million families. They lived in fear and poverty. Farmers who owned land and worked it with family members or hired labor were more independent. They believed that farming gave them a way to make a living as a family in an era before agribusinesses and big farming sent many of them into debt. The greatest prewar differences were between those who owned the land they worked and those who were landless, the tenant farmers and sharecroppers who were often seeking more productive land to work. For their families this meant a seemingly endless series of moves from one substandard small house without indoor plumbing or electricity to another.

During the interwar years, many farmers continued to keep their own seed corn and exchanged it with neighbors, but science was beginning to make inroads here, too. Hybrid corn experiments were conducted at Michigan Agricultural College during the 1870s, and by the 1910s continuing experiments at agriculture research stations demonstrated that hybrids could outproduce the older open pollinating varieties. By the early 1940s, hybrids represented a majority of the seed corn planted, which started farmers down the path to dependency on commercial sources of seed along with decreasing genetic variety. Hybrid seed developers such as Iowa's Roswell Garst developed seed corn that he sold from farm to farm beginning in 1927. By 1931, the agribusiness firm of Garst and Thomas was a major dealer in high-yield and hybrid corn that eventually became the Golden Harvest brand.

WORLD WAR II

During the early war years, the Roosevelt administration encouraged the production of critical outputs. Late in 1942, Congress passed legislation that provided for at least 90 percent of parity for basic commodities, parity being based on the value of those products from 1910 to 1914. Agricultural prices began to rise, and some were held in check by the administration to prevent inflation. By mid-1941, the demand for farm produce among both the US and British militaries increased farm purchasing power by about 25 percent.

One of the war's greatest blanket deferments came in the fall of 1942 when Congress, under pressure from the Farm Bloc, passed the Tydings Amendment. It exempted about two million farm workers from conscription. Still, the exodus of farmers from the land continued, especially among the young. Labor shortages on farms became a common problem despite the deferments. An estimated 20 percent of the prewar workforce entered military service. In the South alone just over 20 percent of the farm population left the land between 1940 and 1945. The vacant roles of military men and women had to be filled at home to meet production goals and the labor shortage was often filled by women. In 1945, the USDA reported that just over 22 percent of all agricultural workers were women, up 8 percent from 1940. The Women's Land Army of America (WLAA) was a major contributor of agricultural workers. Between 1943 and the end of the war more than 1.5 million women worked in the WLAA, the World War II version of the "farmerettes" of World War I. After its establishment in 1943, its women cultivated almost every crop in high demand, weeding, hoeing, and picking fruit as well as shearing sheep, raising chickens, and working in canneries. They were paid on regional scales with the Northwest having the highest per hour rates of between sixty and ninety cents, while the Southeast had the lowest, frequently only twenty cents an hour. The South opposed working WLAA women in the fields in part due to the negative stereotypes of women field hands, but by the end of the war several hundred thousand worked in the fields of the South and Midwest.

Farm women also found work in nonfarm factories and joined the migration of rural folk to wartime manufacturing centers and hundreds of military bases. Animals and crops with high fat and oil content were needed because their high caloric content and shortages in fat were a concern among war food production planners. The USDA encouraged the increased production of hogs for lard and pork meat and more peanuts and soybeans. The Hormel meat processing corporation alone produced fifteen million cans of Spam per week. To meet its goals, the firm bought on average 1.6 million hogs each year. An estimated 90 percent of this output went to allied military forces. Cattle fattening days were cut from between 90 to 180 to only 30 to 90 days to speed up the supply of wartime meat. Partly for this reason the agricultural sector of the economy, which started to slowly improve early in the war, became one of the biggest gaining sections of the nation's economy by 1945.

Another reason for an improved agricultural economy was the emergence of the Farm Bloc. It represented agribusinesses with political clout in Washington, DC, the center of wartime planning and defense contracting. Over half a million farmers belonged to the American Farm Bureau Federation. The biggest agribusinesses appreciated government contracts and sought them out but wanted little or no government interference in their internal efforts to fill wartime military orders. Most of all they wanted cheap labor, low operating costs, and increased prices for their goods. Increased mechanization was essential if the agricultural sector were to replace the men and women who left for military service or to work in industrial assembly lines. The tractor was part of the answer. By 1945, a USDA census reported that just over two million tractors were operating in the fields of the North, South, and West.

From the viewpoint of government planners and economists, the Great Depression and both world wars had left the agricultural community with something of a tabula rasa. Most of the landless sharecroppers and tenant farmers were gone from the land or would be in another fifteen or twenty years, heading for growing urban centers throughout the nation. Small family farmers held onto their property for another decade or two, but by the 1970s and 1980s they, too, were displaced by industrial farming.

By the 1950s, the changes that were explored in this chapter were apparent in farm country throughout the United States. Outmigration, mechanization, highway construction, and farm consolidation were all obvious in the country and in town. The dirt roads that led to farming sections were lined with empty tenant houses, leaning outbuildings, and empty barns. Farm folk left for wartime service, to work in cities and industrial plants, and did not plan to return. One southern farmer recalled that four out of five of his grown children were somewhere in the North. If you followed the roads to town, the transition was felt there as well. On a main street that once was fronted by a half dozen grocery stores maybe one store remained and the rest shuttered. The mule barns and pens were empty. The town folk were losing their countryside customers.

The farmers who worked the land before World War II looked back on an age of animal power that many were happy to leave behind. For them, the turning point was the arrival of tractors as wartime production of tanks, jeeps, and trucks shifted to farm machinery and automobiles. The bright new green and red tractors seemed to appear magically on railroad station platforms before they were moved to the tractor dealer's lot. The more complicated cotton pickers and combines were even more fascinating to watch as they rolled by from the countryside into town after a day in the fields. These costly machines were symbols of rising agribusinesses and the elite farmers who could afford to buy them to work on their new and expansive consolidated holdings.

Animal power had fueled America's farms since the arrival of the Euro-Americans. The empty mule and horse barns were reminders that agriculture as they and generations of their ancestors had known it had turned a page. For several decades a few of them, even in town, kept a horse or mule and a small wagon shed and plowed garden plots for families who still wanted to grow some of their own food. For someone born after 1945 and living in town, these men and animals turning the dirt seemed like players in a living history demonstration. It was their way of holding onto a farming past that had been their way to make a living, providing for their families, and growing what their household and their animals needed for food. The new way of farming represented by the machines was not their way and their arrival soon divided farmers into social groups: those who could afford industrial farming and those who could not and were on their way out.

It is important to keep nostalgia in check when looking back on the prewar era. Some people left family farms with a dislike for the life they had led. Many did not tend to see themselves as victims of larger and overwhelming forces that changed rural America. One Texas farmer recalled during the early 1980s that he "disliked" farming very much. It seemed that work never ended. Crops, fences, buildings, and livestock always needed attention. Meanwhile, his peers in town did not have to work as much, or, if they did, it was not the exhausting physical labor he experienced. A South Carolina farm family had no choice in their departure from the rural countryside. After they lost much of their property during the post–World War I agricultural depression, the sharecropping family decided to leave the farm behind and moved to a textile mill village to find work.

For African Americans, racial oppression and the fear of violence, especially lynching, were reasons for leaving. Landless farmers such as one Texas cropper never felt they got a fair shake from landlords. Even if blacks stayed on the land, they risked abuse and violence for little in return once the costs of farming on shares were deducted. One said, "They were taking it all away. Black man didn't have a chance." These sentiments reflected the thoughts of thousands of black and white landless farmers who left the land after World War II. Those who had seen a larger world beyond the isolated farming communities they knew as children were in no hurry to return. Military service gave many of them an opportunity that their families had never known—attending college on the GI Bill, buying a home, and entering a profession in towns or cities where their children had a brighter future than the one they had known. Compared to the misery and poverty of farm life during the Great Depression, town life seemed like the gateway to middle-class status. But the future outlook for a new generation of young farmers was not bright; the continuing decline in the number of farms and the consolidation of acreage into big commodity farms made acquiring land increasingly difficult. Big government's plan to move hundreds of thousands of small farmers off the rural landscape had worked extremely well, but there was no plan to move them back onto farms once World War II and the Great Depression had passed.

7

Get Big or Get Out

As the nation emerged from almost thirty years of world wars and depression, farmers looked to the future with optimism. Many of the old barriers to successful farming had been eliminated. Millions of farm workers left the land and would soon be replaced by mechanization. Large farms appeared from the consolidation of smaller ones, the vanishing symbols of the old tenant and sharecropping systems. The science and technology used to win the wars now turned to producing chemical fertilizers and pesticides. Overproduction of farm produce, which had led Roosevelt's administration to the radical act of calling for killing hogs and plowing under cotton, was now managed by a small army of federal and state bureaucrats whose job was to allocate crop acreage and monitor production staying within limits. Farmers who owned land and could afford the high input of large-scale industrial farming could realistically envision an era when the gap between farmers and town folk narrowed. Over the next forty years, farmhouses began to look more like those in the suburbs, ranch-style homes with paved driveways and garages. With school consolidation their children would go to high school in the same classes as urban children, wear the same type of clothes, and they would drive family cars that were similar to those in town. Many of the symbols of an inferior rural society—dirt roads, one-room frame schoolhouses, small and dilapidated homes—were falling by the wayside. Rising expectations led farmers to believe their income would at least equal, if not exceed, that of those who decided to find work in booming postwar factories rather than returning to the farm.

As World War II ended, Secretary of Agriculture Henry Wallace looked toward the future and wrote: "The wisdom of our actions in the first three years of peace will determine the course of world history for half a century." Wallace's influence during the final years of Roosevelt's administration waned after he was replaced as vice presidential nominee on the 1944 Democratic party ticket by Harry Truman of Missouri. When Truman became president upon Roosevelt's death, Wallace slipped further from the center of power, and so did agriculture. Truman replaced Wallace as secretary of agriculture. During the early Cold War years American agriculture, which had been an important part of feeding the allied armies and home front civilians, was pushed to the margins of US global strategy in favor of the science and technology needed for Cold War nuclear weapons. Agriculture was still important during the Cold War era to both support friendly nations such as those in Western Europe aided under the Marshall Plan, where the spread of communism was feared, and to punish new communist regimes, such as Cuba.

In 1954, the Agricultural Trade Development and Assistance Act authorized the secretary of agriculture to accept foreign currency to repay up to $700 million in commodities sent to friendly countries. This act was commonly called Public Law 480. It eventually covered more than ten programs such as food for peace and third world agricultural development projects. The general theme of postwar federal economic policy was a larger free market role and a smaller place for the New Deal legacies. Congress approved supports for some commodities until 1949. When postwar prices slumped as they did in 1919, farmers sought to extend economic support. Later, at the end of the Korean War, support was no longer needed and with rare exception, American farmers produced far more than the market demanded until 2005.

During the 1950s and 1960s, several important trends were apparent. The availability of tractors and other farm machinery reduced the farm labor force by about 50 percent. Farm consolidation was rapid in the wake of New Deal crop restrictions intended to reduce overproduction. Rural outmigration that took place during the 1930s and 1940s made it difficult for farm operators to find labor. This was true especially in the South where cotton depended upon black labor. One agricultural engineer understood as early as 1946 when he observed that "much of this labor is not returning to the farm . . . the cotton farmer is forced to mechanize." The same engineer noted that the new machines did not force out labor but replaced the workers who already had left the farm. An estimated four million blacks had left the South before the growing use of machines made up the labor gap.

The amount of the nation's farmland grew on an almost continuous basis until the 1950s when a downturn began. During that decade, land in farms dropped by more than forty million acres, most of it in the eastern part of the country. By 1960, farm acreage in the East had fallen to World War I levels, much of it taken for urban expansion, abandoned and fallow, or planted in trees. Most of this land was agriculturally productive. This stalling on the farm front along with the removal of the World War II high demand for food crops foreshadowed a long period of lingering doubt about lasting farm prosperity. Would the postwar depression that began in 1919 be repeated during the new postwar era?

During the 1950s, many families had their weekly supply of eggs and milk delivered to their front doors by people they knew. Families also knew where their farm produce came from. Half a dozen family-owned grocery stores lined main streets and sold food to town and rural folk. But things began to change. More often families drove about ten miles to the county seat town with its new modern supermarket. Small farms and country stores seemed old, dirty, and outdated. More and more Americans trusted supermarkets for food because their products were deemed safe by food inspectors and the brands of the products they sold were recognizable. One such store was the Piggly Wiggly.

Piggly Wiggly was the nation's first supermarket. Its first store opened in Memphis, Tennessee in 1916. It was the brainchild of grocer Clarence Saunders. Traditionally, women took a list to the grocery store and clerks filled the list with groceries from a storage room. Piggly Wiggly offered the first true self-service set up with aisles and checkout counters. Empowered shoppers filled their own baskets with the individually priced name brands they preferred. The backroom order clerks were eliminated, and the cost of products declined. In 1921, Piggly Wiggly offered seven types of flour. As one magazine advertisement declared in 1929, "Make your own decisions—within easy reach, on open shelves and stands, the choice foods of the world are waiting to be looked over at Piggly Wiggly. Beyond the turnstile, a land of adventure!" The supermarket was a progressive reform that empowered women to make their own choices and save money by deciding for themselves the brands that fit their table's budget and taste.

Piggly Wiggly was perfectly positioned to take advantage of the migration of farm families to larger rural towns and cities, which only accelerated during the early twentieth century. The country life movement, a Progressive-era undertaking that grew out of Theodore Roosevelt's Country Life Commission, hoped to improve farm life by educating women on scientific farming, home economics, and health care for women and children on the farm. Farm mechanization would save labor for women as well as men allowing the "urban homemaker ideal" to take root in the countryside. As historian Elizabeth Ann Ramey concluded, however, "young farm women were leading the charge to the city." Tired of the long hours and isolation of farm life, they were ready for a change and supermarkets gave them control over an important part of their lives.

During the 1920s and 1930s Piggly Wiggly's radio advertisements combined the claims of their newspaper advertisement texts into radio scripts featuring country slang and music. It was not unusual to find a supermarket on the town's major street, and in the case of a Piggly Wiggly in Americus, Georgia, next to the motion picture theater, guaranteeing a steady flow of farm families by both doors.

By 1932, Piggly Wiggly alone had more than two thousand stores. It's understandable why by the 1950s local food sourcing was drying up given the rise of frozen foods after World War II. The supermarket chain thrived in the South and Midwest, especially in county seat towns. The food choices were greater in chain stores but rarely local or produced in the same part of the state. Farm families continued to grow garden crops and livestock for home consumption, but more and more town families turned to grocery stores with row after row of canned goods, boxed cereals, and bagged flour and rice to stock their pantry.

According to historian Paul K. Conkin, agriculture experienced such a transformation after 1950 that he has described it as an "agricultural revolution." He wrote that "very few crops failed to experience an almost unbelievable burst of productivity gains," adding that the largest gains were in the productivity per unit of labor. This change continued until the end of the twentieth century. Conkin believed that machinery, electrification, chemical inputs, and plant and animal breeding were all central to the rate of growth in labor productivity. The impact of improved hybrid grain varieties, synthetic fertilizers, and chemicals resulted in such tremendous gains that they were described as a "green revolution." The high cost and large scale of industrial farming would mean that only the wealthiest farmers could afford to participate in the agricultural revolution. That reality led President Nixon's secretary of agriculture Earl Butz to declare "Get Big or Get Out" to small family farmers.

Prior to the 1950s, many farmers practiced what was called traditional farming. By that historians mean they used animal and human power, sources that had not changed since the Euro-Americans arrived. They raised crops to feed those animals and used their manure for fertilizer. Most of these farmers grew mixed crops and a variety of livestock. Crop rotation was necessary to maintain soil fertility. Corn was the basic food crop for people and animals, but many farmers grew one cash crop such as tobacco, cotton, or wheat and sold it on local markets. Often the success of this one cash crop meant the difference between being able to pay debts and taxes and continue into another year of farming or failure. Too much or too little rain could set the farm back. There was little a family could do about it except borrow money for supplies for the upcoming year unless the barns and smokehouses were full. Even into the 1960s many small farmers continued along the traditional farming path.

According to the *New York Times*, Butz negotiated a major change in federal farm policy while serving from 1971 to 1976 as secretary of agriculture. President Nixon told Butz to make food cheaper for American consumers. In 1972, Butz brokered a huge grain deal with Russia that emptied much of the US grain surplus but created a problem of how to make up the shortage. Butz's answer was for agriculture to get big. He became the voice of the nation's agribusiness establishment and a champion of corporate and factory farming and the use of chemical fertilizers and pesticides as well as hybrid seeds.

Agronomist and humanitarian Norman Borlaug is often called the father of the green revolution. Borlaug received a doctorate in plant pathology and genetics at the University of Minnesota and undertook agricultural research in Mexico. There he developed semi-dwarf and high-yield wheat varieties that greatly improved food security there and in India and Pakistan. Borlaug hoped that increasing crop yields by using NPK (nitrogen, phosphorus, potassium) fertilizers that were abundant as the nation's wartime chemical industry transitioned to peacetime use would decrease deforestation and minimize environmental impact on the soil in developing countries. Borlaug hoped peasants in nations such as India and Pakistan would benefit most from his work, which was recognized by a Nobel Peace Prize in 1970. Borlaug's mantra was "Give the farmers more fertilizers." Pushing fertilizers was an important part of selling new genetically modified hybrid seeds that were responsive to the NPK plan. Chemical farming destroyed many of the organic nutrients in the soil.

Organic farming leader Alfred Howard's fear that the abundant postwar use of chemical processes, such as fixation of nitrogen, would lead to a seed-fertilizer revolution that would culminate in dying soil had become a reality. Agribusinesses were major domestic players in the chemical farming revolution, which only increased soil toxicity and trace elements due to farm runoff. How long had this process lasted before the Green Revolution? Wherever deforestation and prairie busting took place it was only a matter of time before natural organic replenishment of the soil was lost and chemical input was needed. This was certainly true in the Deep South where cotton production would not reach its peak until the early twentieth century. It was also true in the Dust Bowl of the 1930s, where grain monocultures, deep plowing, and chemical fertilizers killed soil nutrition.

FARM CRISIS

By 1970, real farm income reached $48 billion and within three years almost doubled at $92 billion. It appeared that Earl Butz's "get big" agricultural model was paying off in farm country in ways no one could have anticipated. Commodity prices continued to increase due in part to high demand in export markets, the increasing value of farm real estate, and easy credit available to buy more farmland and equipment. The boom was on to plant on more land worked with more equipment. During the 1970s, farm real estate debt increased from $29 billion to $79 billion and total farm business liabilities almost tripled. The idea that the boom could end and leave farmers overexposed was not unheard of in farm country. One Iowa banker said, "For any farmer who has become overextended,

I am sure it is going to be hell." But many farmers had bought into the idea that bigness in agriculture was the way to future prosperity. As long as the returns on their commodity crops allowed them to pay their debts and maintain an improved socioeconomic status, few questioned the Butz's philosophy.

The 1970s and its years of speculative excess could not last forever. In the fall of 1979, the Federal Reserve Board tightened its monetary policy to bring inflation under control. This was not a repeat of the expected agricultural cycle of one year's crop overproduction leading to low prices followed the next year by decline in production and a return of better prices, this was something different. Inflation, high oil prices, the US trade embargo, and the Federal Reserve Board's decision all added up to a major economic crisis.

Farm income went down as fast as it went up ten years prior. Between 1980 and 1983, real farm income dropped from $23 billion to about $8 billion. The Farm Credit System saw its first loss since the Great Depression, due to overproduction brought on by the nation's own Green Revolution fed by hybrid seeds, synthetic fertilizers, mechanization, and staple monoculture production. Higher oil prices and the trade embargo with Russia were also important factors. The crisis was felt everywhere, but it was centered in the Midwest, described by one historian as one of the most developed landscapes in the nation. It was a place where "the industrial ethos became an article of faith for farmers during the post-war period" and big agriculture was the mantra during the 1970s. The crisis of the 1980s was the worst for farmers since the Great Depression. Prices dropped, loans were called in, and interest rates doubled. Writer Debbie Weingarten likened the 1980s crisis to a "wrecking ball in rural America."

According to historian J. L. Anderson, farmers in Iowa had accepted hybrid seeds during the 1930s and 1940s, which helped set the stage for the use of chemical fertilizers after 1945, especially nitrogen and phosphates. During the 1940s and 1950s antibiotics and growth hormones were introduced to cattle after farmers became aware of them from county extension agents, farm journals, and other media. Due in part to postwar labor shortages and rural electrification, "push button" farming appeared in the dairy industry. High investment costs forced farmers to increase the size of their herds, a process that was well underway in Iowa by the 1970s. There, investment in the Green Revolution model had helped achieve Butz's get big plan for US agriculture. Due to investments in land and equipment during the boom years, farm debt in those areas doubled between 1978 and 1984. Meanwhile, in some areas of the Midwest the value of farmland dropped by 60 percent during the early 1980s.

Why did farmers fail to organize themselves during this crisis? Some historians believe that farmers who followed the bigness path now viewed themselves as businessmen, members of the middle class with modern homes and the same aspirations as bankers, agribusiness men, and dealers in machinery and fertilizers. They had allied themselves with people who they believed had mutual interests. To revolt against the town elites that controlled industrial farming as poor farmers did during the Populist revolt of the 1890s would alienate the same people they depended on for credit and market access and be against their self-interest.

Race was also an issue that kept farmers from uniting. White farmers wanted to see their ties to bankers, agribusiness men, and government lenders and federal and state programs as a relationship that largely excluded blacks. In 1997, Timothy Pigford and four hundred other African American farmers filed a class action lawsuit against the USDA. The plaintiffs claimed that between 1981 and 1996 the agency had discriminated against black farmers seeking loans to weather hard times and named agency head Dan Glickman as defendant. Black applications for family farm loans to support the purchase of seed and fertilizer were lost in the shuffle. The *Pigford v Glickman* case in 1999 recognized blacks had been denied access to USDA farm programs that would have benefitted them and let them remain a part of the agricultural community. Because a farmer's credit was used to decide whether an application was approved or not, black farmers were especially hard hit. Many lost their farms due to tax sales.

Eventually, more than $2 billion in payments was made in an effort to rectify this wrong in two settlement stages. The payments to what would grow to thousands of farmers was the largest civil rights settlement up to that time. This history of racial discrimination was especially true in the South, where segregation was a matter of course and reached far beyond the 1981 beginning date of the lawsuit. There, a handful of county-level agency committee members with programs such as the Soil Conservation Service, for example, were not only white but frequently among the largest farmers in the county. By 1992, black farmers in that region had decreased by 98 percent and their committee representation was estimated at 1 percent or less. But in the Midwest, where the percent of black farmers was historically low, there were no African American committee members. As a result of this case, others were filed against the USDA representing American Indians and women farmers. Gradually, the numbers of minority and disadvantaged farmers began to increase. The 2008 farm bill, for example, contained funding for programs to specifically begin a process of correcting these wrongs.

The general feeling that seemed to persist among farmers was one of helplessness. Their numbers had dwindled since the beginning of the century to such an extent that they were powerless to bring about change themselves and could not depend on state and federal leaders of the agricultural establishment to champion their cause. Farmers themselves were divided about rejecting a culture of agricultural "bigness" that they so recently believed would bring them prosperity and a permanent seat at the middle-class table. The elite farmers at the top of the industrial farm ladder indicated that such upward mobility was possible, and then some. Between 1974 and 1992 the number of farms whose value of sales exceeded half a million or more increased from 11,412 to almost 47,000, while those whose sales fell between $100,000 and $499,999 doubled. Members of those groups saw no reason to rock the boat and held the most sway in the major farm organizations and the farm lobby in Washington. Ultimately the farming elite and the agribusiness establishment sought to control the future of American farming through periodic farm bills and the North American Free Trade Agreement.

FARM BILLS

The origins of many farm bill programs can be found in the Great Depression of the 1930s and especially the Agricultural Adjustment Act (AAA) of 1933. Commodity price supports, import restrictions, crop insurance, and production controls all reshaped an agricultural landscape that before World War I was largely a free market world. After World War II most efforts to return to the pre-Depression philosophy were considered "reform," but there have been few of these, especially in years when commodity prices have fallen and when the farm lobby has placed pressure on Congress to not only keep farm bill revenue streams, but to also increase and expand them. In 1996, Congress passed the Federal Agricultural Improvement and Reform Act, called by some the Freedom to Farm Law, which removed many of the AAA's crop controls. Farmers were free to exercise their own discretion in crop planting and marketing. By the end of the decade, however, Congress changed direction with a number of supplemental farm bills that ended up costing not $47 billion but $121 billion. Another reform in 2002 increased subsidy payment by almost 75 percent over ten years. The farm lobby was so strong that in 2008 Congress overrode a presidential veto by George W. Bush and added even more subsidies.

During the eighty years since the Great Depression, subsidies have altered the American farm scene. Small farmers who might have represented an alternative to large commodity operations have all but

FIGURE 7.1. Empty farmhouse, 1972. Mechanization and farm consolidation left many homes abandoned. Photo by author, copyright 1972

disappeared. The idea that the average farmer operates a small family farm is a myth, as are old concepts such as a free market and supply and demand. Indeed, the new American plantation belt of the Midwest has the lowest percent of family farms by state in the nation. President Eisenhower's warnings about the dangers of the military-industrial complex are just as appropriate for the present-day agricultural-industrial complex with farm bill after farm bill funneling billions into farm country each year in the forms of agricultural subsidies, crop insurance, price loss coverage, and federally funded research and development for the agriculture industry. It all adds up to one of the largest wealth redistribution schemes in American history, one that effectively removed the nation's most disadvantaged farmers from the agricultural landscape.

FARMS ON THE MOVE

During the post–World War II era, the geographical distribution of farms continued to change. Early in the nation's history the crop belts extended in a generally westward pattern. In 1950, about half of the farm population of the United States was in the South and around one-third in the Midwest. Thirty years later these regional roles had reversed. By 1980, about half of the farm population was in the Midwest and almost 30 percent was in the South. Obviously, mechanization and rural out-migration played major roles, especially in the South where tenant farming, share cropping, and the decline of African American farmers reduced the number of farmers in the region. These farmers generally did not move to another region to farm and often left farming altogether. By the end of the 1980s, 97 percent of the farm population was white.

NEW PLANTATIONS

Writing in 2008, Conkin described the concentration of farm sales to a commercial farming elite as "scandalous." Farms with sales of more than $100,000 per year sold 89 percent of farm products leaving only 11 percent for the other 1.8 million farms in the nation. Farms below the $100,000 annual sales mark usually needed at least one family member working off farm in nonfarm work to make enough total income to stay afloat. The true elite according to the Department of Agriculture earns sales of more than $250,000 per year. There were about 160,000 of these commercial farm operations in 2002 and they received about three-quarters of all farm sales and government payments. In 2018, there were 239,370 farms with sales of more than $250,000 as consolidation continues.

Another concentration of agricultural wealth in our nation's history, one also controlled by a white male elite with political power and influence in Washington, comes to mind: the plantation elite of the pre–Civil War South. That elite's money crops helped push the Plantation Belt's major commodity crops—cotton, hemp, sugar, and tobacco—westward during the Early Republic. In 2012, only two southern states, Texas (third) and North Carolina (eighth), were in the top ten in the new concentration of farm wealth. California led the rest with Iowa, Nebraska, Minnesota, Kansas, Illinois, Wisconsin, and Indiana following in that order, for a total of 62 percent of the value of all farm products sold. For purposes of comparison, cotton, at its peak as an export commodity, was about 50 percent.

What do these new plantation areas, mostly in the Midwest and Upper Midwest, grow? Mainly wheat, corn, soybeans, poultry, and hogs. What else do they share in common? They are overwhelmingly white states racially and majority red states politically. Historically, they were among the last states in the Midwest and North Central states to be settled and sided with the Union during the Civil War. Collectively, they represent the heartland of the Republican Party with its legacies of free soil, free labor, and free men.

Soybeans are one example of crop migration to the Midwest. Soybeans were first planted in the present-day United States in 1765 in the colony of Georgia. They grew well in the South and were used as forage for farm animals. In 1904, African American scientist and inventor George Washington Carver experimented with soybeans along with peanuts and sweet potatoes, as well as many other crops. He recommended that southern farmers try a three-crop rotation of nitrogen producing peanuts, soybeans, and sweet potatoes over two years and plant cotton in the third year to regenerate the soil. Cotton yields increased. During World War II soybeans were used to produce meat substitutes, lubricants, meal, and plastics and fed to poultry, pork, and cattle. With the arrival of the Green Revolution, herbicide-resistant soybean hybrids were developed and became a staple commodity crop especially in the Midwest, where Iowa, Illinois, Indiana, Minnesota, and Nebraska were leading producers, with the vast majority of the crop turned into meal and vegetable oil.

The Midwestern Plantation Belt received a major head start where the Green Revolution is concerned. Because of its relatively flat terrain it was among the first areas of the nation to experience widespread use of mechanization and transportation systems not dependent on natural levels of rainfall. According to Don and Phillip Paarlberg, Midwestern farmers managed to grow as farm populations in the other areas of the nation declined. They also broke with tradition by embracing science despite the "natural conservatism of farm people." They were not slow to adapt chemicals to farming, embracing hybrid seeds during the 1930s and 1940s. By 1946, DDT was already being used. In the 1940s and 1950s in Iowa, starter fertilizers were being used with as many as 60 percent of farmers using them by 1960.

The rise of the new Plantation Belt with its large-scale farms depended on partners to feed the wonders of science and technology onto the fields. Some observers have described them collectively as an agricultural-industrial complex resembling the military-industrial complex Dwight Eisenhower warned the nation to guard against in 1961. Farmers depended on integrated food conglomerates, scientific research centers, and major nonfarm entities such as Monsanto, Bayer, and Cargill to create new hybrid seeds and fertilizers and pesticides to feed and protect them. These groups, forming an agribusiness establishment, lobbied hard in Washington to push forward the next generation of scientific and technological advances led by champions such as Earl Butz. By controlling the environmental agenda and gaining subsidies for their initiatives in farm bills of the last forty years, billions in farm bill subsidies have gone their way with no end in sight.

For purposes of comparison, the commercial farmers who make $250,000 a year make about the same amount as what the *New York Times* described in 2015 as an "elite group" in US society representing the highest 5 percent of income. There were about 160,000 commercial farmers at the turn of the last century. This comparison is not intended to denigrate their success. It merely points out how concentrated wealth is in modern agriculture. They have had a lot of help along the way. After commodity prices fell in 1996, the federal government started to send about $20 billion a year to farmers. The big commodity farmers received about 75 percent of this largesse between 1995 and 2010 in the wake of the Freedom to Farm Act, which decreased the safety net for farming. According to Conkin, critics of this income and support structure would say "contemporary American agriculture is a scandal."

There is little chance that this situation will change soon. Farm bill subsidies favor the commercial farming group that produces the largest commodity crops. They are as resistant to change as southern planters who were free trade and antiemancipation champions. They and their collaborators in agribusiness, multinational seed, fertilizer, and pesticide corporations, and the farm lobby have shaped the farming landscape to suit them. By 2007, eight commodity crops led by corn, soybeans, and wheat accounted for almost three-quarters of the nation's cropland and their growers received about three-quarters of all government farm subsidies. NAFTA has played a major role in this story since the Farm Crisis.

NORTH AMERICAN FREE TRADE AGREEMENT/ UNITED STATES–MEXICO–CANADA AGREEMENT

The history of the North American Free Trade Agreement (NAFTA) goes back at least to the 1979 presidential campaign and was one of candidate Ronald Reagan's proposals. During his campaign Reagan told voters he hoped that North America could come up with its own version of the European common market. In 1984, Congress passed the Trade and Tariff Act without congressional debate and the power to reject specific proposals. In 1989, the Canada-U.S. Free Trade Agreement began. Although President Bill Clinton did say that NAFTA "means jobs," he did not initiate the controversial agreement. His predecessor George H. W. Bush, and his administration did. President Bush initialed the agreement in August before the presidential election of 1992 the following November. He also negotiated with Mexican president Salinas, whose country had imposed tariffs on US imports that were 250 percent higher than those the United States imposed on Mexican goods.

President Bush believed the deal would be viewed favorably by voters during his campaign, but he lost. He signed it in December before leaving the White House. The bill was supported by both parties, with more senate Democrats voting against than for it. Farmers hoped NAFTA would bring lasting stability and prosperity to rural America thus ending their troubled search for economic success that had eluded them since the 1970s. It was opposed by organized labor, which feared job losses.

In some ways NAFTA went against the free trade philosophy of American farmers. During the nineteenth century, and especially in the South, farmers such as cotton growers wanted to ship their crops abroad to England for use in industrial textile centers such as Manchester. In return they expected no tariffs or at least low ones on the finished goods they imported from overseas. Northeastern manufacturers, on the other hand, wanted high protective tariffs to safe guard them from the competing European manufactured goods. NAFTA's goals included what amounted to a closed trading system based on the free trade idea.

The trade agreement came on the heels of the worst depression in farm country since the Great Depression. Crop prices fell. Farmers were unable to make mortgage payments. Foreclosures followed as did more farm consolidation. Stress in farm states reached new highs, as did farmer suicides. This was a picture at odds with the nostalgic images of family farms and farmers.

Understandably, the complex agreement was soon opposed by many farmers. Some feared that the agreement took away too many farm safety nets, including domestic price supports and loans for commodity production. The removal of these farm safeguards left the nation's farmers vulnerable to crops dumped from Canada and Mexico since protective tariffs were removed by NAFTA. At the same time, export subsidies for commodity traders and brokers, the same agribusinesses that pushed the agreement through Congress, remained in place.

After seven years some critics of NAFTA's new model of export agriculture, which some hoped would cure the farm ills of the 1980s, believed its legacy was "lost farms and rural crisis." Before the agreement, US trade surpluses in agricultural products between the nation and Canada and Mexico reached $203 million during the early 1990s but dropped by almost $1.5 billion under NAFTA. By 2007, corn, cotton, and wheat exports dropped, and prices fell between 20 and almost 40 percent. Some markets did grow, but these were mainly domestic markets and even there the nation's farmers competed with those from Canada and Mexico, just as their farmers competed with exports from the United States. The US International Trade Commission concluded that the value of the nation's grain and cereal exports dropped by 31 percent during the late 1990s. In all three partner countries income for small farmers declined.

Large agribusinesses, however, reaped benefits including greater control over markets by playing off farmers in all three North American nations against each other in a free trade plan with no tariff protection for farmers. The agreement also included wide international intellectual property protection among the three partner nations for some genetically modified seeds and plants. The upshot is that the elite agribusiness and science and research organizations now exercise much more control over almost all aspects of farming from seed research and development to controlling where harvested crops are sold. In the case of NAFTA, both farmers and their representatives in Congress had little input or control in forming the policies that have changed their lives. In September 2018, the NAFTA partners agreed to the United States-Mexico-Canada Agreement (USMCA), which strengthens the partners' manufacturing and automotive outputs.

THE NEW CENTURY

By the end of the twentieth century the number of farms continued to decline. Butz's "get big" strategy scraped hundreds of thousands of people off the agricultural landscape. In 1970, there were approximately 2.7 million farms in the nation with farmers representing 4.6 percent of the US labor force. By 1990, there were about 2.1 million farms and farmers accounted for 2.6 percent of the labor force. The loss of more than a half million farms over a twenty-year span reflected the marginalization of agriculture as a way of life and as an industry as the George H. W. Bush administration began preparations for NAFTA, including the removal of safety nets represented by commodity loans and crop supports. The exact number of farms over time is difficult to assess since in 1974 the USDA redefined "farm" not by acreage but by the value of farm goods sold. Selling $1,000 of agricultural goods in a year qualified an operation as a farm.

The first farm census of the new century was taken in 2002 not by the Census Bureau, but for the first time by the Department of Agriculture's National Agricultural Statistical Service. Their census revealed that the number of farms in the nation was about 2.1 million, approximately the same number as 1990. Critics of NAFTA estimated in 2001 that about thirty-three thousand farms producing below $100,000 a year disappeared since 1993 in that category alone. They claimed the trade agreement often benefitted the farming elite and industrial farming where farm owners do not have complete managerial control of their operations due to contracts with large corporations operating poultry and pork factories.

The farm landscape of the early twenty-first century could not have been more different than the one confronting Europeans at the point of contact during the sixteenth and seventh centuries. First, matriarchy's leadership role in agriculture was replaced by patriarchy. About 90 percent of the nation's farmers are men. Decisions made by native women regarding seed selection and conservation, knowledge that was beneficial to the first European transplants, is now controlled by corporate scientists at research and development facilities. Their new hybrids are protected by patent laws. Second, African Americans have all but vanished from farming, accounting for only about twenty-nine thousand farm operators, including owners and tenant farmers in 2002. The decline of black farmers in the South did not result in gains of farmers in other regions due to their migration to areas such as the Midwest. Rather their experience as farm owners and laborers left them with little hope for a future in agriculture. Near the end of his life, Alabama tenant farmer Nate Shaw recalled that only one of his children decided to try farming, the others migrated to Ohio, New York, and Philadelphia. Cotton, the crop their father farmed on rented land, was gone. The South had fewer acres in cotton in 1960 than Texas alone grew on the eve of the Great Depression.

Less than a decade after NAFTA, cotton, once the greatest crop of export value in the nation, accounted for less than 5 percent of the value of all crops sold. Meanwhile, cotton production in India, which had been declining, reversed course with the help of new hybrid seeds, which in turn needed pesticides, both bought on credit by peasant farmers. Cotton growing expanded to such an extent that food crops were displaced. But when the cotton crop failed during the late 1990s, more than four hundred Indian cotton farmers killed themselves. This scenario was played out in the US South during the late nineteenth and early twentieth centuries. Tenant farmers and sharecroppers could only receive credit for cotton and therefore planted mostly that crop. Their food supply often was drawn from the country stores of landlords and furnishing merchants in tin cans and sacks of corn meal, much of it produced in the Midwest and of poorer quality than garden crops. Their ability to feed themselves worsened as grazing land, fresh water supplies, and fish and game dwindled as cotton farming continued to expand. Rural families in both nations experienced roughly the same fate.

ORGANIC FARMING

The social history of American farming did not have to end with millions of former farmers dispossessed and dependent upon other sources for food and a small group accumulating the wealth. Nonchemical farming was the birthright of the nation's farmers and those the world over. But the timing for organic farming on a large scale was not ideal with the "get big" model taking hold during the postwar era. Earl Butz said, "Before we go back to organic agriculture in this country, somebody must decide which 50 million Americans we are going to let starve or go hungry." The agribusiness establishment was determined to find buyers for its chemical farming products and the organic movement became the straw man in its argument.

In Europe the foundation for the organic movement dated at least to World War I. After World War I, what united its leaders was concern over the rise of chemical farming when military use of cheap nitrogenous explosives and poisonous gases was banned by the Geneva Protocols. These chemicals were repurposed during peacetime to agriculture by their manufacturers in a wide variety of artificial fertilizers and pesticides. Many of the leaders of the organic movement published their concerns in articles and books. Ehrenfried Pfeiffer's *Bio-Dynamic*

Farming and Gardening was published in 1938 prior to his relocation from England to the United States. Albert Howard, an English botanist and organic farmer, spent much of his post–World War I years as an agricultural advisor sent to assist Indian farmers by running the government research station at Indore. Howard concluded that he could learn more about organic farming from Indian peasants than he could teach them, the main lesson being that healthy soil, was the key to healthy villagers, who understood the value of the links between ecology and agriculture. Howard warned during the 1940s of unleashing chemicals on the soil. "Agriculture must always be balanced," he wrote during the 1940s in *Food Shortage and Agriculture*. "If we speed up growth we must accelerate decay. If . . . the soil's reserves are squandered, crop production ceases to be good farming. . . . The farmer is transformed into a bandit."

Howard was not alone. Eve Balfour's book *The Living Soil*, published in 1943, recorded her and her sister's work in what was described as the first side-by-side trial of organic versus chemical farming, which was called the Haughley experiment, named for their farm. The person generally credited with coming up with the term "organic farming" was a farmer, philosopher, and writer named Walter James, Lord Northbourne. A survivor of the horrors of World War I, James published his book *Look to the Land* in 1940 and set out his concept of "the farm as organism." At his farm at Kent, England, he tested many of the ideas of other leaders in the movement, including Rudolph Steiner. He saw the central issue as "organic versus chemical farming" and explored the philosophy of the movement rather than detailing the nuts and bolts "how to" approach. He clearly expressed the threat of chemical farming, centralization of decision making, and its impact on traditional farming and food. He warned that farming should not be viewed as "a mixture of chemistry and cost accounting" and turned into a "modern business, in which speed, cheapness, and standardizing count most." The *English Agricultural Journal* said of *Look to the Land*: "This book sounds an alarm."

Unfortunately, the alarm was lost in the din of postwar mechanization, chemical fertilizers, and industrial farming. During the early 1990s, a Midwestern farmer, for example, started out what had become the normal way to farm after he bought his place. He bought chemical fertilizers and pesticides and tilled the soil. Bad weather and other set-backs soon left him ready to get out of the business. He admitted that while he was a farmer he really didn't know much about soil and how it worked; he eventually figured out that his soil was almost dead. He soon became a major champion of regenerative farming. A major problem for this farmer and others was that his soil had lost much of its carbon content. Deep plowing and tillage had historically gutted the land of carbon, which disappeared into the air instead of feeding plants. Stopping tillage, planting cover crops, and grazing livestock were among the steps taken to begin reversing the carbon loss.

Sir Alfred Howard was not the only person concerned about the relationship between society and science and industry. During his farewell speech to the nation in January 1961, President Dwight Eisenhower cautioned Americans against the domination of government policy decisions by the "scientific-technological elite." Most citizens probably thought he was talking about growing deficits incurred by the external threats to the American way of life posed by the Cold War and the ties between what he called the "military-industrial complex," and he was. But there were also internal threats to society. He continued, "We . . . must avoid the impulse to live only for today, plundering for our own ease and convenience the material assets of our grandchildren." One of those material assets was farmland and the rate of abandonment rose with each decade as industrial farming expanded. The state of small family farms changed dramatically due to the policies Butz championed. Despite technological advancements, such as tractors, which numbered almost five million by 1960, there have been periods of depression where farmers have made less than the national average. The exceptions are years of the early twentieth century before 1920 and the World War II and Korean War years.

At the beginning of the twentieth century farmers kept their own seed corn and exchanged it with neighbors. They did the same with other seed crops. These were open pollinated varieties and farmers traded their favorite and most productive seeds among themselves. While hybrid seeds became popular during the 1920s and 1930s, their history dates back further, at least to the 1870s and experiments at Michigan Agricultural College. Crossing two pure lines provided new strains that outproduced open pollinated seed. By the beginning of World War II hybrids made up the majority of seed corn planted by farmers and were bought from seed companies. This was a quick transition that started farmers down the road to dependency on commercial sources for seed and led to less genetic variety, but heirloom varieties still existed within human memory and farming practice of older farmers used to working with farm animals rather than tractors. The small farmers of the South and Midwest were as close to the millions of Indian peasants as the nation's landscape could find. Such farmers grew farm gardens and food crops such as corn and vegetables with few chemicals and little or no mechanization. Tenant farmer Nate Shaw said, "I didn't never want for no vegetable, what I had I growed em." These included collards, cabbage, potatoes, tomatoes, okra, beans, squash, and onions. He also had chickens and cows for eggs and milk and killed hogs in the winter to put meat on the kitchen table.

But many of these small farmers were located in what economic historian Ross Robertson described during the 1950s as agricultural "trouble spots." These included the "one-hundredth meridian" states subject to drought and wind damage, deforested sections of the Great Lakes and the Appalachian Mountains, and especially the South, where "agricultural distress has been most severe." Although the great migrations of the Depression and war years had moved about one and a half million people off the nation's rural landscape, many of them moved back, as many as half of those in the South returned. Robertson concluded that during the early 1950s, about half of the nation's farm population was in the South, farming small tracts of land with annual income of less than $2,500 with about one tractor to every seven farms. The long periods of agricultural depression that stretched back to the post–World War I years persisted here. For government planners these small and often poor farmers were obstacles to efficient and mechanized large farms growing commodity crops.

Government planners saw part of the answer in acreage restrictions with price supports and a soil conservation program, the latter diminishing "the element of subsidy in the public mind." Small farmers with less money for inputs such as hybrid seeds, fertilizers, and mechanization favored harsh restrictions on acreage coupled with high support prices, while larger and better-off farmers were less concerned with price supports so long as they could plant as much acreage as they wanted, wishes reflected in the "get big" mentality. Robertson wrote during the 1950s that agricultural economists contended that such farm policies could become barriers to solving farm problems.

It did not have to turn out this way. By 1945, there was a clear alternative to becoming a "chemical farmer" dependent on hybrid seeds, toxic fertilizers, and deadly pesticides. It was called organic farming and its twentieth-century roots reached back to post–World War I in Europe, Albert Howard, and many others. In America, J. I. Rodale used the word to describe Howard's ideas expressed in *An Agricultural Testament*. In 1941, Rodale bought a small farm in Pennsylvania with "eroded . . . land and broken-down buildings." His goal was to create a test farm to put organic farming ideas to work. According to his son Robert, who was eleven at the time, they bought cattle mostly for manure, "made piles and piles of compost," and demonstrated that the "best way to convert land from the old high-input pattern using chemical methods" was to use "crop rotations and organic practices."

But under the "get big" philosophy of the 1970s, organic farming's beginnings were lost in a flood of chemical fertilizers and pesticides. Anyone hoping today to repeat the Rodale experiment would need to find land that would go through a three-year transition when no organic banned substances are used to reach certification or purchase certified acreage. In 2014, more than 122,000 acres of farmland was moving toward organic status, in part because almost 40 percent of organic farms were planning to increase their production. About two-thirds of all organic farms are following Rodale's path of using green or animal manures and using buffer strips to protect organic acreage from nonorganic acres. The top five production practices of organic farms in 2014 were green manures, buffer strips, water management, organic compost, and no- or low-till cropping.

Today, the organic farming centers of the nation are in the North and along the West Coast where ten states each reported to the USDA more than five hundred certified organic farms. In 2016, California lead all states in the number of USDA-certified organic farms in the nation followed by Wisconsin, New York, Pennsylvania, and Iowa. Almost all sales went to wholesale markets. Of the top ten organically grown commodities, milk is by far the leader accounting for twice the sales value of eggs, which finished second. Organic sales increased by 23 percent from

2015 to 2016 with six southern states reporting sales increases of more than 100 percent. The total organic sales on US farms and ranches in 2016 was $7.6 billion.

8

The Future: What Kind of Agriculture Do You Want?

Control, consolidation, and chemicals are the key themes to the story of agriculture in the United States. Since beginning this book, one of the largest mergers in our nation's farming history took place during 2017 and 2018. The "Big Six" agricultural chemical and seed corporations merged into the "Big Three": Dow-Dupont, ChemChina-Syngenta, and Bayer-Monsanto. Collectively, these giant agricultural corporations controlled an estimated 60 percent of the world's market.

When the "Get Big or Get Out" era began during the early 1970s, there were about seventy independent corn seed companies according to John Hansen, president of the Nebraska Farmers Union. By the time of the mergers there was "hardly a handful left." Consolidation left greater control in the hands of fewer people and fewer choices for farmers in seeds, chemical fertilizers, and pesticides. In farm country the event caused fear that there would also be less competition. As Hansen said, "I don't know of any merger, ever, in the last 40 years that has produced a benefit to a farmer." The goal, he continued, was to decrease corporate competition, increase market share, and control price margins. Steve Johnson, the Nebraska Farm Bureau president, likewise believed that "There is always some concern when consolidation takes place about the competition in the marketplace." There was little belief that relief might come from Washington, DC, in the form of updating and enforcing the antitrust laws especially when the administration seemed committed "to turn big business loose from government oversight." One journalist asked after the merger of Bayer and Monsanto was completed, "What kind of agriculture do we really want?"

How did our story end this way? It began when Euro-American explorers discovered an agricultural landscape that was old, ordered, and managed by American Indian women. John White's 1580s watercolor painting of the Indian town of Secotan on present-day North Carolina's Outer Banks shows a main street through the center of the village flanked on both sides by houses and fields with a variety of plants in what appears to be both communal and family plots. This arrangement was efficient enough to feed the native population except in times of drought or other natural failures but was not plentiful enough to sustain both Indian and Euro-American populations for any length of time. Gradually over centuries the native population was pushed westward onto semiarid lands of the Trans-Mississippi West and confined to reservations. By 1800, crop regions were well defined in the eastern United States, white men had replaced Indian women as farm owners and managers, and enslaved African Americans were the major farmers of commercial crops.

This was certainly not the ending that American Indians wanted, to be violently driven from farming lands they had cultivated. Amerindians have been farming the soils of North America for thousands of years. Euro-Americans had worked the land for about five hundred years and for much of that time, according to some historians, the tools farmers used had changed little since biblical times.

Nor was it the ending that African Americans wanted, to be forcibly removed from their homeland and driven by abuse, fear, and violence to farm others' farmland for generations. And it is not the ending that traditional family farming agriculture embraced, one now controlled by big agricultural processors and distributors tightly integrated from seed to shelf. It is the ending envisioned by Big Business and Big Government enamored with big profits, efficiencies, and new technologies, one where GPS data-guided machines read the fields better than humans.

Why farm? Given the shrinking presence of farmers in American society, less than 2 percent of the population, it is a question we should ask today. It is far from the easiest way to make a living. Wendell Berry concludes that "they must do it for love." They loved to watch plants and animals grow, to work outdoors with their family and children, and gain a sense of independence, not to mention "live at least a part of their lives without a boss." Good farmers, Berry went on to write, are "stewards of Creation." They conserve soil and water, wildlife, and scenery. "Every man is called to be an artist" and the small family farm is one of the last places to practice the art of agriculture. Michigan farmers were asked this question in 2014: "I farm because . . ." Their responses were similar to Berry's conclusion. They farmed because it was a passion, it was rewarding and self-gratifying being stewards of the land, watching plants and animals grow, and to feed others.

Berry's writings bring us back to the central question of why farm? Bumper stickers tell us "If you ate today, thank a farmer," so providing food is one very important answer. Early American colonists could have thanked an Indian woman farmer for food since their own agricultural adventures led to "starving times." But since the beginning of the twentieth century, science and technology transformed traditional ways of farming and our landscapes like never before. By the end of the last century less than 2 percent of the nation's population farmed compared to about 32 percent in 1920.

Major export crops such as cotton, which once represented almost half of the export value of American agriculture, had fallen to 5 percent by 1998. The landscape emptied itself of farming people and their visible legacies—houses, barns, fences—began to fade and fall away. The soil itself was dead or dying, losing its natural nutrients after decades of chemical fertilizer and pesticide use. Farming as an industry now represents less than 5 percent of the gross domestic product. Farming like many industries has some dark secrets shaped by control, consolidation, and chemical agriculture; deforestation, slavery, peonage, soil and water pollution, rural segregation, and violence are just a few discussed in this book. Corn is now the nation's major crop, but about 75 percent of it is used for bio-fuel and animal feed, not food for humans. Little wonder that defenders of the contemporary industrial farming landscape use stories about the family farm and feeding the world as window dressing.

FAMILY FARMS

In January 2018, Secretary of Agriculture Sonny Perdue stated that 99 percent of the nation's farms were "family farms" in a Nashville speech before the American Farm Bureau Federation. When many Americans think about traditional family farms, they think of a couple with their children living in the same home, sometimes with kinfolk. And when they think of the agriculture practiced by the family, its goals are to feed, clothe, shelter, pay off debt, and give their children a better life than the one they experienced. What is a useful definition of family farm today? How will the family farms remain given the dominance of industrial agriculture in the marketplace? Historian Paul Conkin listed some important criteria of family farms in 2008: "a family owns, lives on, and works on a farm; gains most of its livelihood from farming; and, perhaps most critical, makes all the important decisions about the farming operation."

Over the course of American history millions of people have farmed but would not be family farmers under Conkin's definition. These include millions of enslaved African Americans and Amerindians, white indentured servants, sharecroppers and tenant farmers, migrant workers, prison farm workers, and hired hands of all description. They were all farm workers but did not make the "important decisions." At no time in our nation's history have 99 percent of our farmers met all of these criteria. Conkin noted that most twenty-first-century operations listed as family farms did not meet these criteria. Almost one-quarter of the principal operators do not live on the farm or make half their income from farming, and on large contract operations managerial control lies beyond farmer control and with corporate headquarters.

According to the USDA in 2016, "small farms" and "family farms" are terms used to describe a group of farmers that operate 48 percent of all farmland, account for 20 percent of agricultural sales, and earn only 5 percent of the nation's net farm income. Southern states such as Tennessee led the nation in this category, especially states with a legacy of sharecropping and tenant farming such as Alabama and Oklahoma. This region also led in retirement farms, where the principal operator has retired, has low farm sales, and is often a woman. In contrast to Conkin's findings, the USDA found that only 3 percent of the nation's farms were not family farms in 2012.

In some respects small farms, while earning only 5 percent of the net farm income, could offer the greatest hope for diverting the farm landscape from the high chemical fertilizer and pesticide inputs that have damaged the organic structure of farm soil since World War II. Industrial farms are high in inputs of water and chemical fertilizers and pesticides. Traditional farms sought alternative methods of fertilizing and killing pests, including allowing chickens to free range in pastures and collecting manure from livestock. They also stressed raising as many vegetables as possible and carrying these over through canning and banking. Sustainable and organic farming fit the small and local models and ignore the fencerow to fencerow admonitions of the large industrial farm generation.

However, for farmers to begin to follow this path they must control day-to-day decision-making. Do the nation's farmers control their own destiny any more than the landless farming families of the past? If they are not making the major management decisions on their lands they do not have stewardship responsibilities. They may make a good living following the direction of corporations who sell hybrid seeds and determine the types of inputs based on legally binding contracts, but they cannot control the use of environmentally damaging chemical fertilizers and pesticides. As Conkin wrote, they do not depict "farmers as responsible citizens" and in Berry's words do not represent the "good farmer." Their world may not be "serfdom" as one observer wrote but it is also not a world of free choice and independence of the Jeffersonian farmer. As Joel Salatin wrote, "the tragedy of our time is that cultural philosophies and market realities are squeezing life's vitality out of most farms."

Since the farm crisis of the 1980s, even more farm consolidation has taken place. In 1991, larger million-dollar farms with more than $5 million in gross cash farm income (GCFI) accounted for about 13 percent of production. By 2015, their production share rose to 23 percent. During the same period large farms making between $1 million and just under $5 million GCFI increased their share from 19 to 29 percent. There were about two million farms in the United States in 2018, a loss of approximately two hundred thousand since the Great Recession. The median income for farm operators was $76,700 "practically the same as that for U.S. households with a self-employed head ($78,400)." Consolidation and large farm control of market share has not slowed down.

At the beginning of the last century most family farm laborers were family members. Conkin placed the number at ten million family members who worked and lived on farms, not counting children and housewives who nonetheless performed farm work. These farm operators employed about 3.5 million hired hands, who lived on farms and accounted for about one-quarter of all farm workers. Even when family farms were more common a century ago, about 25 percent of the workers were not family members. A major trend of the twenty-first century is the growing use of Latino migrant workers. In the Tobacco Belt of Kentucky, the transitional decade of the 1980s replaced white and black workers with Latinos The Latino population of Kentucky increased by about 300 percent between 1990 and 2006, mostly among tobacco workers. Berry wrote that this group of workers resembled pre–Civil War slave labor in that they formed a "racially denominated and subordinated class of menial laborers working without either a proprietary interest in the crop or equity in the land." As much as 75 percent of the total labor hours in this industry were performed by these workers, many of them undocumented. The recent past gives us no certainty that this trend will not continue or increase. In 2016, about 130,000 visas were issued to migrant workers under the H2-A program. That number increased by 15 percent to two hundred thousand in 2017.

FARM BILLS OF THE 2000S

Food security is important in the sense that we have enough food to prevent hunger, but it is also important that the food we eat does not damage our health. We could start with major government decisions on farm programs that will be supported by billions of tax dollars—the farm bill. From the Great Depression into the 1950s and 1960s, farm bills were considered and passed on a periodic basis by Congress. Beginning in the 1970s and continuing into the 1980s, farm bills became more routine and appeared around every four years unless there were delays. At the same time, the number of Americans living on farms continued to decline, from 32 percent in 1920 to only 1 percent in 2020. The cry "Get Big or Get Out" supported by a half century of government-subsidized commodity farming changed the nation's farming landscape.

The first farm bill of the new century was in 2002. Along with peanuts, the bill added around sixteen crops eligible for loans with rates set
by Congress. Another ten crops were guaranteed five-year subsidies. In
2007, the next farm bill was estimated to cost about $300 billion over five
years. But farm prices in the United States increased in early 2008 and
"led to a global food crisis and a rapid increase in food prices." Given
the high farm prices, the subsidies seemed unnecessary, particularly since
about one-quarter of the corn crop was diverted to ethanol production,
which Conkin believed "irresponsible, or even immoral." The Bush
administration proposed lowering the commodity payments cap to any
individual farm whose adjusted gross income exceeded $200,000, a tre-
mendous drop from the existing $2.5 million income cap. Dropping the
cap would have saved taxpayers about half the commodity program's
expenses. The Bush White House called the bill "bloated." It argued
that taxpayers should not subsidize the agricultural elite, including doctors, lawyers, and agribusiness men who owned farms and belonged to
the top 2 percent of theAmerican social structure. Industrial farm interest pushed back and both houses of Congress passed the bill with large
enough majorities to defeat President Bush's proposed veto. This bill set
farm subsidies and policies through 2012.

Even farm bill subsidies do not ensure that the support will be distributed equitably. Data from 2018 indicate that about 60 percent of the
nation's farmers did not receive subsidies. Clearly, the farm bill era has
pledged more and more federal support for fewer and fewer farmers.
Why? Because the major beneficiaries of the farm bills, the elite farming
operations, see no need to change a process that has helped them get bigger and drive small farmers into the margins of agricultural production
or out entirely.

Part of the increase can be explained by the successful lobbying efforts
of groups representing farmers. Foremost among these is the American
Farm Bureau Federation, which was founded in 1919 as a nongovern-
mental organization. Farm Bureaus were organized at the county level in
all fifty states and Puerto Rico. In 2005, for instance, about two hundred
thousand people belonged to a Farm Bureau chapter in all eighty-five of
Ohio's counties. These groups became the political voice of farmers at all
levels and championed many of the initiatives taken up by the New Deal,
including rural electrification and crop insurance and subsidies.

Another problem is that the voting public does not follow farm bills or understand what they control. Tom Vilsack recalled, "When I became U.S. secretary of agriculture in January 2009, I learned quickly that the bill covers much more than farms and farmers. In fact every farm bill also effects conservation, trade, nutrition, jobs and infrastructure, agricultural research, forestry and energy." The farm bill, he continued, "affects everyone living in the United States." Farmers received credit and are protected from farm losses and natural disasters, such as hurricanes and drought, with crop insurance. Specific commodity growers receive payments if they are beset by low yields or low prices. The nation's farmers exported about 20 percent of their agricultural production, which accounted for around 30 percent of their farm income in 2017. About 80 percent of the 2014 Farm Act outlays were marked for nutrition programs for low-income citizens through the Supplemental Nutrition Assistance Program (SNAP). Urban representatives in Congress support the farm bill because it is largely a food program for disadvantaged citizens. Part of that story goes back to federal government decisions during the 1930s and 1940s to move landless farm workers off the rural landscape without developing an urban plan to find homes and jobs for them. Economist Gavin Wright wrote over forty years ago that tenant farmers "poured into the cities in the 1950s despite the fact that job prospects were no longer favorable, particularly for blacks." They moved to cities where friends or relatives lived but the "economy had relatively little use for them."

The Agricultural Improvement Act of 2018 was passed and signed into law in December 2018 and will remain in effect through 2023. It increased spending by less than 1 percent. Much of that funding supports the staple commodities program. Staples destined for some export include corn, soybeans, feed grains, peanuts, rice, cotton, and dairy products, among others. Over the past fifty years, and especially during the Cold War era, Americans were led to believe that this type of support was necessary and worthwhile to feed the hungry of the third world and create food security in regions vulnerable to communism. But most of these staple commodities did not end up in the third world, but did in places such as Canada, the leading consumer, and Australia, among others.

Another problem with the nutritional program is that "cheap and unhealthy food choices" find their way into SNAP, including many artificial food additives with elevated sugar levels resulting in obesity in children and adults. Corn is still the number one crop in US agriculture, accounting for more sales than soybeans and wheat combined. It is the major source of high fructose corn syrup that finds its way into soft drinks and other fast foods.

In 2016, SNAP helped approximately forty-four million Americans with food support. It appeared almost certain that the 2018 bill review would include requirements that able-bodied adults without dependents work, and that people who receive assistance be barred from buying "soda or other foods that are considered unhealthy." Under consideration as well are opportunities for senior citizens to buy fresh vegetables at local markets and to make fresh produce available to school children. But many of those concerns were set aside after discussions of the bill stalled in May 2018. As it passed in December 2018, the Farm Act's nutrition funding, which includes the SNAP program, accounts for 76 percent of the farm subsidies, 9 percent to crop insurance, and commodities and conservation each receiving 7 percent.

Throughout the Earl Butz years big farming was championed as a necessity in order for America to feed the world and become the globe's farmer as well as its policeman. These two ideas went hand in hand, since the logic held that hungry people in the third world were more likely to reject capitalism and become communists if American agriculture did not feed them. Industrial farming has not solved world hunger, saved family farms, or preserved the free market system. It can be argued that it has done precisely the opposite by producing food monocultures, replacing family farms with neoplantations, and destroying free trade-with government-supported subsidies for the wealthiest farmers and agribusinesses.

The 2018, reauthorization of the farm bill offered an opportunity to support innovative programs in alternative and organic farming, which at present represent only a small fraction of the total farm bill budget. The National Farmers Union has called for greater support for minority and disadvantaged farmers, veterans, and youth in the 2017 discussion of the farm bill's reauthorization. Efforts should be made to fund programs that move sustainable and organic farming ahead of industrial farming by reducing the bloated commodity subsidies that go to the wealthiest farmers. After fifty years of Butz-style agriculture, it is time to move away from killing the soil, polluting water, and feeding SNAP recipients junk food. Ideally, organic foods and not pizza, soda, and burgers would be the lunch options of school children, where obesity is high, and support healthy diets not dependent on what comes off the end of the industrial farming food chain. Is this the food output that US citizens want for billions of dollars consumed by farm bills?

It is doubtful that this will happen without tremendous pressure on the farm lobby. It was not until 1990, almost fifty years after J. I. Rodale began his experimental organic farm in Pennsylvania, that Congress passed the Federal Organic Foods Production Act after it took a panel "a decade to complete its work because of contending factions." Beginning in 2002, organic farmers who sold more than $5,000 in crops had to be certified by the Department of Agriculture before displaying an organic seal. The cost of certification can reach up to $2,000 and in 2014 amounted to a total of $19 million. Washington, DC, moves slowly especially when it comes to changes in agriculture and the Midwest's heavily subsidized commodity economy. The 2018 reauthorization did include important steps to increase women, minority, veteran, and sustainable and organic initiatives, as well as including some of the provisions of the 2018 Hemp Farming Act.

In January 2018, Secretary of Agriculture Sonny Perdue told the nation in a USDA press release that he had traveled to thirty states "listening to the people of American agriculture about what is working and what is not." He went on to describe the broad principles that will be used as a "road map" to let Congress know that he has heard from "the hardworking men and women of American agriculture." Among the eight legislative principle areas, each with multiple talking points, "Management" came last but its number one talking point was: "Provide a fiscally responsible Farm Bill that reflects the Administration's budget goals."

It is doubtful that the 2018 farm bill will provide a new road map to the future for American agriculture. That is unfortunate because it could. Wealth generated by American agriculture is very top heavy largely because of congressional boons to industrial farming, corporate agriculture, and science and research funding. Conkin wrote that "the concentration at the top is remarkable or, some would argue, scandalous." After eighty-five years of farm bills that concentration of wealth may be the collective farm bills' major legacy to American society. Millions of small farms that could have allowed rural families and their descendants to feed themselves are now dependent on congressionally approved food programs. This is the same legislative body that decade after decade helped move small farms off the land while at the same time lowering farming risks for the agricultural elite through crop subsidies and insurance, trade support, and marketing.

Although rural development and greater broadband availability are two of the current 2018 farm bill's measures, neither of these are new. Since 2009, rural citizens have had increased access to home loans, better broadband access, and help finding second income nonfarm jobs that support farm households. The internet is not the solution to the rural crisis. Getting more people who love nature and farming back on the farming landscape, people such as Wendell Berry and Joel Salatin, would be a big step in the right direction. Rural America needs a big fix, not a quick fix, not after what it has been through over the last half century. It needs a massive transfusion of low-input farmers who will not kill the soil and water but hold and regenerate a space for the commonwealth—a resettling of American forgotten places.

In 2017, about forty-six million rural people, around 15 percent of the population, lived on 72 percent of the nation's land area. On the other hand, almost 81 percent of the population lived in cities. Among those living in rural areas a generation shift is on the horizon. About 90 percent of US farmers are white men and their numbers are declining. The average age of the nation's farmers is almost sixty and the age has been climbing since the 1990s. Thirty-one percent of principal farm operators are sixty-five or older. The role of mechanization in allowing farmers to work longer with less physical labor is an important factor in the last century. Doubtless many of these farmers will turn their farms over to younger family members.

WOMEN AND MINORITY FARMERS

Gains in new farmers are already coming from more diverse backgrounds according to the USDA, although "new" does not necessarily mean young. Asian Americans and Hispanics are among the fastest growing minority farm groups followed by African Americans and

FIGURE 8.1. Indiana barn: a symbol of disappearing small family farm agriculture. Painting by Glenna Pfeiffer, copyright 2019.

American Indians. Reclaiming the rural landscape is an opportunity to create more diverse populations in areas that have witnessed major out-migration since the Great Depression.

According to the USDA, several encouraging trends are visible. Despite the dominance of industrial farms in in the marketplace, most farms are small, their average size around 444 acres in 2017. Their numbers are growing. Many farmers and ranchers are selling directly to consumers, often through farmers markets, and more would if barriers to direct marketing were lowered. Consumers are now seeing their food producers face to face in much the same way the egg and milk men of the 1950s small towns. About one in five of these new farmers have less than ten years of experience on the job. The major impediment to young farmers is money to buy land, which often is not the problem for young people in established farming families who can work family-owned land and often inherit it as well. In some ways this pattern resembles the barriers young farmers faced at the beginning of the twentieth century when farm tenancy reached its peak.

It is difficult to gauge the involvement of women in agriculture over time even during the post–World World II era. The agricultural census first asked the gender of the principal farm operators in 1978. Women were the primary agriculturalists in American Indian communities and were directly involved in farming activities throughout the nation's history. They were often responsible for the same farm duties as earlier Indian women and children, planting, cultivating, picking, and guarding garden crops and tending farm livestock. In time, women drove tractors, baled hay, and helped repair farm buildings. At first glance it would appear that women are regaining their traditional roles as farmers, but the unreliability of data makes it difficult to assess true progress, making reliable comparisons over time difficult.

USDA research suggests that the number of women farmers increased from about 5 percent in 1978 to around 14 percent in 2007. But it is possible that this apparent growth is due to prior undercounting of women farmers before 2002, when it appears that women were more than twice as likely to be missed by the census than men. By 2017 women were involved in decision-making on 56 percent of US farms and accounted for 36 percent of the country's farmers. Women are making inroads but the average female farmer on a very small operation makes an average of only $2,560 per year while the average male farmer makes almost $43,000. Like many farmers regardless of gender, their survival often depends on additional nonfarm income and it remains difficult to find financial independence by farming alone.

Most farms where women are in charge of the day-to-day operations are small in terms of value of sales. By 2007, three-quarters of the approximately 306,000 farms operated by women had sales of less than $10,000. The larger commercial farms operated by women had sales of more than $100,000 and were concentrated in grains and oil seed, poultry and eggs, and beef and dairy operations. Women-operated farms with sales of over $1 million represent 21 percent of women-operated farms but generate 72 percent of sales. Women who are the principal farm operators tend to be slightly older than men and are more highly educated, with 32 percent of women having a college degree compared to about 23 percent of men. Fewer than 3 percent of the two hundred thousand commercial farmers today are women.

Women were better represented on the farming landscape in New England, the West, and the Southwest. Texas had the most women farmers while Arizona, with 45 percent of its state's farmers, led all states proportionally. However, the nation's women controlled only 7 percent of farmland and had only 3 percent of farm sales. Their farms were small. Eight out of ten were less than 180 acres and seven of ten had sales of less than $10,000 per year. Unless they had off-farm sources of income, they were well below the poverty level. About half of women farmers were involved in a combination of crop growing and beef cattle. Others raised sheep and goats and grew grain and oil seeds. The average age of women who were primary farm operators was sixty.

Today the percent of American Indians who are principal farm operators in the nation, meaning those who make the daily farm decisions, has increased by 9 percent between 2007 and 2012. They are trying to make their voice heard as Congress takes the farm bill into consideration. A leader in the effort, Janie Simms Hipp, director of the Indigenous Food and Agriculture Initiative at the University of Arkansas, said the various Indian Nations, which is their treaty status historically, want to at least be considered as states and receive access to USDA farm support programs in the 2018 farm bill. Most American Indian farmers and ranchers in 2017 who operated a total of 58,199 farms and ranches in the United States are located in the Four Corners region of the Southwest and in Oklahoma.

As late as the 1920s, African Americans made up 14 percent of all American farmers. They owned fifteen million acres of land. By that time the Great Migration had already carried away half a million southern blacks. But it could not account for the millions of African Americans who left the region, only those working in cotton farming, where the boll weevil made inroads. Interviews with blacks who migrated after the boll weevil and mechanization took hold did not specifically single out those occurrences as reasons for leaving, though they may have played a role. Isabel Wilkerson, author of *The Warmth of Other Suns,* concluded that the "act of leaving itself" and the decision to be free of the past of racism, lynching, segregation, and exploitation was "its own point" no matter where they went or what happened to them afterward. And for those who remained in the South, perhaps Alabama farmer Nate Shaw expressed their view when he said that he felt "a certain loyalty" to Alabama because he was born there and had "sowed my labor into the earth." He stayed knowing "it's too late for me to realize it now, all that I put into this state. I stays on if it gives em satisfaction for me to leave and I stays on because it's mine."

THE NEXT GENERATION

The leadership will have to come from America's younger generations who not only care about their own health, what they eat, who produces it, and under what conditions, but also care about the health of their communities. Wendell Berry believes that the good farmer is a conservationist. The good farmer conserves the soil, water, wildlife, and open space. He has written that the best place to practice this type of stewardship is on small family farms, which he has also written is becoming rarer. It will be up to the next generation of younger and more diverse farm population to follow this path; it gives those farmers more freedom to reject the major tenets of chemical farming. It takes commitment to grow an acre of organic food on the rooftop of a building in Brooklyn, New York, by a group such as the Brooklyn Grange. It also sets an important example that where there is a will people can grow food and receive the satisfaction that they controlled the process. There is a new wave among young people to start urban gardens, a backyard raised bed, an urban vertical garden, a chicken and egg operation in a city backyard, and community food coops.

Comparatively few American Indians, African Americans, women, and young farmers benefit from the massive farm bill subsidies. Farm bill subsidies will go to the small elite group of commercial farmers who have profited from federal subsidies for as long as farm bills have existed. Their suppliers of seeds, fertilizers, equipment, insurance, and state and congressional representation do not want to change farm business in Washington, DC, either.

How will the farm lobby's stranglehold on American agriculture be broken? It will take a massive effort on the scale of the civil rights movement to restore opportunities to those who have been driven off the nation's farming landscapes regardless of region for over a century. This movement's leadership will not come from baby boomers; this generation is passing from the national scene. Another way to approach this issue is to ask another question: What is the purpose of American farming? Is it still to feed the world as the industrial farming community has argued for half a century, or is it something else? Is it to provide every citizen with healthy food? Joel Salatin noted that as late as 1946 almost half of the produce grown in the nation came out of backyard gardens. Today, 95 percent of the food bought at grocery store chains is likely produced in another state.

There were approximately fourteen thousand organic farms in 2016, far too few. The Northeast, upper Midwest, and the Northwest are the nation's leading organic farm regions with California and Wisconsin being the only states with more than one thousand organic farms. For organic farming to play an important role in any rural redevelopment plan it needs to increase in states where small farms represent more than 85 percent of all farms, notably in the South and New England. It is not encouraging that the USDA has been studying beef and poultry organic rules for more than twenty years with no ruling yet. The 2012 farm bill did extend crop insurance to organic farmers, but it was not as comprehensive a policy as those available to major commodity growers. It also included a young farmer's initiative, but they need sustained support measured in billions of dollars.

The future farmers of our nation will have to be young but there are severe barriers that they have to overcome in order to inherit farmland. The average farm today is about 444 acres and in 2019 the average cost of farmland was $3,160 per acre. That is a high cost for anyone and especially for young people who want to make farming a way of life. It was not cheap in 1950 when the average acre cost about $650. Some defenders of industrialized farming argue that mechanization, precision farming, and other new technologies, including autonomous field machines, will mean the nation will need even fewer farmers.

One of the principles of the 2018 farm bill is that rural development will help communities create "a quality of life that attracts and retains the next generation." The best chance to attract new farmers to rural areas may be small-scale farming with low-cost inputs. If we were writing a guide to prospective small family farmers heading west, for example, the type of guide that was popular in the nineteenth century, one piece of advice might be go west to states where small farms are common. That area would not include the Midwest and North Central monoculture plantation states where small family farms are less common and where land, equipment, fertilizer, and pesticide costs are high. California would also be dominated by large landholdings. West Virginia and Tennessee, on the other hand, look promising. Their eastern Appalachian landscapes are hilly and less friendly to self-driving tractors and are comparable to Alabama, Oklahoma, and New Hampshire in that small farms account for more than 90 percent of the total.

Organic farming produces quality produce free from GMOs, chemical fertilizers, and pesticides. Based on levels of pesticide use by state, California and Florida would be difficult places to begin organic farming and local food movements. Both of these states have large congressional representation, and with more of the nation's population moving south and west, their power in Washington will only increase. Both these states are also leaders in the H2-A visa program, which provides agricultural work to nonimmigrant foreign agricultural workers when domestic help will be in short supply.

Despite the banning of DDT in 1972, the use of insecticides and pesticides continued at high levels as American agriculture entered a new century. These chemicals alter ecosystems, some are toxic to humans, and others concentrate in the food chain. According to the National Pesticide Use Database two farming regions used far more insecticides in 2002 than any others: the Southeast and the Pacific Coast. In the Southeast, Florida led all states in the region and in fact all states in the nation with more than fifty-eight million pounds of insecticides per year largely for citrus production. Texas, Arkansas, Georgia, Mississippi, and Louisiana all used between two and five million pounds, largely on cotton crops. Along the Pacific Coast, California, Washington, and Oregon made heavy applications of insecticides, with California's total of twenty-nine million pounds more than doubling Washington state's total, mostly for fruit production. Oregon used almost three million pounds, about the total of Arkansas in the South. Citrus, cotton, apples, corn, and almonds were the top five insecticide crops. But when the category of "other pesticides" is added to control other "pests" such as weeds, potato producers used ninety-four million pounds of "other pesticides" in states such as Idaho, where use increased from more than fifteen million pounds in 1992 to more than thirty-three million pounds in 2002.

Even if the peopling of such spaces were successful, the new farmers would have to grow something that they could sell. As many critics of current farm policy have observed, government at all levels has put in place regulations that restrict market access to small farmers. These regulations favor industrial farming over traditional small farming methods, including sustainable and organic farming. Industrial farming has been harmful to rural America not only by pouring chemicals into the soil, air, and water, but in their control of farm decisions through contracts as well as their negative social impact on small towns. Mechanization decreased the demand for farm labor and the rural population decreased. With financial troubles, small farmers and farm laborers bought food and clothing in small towns often on credit. On the other hand, large-scale commercial commodity farming operations often bought their equipment and supplies wholesale and out of the area as well as the services of banks, insurance companies, and lawyers, which were located in cities. As small farms declined the rural markets for their bankers, grocers, doctors, and feed and seed suppliers vanished. Wealth became concentrated among a smaller number of wealthier industrial farmers who often controlled most farmland and water rights. Their main streets shut down. Schools closed. Small farming towns that once had their power diffused among many smaller farmers and town professionals over time became power-concentrated towns with a few wealthy farmers, farm laborers with low standards of living, and only a post office and elementary school in town. Studies of this process began in the 1940s and continued into the 1970s with no change, and today it has worsened. For the rural economic development listed as a goal of the Trump administration to be lasting and meaningful, this trend and its results must be reversed.

The USDA estimates that chemical farming and ranching are responsible for 68 percent of all species endangerment; chemical farming is not good stewardship. At the same time, much of our nation's industrial agriculture production is unnecessary to feed the country's population and is used for ethanol production. Indeed, larger corn crops have encouraged an increase in ethanol in 2016 and 2017. In 2020, it was estimated that about 40 percent of the nation's corn crop was used for ethanol production compared to 36 percent for domestic animal feed. Another 13 percent was exported, leaving around 11 percent of the total corn crop for domestic human consumption.

There needs to be governmental support for small farmers, including American Indian, African American, veteran, young, and women farmers. The local food movement and organic farming in general are providing opportunities for women and men who want better quality foods for their families and the public's kitchen tables. Given the toxic state of much of our farmland, future farm bills need to begin major support of transitioning such land to sustainable and organic use. Organic food should be the staple of all public school food programs, creating large new markets for organic farmers and ranchers. They should be supported by farm bill funding for starting farmer and rancher programs on small farms of under one thousand acres.

We do not need more corn for food. We need supports in place for farmers who want to move into sustainable and organic farming or try new approaches to agriculture. Some university agriculture departments are establishing programs to help, and they need more state and federal encouragement to change an industrial farming structure they helped put in place since World War II. There were approximately 899.5 million acres of total farmland on 2 million farms in 2018. The agricultural history of the soil on each farm varies depending on its past use and abuse. Since 1945, and the increased use of NPK fertilizer, the soil's natural fertility has declined. Farmers assumed that whatever fertility the soil lost could be replaced by using nonrenewable chemical fertilizers containing nitrogen, phosphorous, and potassium. This so-called NPK mentality displaced the organic cycle in which plants produce nutrients and then return to the soil as organic nutrients. It has been estimated that it took twenty years of this type of nonsustainable chemical fertilization to destroy soil fertility in some farming districts in India. There, prior to World War II, much of the early research in organic farming was done by Albert Howard, who studied composting and other techniques of Indian farmers. Some US farms have been using this type of chemical fertilizer for more than half a century.

UNITED STATES–MEXICO–CANADA AGREEMENT

In 1993, the North American Free Trade Act (NAFTA) set aside most favored nation status tariffs for Canada and Mexico. Under NAFTA, food and agriculture exports to these two partners increased by approximately 450 percent. In 2016, that trade represented $43 billion making

Canada and Mexico the largest export consumers of the nation's agriculture, not poor third world countries with starving populations. Similar
to the political discourse surrounding the reauthorization of farm bills,
the debate over NAFTA's future tells us much about the state of mind
of the nation's farming community. Over the long history of the United
States, farmers have represented a majority of the population until the
early twentieth century, at times as much as 90 percent. But over time
that proportion has dropped to about 2 percent. The rise of urban and
industrial America has continuously marginalized farmers and farming
communities in favor of industrial and technological ones.

Understandably, US farmers, especially those involved in growing
foods high on the list of exports to Canada and Mexico, feel threatened by
talks of ending the trade agreement. Many citizens in "farm country" feel
that any talk of ending NAFTA will endanger "the heart of rural America," a sentiment expressed in a letter to US commerce secretary Wilbur
Ross in October 2017 and signed by eighty-six organizations representing
twenty-one million jobs nationally. The sentiment expressed is that the
Trump administration is using NAFTA and their future as a bargaining
chip while ignoring a sector of the economy that employs more manufacturing jobs than any other.

On January 8, 2018, President Trump became the first national leader
to attend the AFBF annual meeting since George H. W. Bush. More
than 7,500 farmers, ranchers, lenders, and agribusiness leaders gathered
in Nashville, Tennessee, to hear the man they helped put in the White
House. Trump praised farming's legacy. Farmers founded the nation,
tamed the continent, and manned its armies. They epitomized the Jeffersonian yeomen qualities of hard work, grit, and self-reliance. He then
attacked the federal government that placed barriers to their success,
mostly the EPA and the FDA. Declaring "you are forgotten no more,"
he pledged to free farmers from the "burdens" of overregulation and
renegotiate NAFTA, restore crop insurance in the farm bill, which got
the loudest applause, and build the wall to control illegal immigration
and end chain migration.

He also promised to restore hope and prosperity to the nation's rural
areas by increasing internet and broadband service; fix the rural infrastructure of roads, bridges, and waterways; and end the opioid epidemic.
Other than pledging to even the playing field with Canada and Mexico, he

revealed few details about renegotiation. The state of the environment did not appear to be a concern. The conference's sponsors included the major agribusiness and industrial farming suppliers of chemical fertilizers and pesticides that continue to damage the soil's natural fertility. The crowd cheered when he stated he "ditched" an EPA water quality measure.

Unfortunately, policy makers, Congress, and our national leadership have been slow to accept that the climate is warming, that our soil is toxic and dying, and that our water is polluted largely for a high-input corn crop that only about 11 percent of Americans eat. Since World War I, millions of small farmers have left the land due to depression, racism, poverty, and state and federal programs to rid the landscape of small farmers. Through farm consolidation and government subsidies aimed at these small farmers have been replaced by industrial farmers who use the greatest amounts of chemical inputs from planting to harvest. In some respect, tenant farmers such as Nate Shaw were as close to Indian peasants as our country had on its farming landscape. Certainly, we can't become too nostalgic about farm life in rural America, but farmers such as Shaw did feed their families on land they worked and felt a sense of loyalty to that place. Never did he "want for no vegetable," he had his own cows to milk, and he raised and killed "all the meat we could use."

Our soil needs healing and some encouraging steps are underway. The origins of modern no-till farming in the United States have been attributed, among others, to Edward H. Faulkner's *Plowman's Folly*, published in 1943 and a bestseller. He attacked the harmful results of deep plowing, which included erosion, farm runoff, and the loss of natural nutrients and organisms in the soil. He advocated no plowing or shallow tillage. Since the 1980s, the increase in no-till has been "dramatic" according to the *Washington Post*, and especially in soybean and wheat production. Deep plowing and tillage caused soil erosion and allowed greater escape of carbon dioxide into the air. In 2017, only about 21 percent of all US cultivated cropland was in continuous no-till operations.

In 2012, the Census of Agriculture for the first time asked farmers about their practices to conserve farmland by protecting it from wind and water erosion. Since the Great Depression harmful practices that led to the Dust Bowl and deep erosion in the South have been lessened by conservation efforts. The grain boom of the 1970s and its fence row to fence row planting mentality, however, pushed farming onto erodible lands and took conservation backward by decades in some areas. Subsequent measures were taken to correct soil erosion including the use of no- and low-till cultivation. There are advantages to low- and no-till cultivation. It protects the soil against erosion, saves the labor spent on more invasive tillage, and reduces farm runoff by increasing the soil's capacity to absorb water. In no-till, farmers plant crops into the residue of the previous year's crop. Larger farms of more than one thousand acres in size were more likely to use no-till, especially on grain and oilseed crops.

According to the 2012 Census of Agriculture, about 97 million of the nation's total cultivated farm acreage of 279 million was under no-till cultivation, or about 30 percent. By comparison, almost 106 million acres of cropland still used conventional tillage. The increase in less invasive no- or low-till farming is a major step in soil regeneration. Kansas led all states in the number of acres in no-till practice, followed by Nebraska, the Dakotas, Iowa, and Montana. As of 2017, continuous no-till is practiced on only 21 percent of all cultivated cropland. Those most likely to practice no-till farming are principal operators whose main occupation is farming; they account for nine out of ten acres of no-till.

Not all chemicals used on farms are absorbed by plants as they grow. Depending on the condition of the soil, the chemicals can end up as farm runoff carried into streams and rivers with the next rain. The chemical fertilizers and pesticides are flushed out of the small streams and rivers and eventually find their way to coastlines. There they join industrial-use chemicals and dyes from cotton mills and other industrial sites. This high level of pollutants endangers the stability of coastal estuaries, the breeding grounds for much seafood and wildlife. Groundwater is polluted not only by farm runoff but also by household waste due to the lack of rural sewage systems in small unincorporated towns with little or no zoning restrictions. As coastal ecosystems are altered oysters, shrimp, and other seafood forming the foundation of local livelihoods are altered or destroyed.

Forests act like a giant sponge, soaking up and holding water in plants, soil, and wetlands. Evaporation returns the moisture to clouds, where it falls to earth as rain. The destruction of US forests, especially in the woodlands east of the Mississippi River, denied these resources to millions of Americans as rural industrialization destroyed the ecosystems of one species after another. This loss was felt by small, rural farmers first, the people who depended on woodlands for hunting, foraging, grazing, building material, and fuel. Industrial agriculture as we know it today benefitted from this destruction, and the number of flora and fauna we have lost is difficult to determine.

The most pressing need now is to stop the environmental damage to our soil, water, and air. Time matters. Baby boomers spent the first twenty years of their lives in a world where DDT was legal and crop dusting was widespread. But for this to happen a significant part of the farming community must turn its back on industrial farming in order for anything resembling balance to take place. The technological new world represented by autonomous tractors, precision farming, and GPS mapping may help us understand efficiencies like never before, but what will farming mean when more and more human contact is eliminated? What will happen to the spiritual ties, love of the land, and its produce when human beings are moved even farther from the farming landscape? How long can our society last when our guiding agricultural philosophy seems to be "use up everything that we have"?

Almost a century ago a group of southern writers called the "Fugitives" protested a future of agriculture dominated by an industrial ideal rather than agrarianism. Their collected writings were published in a 1930 book titled *I'll Take My Stand*. The farmers of today and tomorrow will make important choices and take their own stands on which agricultural path they want. Will they become a part of the agri-industrial complex that has come to dominate American farming over the past seventy years or will they take an alternative road rejecting extreme industrial and technological developments and become an artist farmer rather than a factory farmer?

Currently, about 80 percent of farm subsidies are earmarked for the nation's largest industrial farmers, leaving little or nothing for small local farmers—women, Indians, African Americans, veterans, young farmers—making the possibility of earning a living wage difficult. Instead, capitalism has worked to move small farmers and landless farm workers off the land. The inheritance provisions of the bill make it easier for Midwestern plantation owners to keep their enormous estates in what one economist has called a hereditary landowning class almost ensuring that only young people who inherit farm land will be able to farm as farm owners. To alter the course of US agriculture, the control,

consolidation, and chemical strategy must radically change if US agriculture is opened to a new generation of American farmers.

Sources

Introduction
Paul K. Conkin, *A Revolution Down on the Farm: The Transformation of American Agriculture Since 1929* (Lexington: University Press of Kentucky, 2009); Rob Nixon, *Slow Violence and the Environmentalism of the Poor* (Cambridge, MA: Harvard University Press, 2013); Wendell Berry, *Life and Work* (Lexington: University of Kentucky Press, 2007); Joel Salatin, *Folks, This Ain't Normal: A Farmer's Advice for Happier Hens, Healthier People, and a Better World* (New York: Center Street, 2011); David Pitt, "Of Growing Concern," *Dallas Morning News,* July 26, 2018.

Chapter One: Beginnings
T. Douglas Price and Ofer Bar-Yosef, "The Origins of Agriculture: New Data, New Ideas," *Current Anthropology*, Vol. 52, No. S4 (October 2011); Lyman Carrier, *The Beginnings of Agriculture in America* (New York: Johnson Reprint, 1968); James A. Vlasich, *Pueblo Indian Agriculture* (Albuquerque: University of New Mexico Press, 2006); Bradley J. Vierra, *The Late Archaic Across the Borderlands: From Foraging to Farming* (Austin: University of Texas Press, 2005); Bruce D. Smith, *The Emergence of Agriculture* (New York: Scientific American Library, 1995); Cynthia Stokes Brown, *Big History: From the Big Bang to the Big Present* (New York: New Press, 2008); Noel Kingsbury, *Hybrid: The History and Science of Plant Breeding* (Chicago: University of Chicago Press, 2009), especially helpful for domestication of plants; James C. McCann, *Maize and Grace: Africa's Encounter with a New World Crop, 1500–2000* (Cambridge, MA: Harvard University Press, 2005). Among the more helpful early recorded observations of Indian agriculture in the Southeast is Samuel Cole Williams, ed., *Adair's History of the American Indians* (Johnson City, TN: Wautauga Press, 1930). John Adair was a trader among the Cherokee and other tribes; Mark Van Doren, ed., *Travels of William Bartram* (New York: Dover Publications, 1955); Lyman Carrier, *The Beginnings of Agriculture in America* (New York: Johnson Reprint, 1968); Lawrence

Clayton, Edward Moore, and Vernon James Knight Jr., *De Soto Chronicles: The Expedition of Hernando De Soto to North America in 1539–1543* (Tuscaloosa: University of Alabama Press, 1993); Claire Hope Cummins, *Uncertain Peril: Genetic Engineering and the Future of Seeds* (Boston: Beacon Press, 2008); Ralph H. Brown, *Historical Geography of the United States* (New York: Harcourt, 1948) notes Indians clearing land and meadows for cattle in New England; William Cronon, *Changes in the Land: Indians, Colonists, and the Ecology of New England* (New York: Hill and Wang, 2003); Charles Hudson, *The Southeastern Indians* (Knoxville: University of Tennessee Press, 1992); John E. Worth, *The Struggle for the Georgia Coast* (Tuscaloosa: University of Alabama Press, 2007); Charles Hudson, Marvin T. Smith, Chester B. DePratter, and Emilia Kelley, "The Tristán De Luna Expedition, 1559–1561," *Southeastern Archaeology,* Vol. 8, No. 1 (Summer 1989); Benjamin Madley, *An American Genocide: the United States and the California Indian Catastrophe, 1846–1873* (New Haven, CT: Yale University Press, 2016); Edmund S. Morgan, *American Slavery, American Freedom: The Ordeal of Colonial Virginia* (New York: W. W. Norton, 1975); Peter H. Wood, *Black Majority: Negroes in Colonial South Carolina from 1670 through the Stono Rebellion* (New York: W. W. Norton, 1975); Richard S. Dunn, *Sugar and Slaves: The Rise of the Planter Class in the English West Indies, 1624–1713* (New York: W. W. Norton, 1973); Carla Gardina Pestana, *The English Conquest of Jamaica: Oliver Cromwell's Bid for Empire* (Cambridge, MA: Harvard University Press, 2017); David Hackett Fischer, *Albion's Seed: Four British Folkways in America* (New York: Oxford University Press, 1989); Carl Bridenbaugh, *Myths and Realities: Societies of the Colonial South* (New York: Atheneum, 1963); David L. Carlton and Peter Coclanis, eds., *The South, the Nation, and the World: Perspectives on Southern Economic Development* (Charlottesville: University of Virginia Press, 2003); Gavin Wright, *Slavery and American Economic Development* (Baton Rouge: Louisiana State University Press, 2006); Jackson Turner Main, *The Social Structure of Revolutionary America* (Princeton, NJ: Princeton University Press, 1965); Charles Joyner, *Down by the Riverside: A South Carolina Slave Community* (Urbana: University of Illinois Press, 1984); Numan V. Bartley, *The Creation of Modern Georgia* (Athens: University of Georgia Press, 1990); Lawrence S. Easley, *Looking for Longleaf: The Fall and Rise of an American Forest* (Chapel Hill: University of North Carolina Press, 2004);

Phillip Greven, *Four Generations: Population, Land, and Family in Colonial Andover, Massachusetts* (Ithaca, NY: Cornell University Press, 1970); Sumner Chilton Powell, *Puritan Village: The Formation of a New England Town* (Middletown, CT: Wesleyan University Press, 1970); Brian Donahue, *The Great Meadow: Farmers and the Land in Colonial Concord* (New Haven, CT: Yale University Press, 2004); William Cronon, *Changes in the Land: Indians, Colonists, and the Ecology of New England* (New York: Hill and Wang, 1983); John Demos, *A Little Commonwealth: Family Life in Plymouth Colony* (London: Oxford University Press, 1970); David A. Taylor, *Ginseng, the Divine Root: The Curious History of the Plant that Captivated the World* (Chapel Hill, NC: Algonquin Books, 2005); Christopher Isett and Stephen Miller, *The Social History of Agriculture: From the Origins to the Current Crisis* (New York: Rowman & Littlefield, 2017); Jonathan Eacott, *Selling Empire: India in the Making of Britain and America, 1600–1830* (Chapel Hill: University of North Carolina Press, 2016); Abbot Emerson Smith, *Colonists in Bondage: White Servitude and Convict Labor in America, 1607–1776* (Chapel Hill: University of North Carolina Press, 1940); Henry Hobhouse, *Seeds of Change: Five Plants that Transformed Mankind* (New York: Harper and Row, 1987); Jennifer Jensen Wallach, *How America Eats: A Social History of U.S. Food and Culture* (New York: Rowman & Littlefield, 2013) provides a helpful overview of food culture; Noeleen McIlvenna, *The Short Life of Free Georgia: Class and Slavery in the Colonial South* (Chapel Hill: University of North Carolina Press, 2016); David B. Quinn, *North America from Earliest Discovery to First Settlements: The Norse Voyages to 1612* (New York: Harper Collins, 1977).

Chapter Two: Crop Regions

O. E. Baker, "A Graphic Summary of American Agriculture Based Largely on the Census of 1920" (Washington, DC: Government Printing Office, 1922); Ross M. Robertson, *History of the American Economy* (New York: Harcourt, Brace & World, 1964); Clarence A. Danhof, *Change in Agriculture: The Northern United States, 1820–1870* (Cambridge, MA: Harvard University Press, 1969); Richard F. Nation, *At Home in the Hoosier Hills: Agriculture, Politics, and Religion in Southern Indiana, 1810–1870* (Bloomington: Indiana University Press, 2005); Bradford J. Wood, *This Remote Part of the World: Regional Formation in Lower Cape Fear, North*

Carolina, 1725–1775 (Columbia: University of South Carolina Press, 2004); on slavery and its central role in the rise of American capitalism, see Sven Beckert, *Empire of Cotton: A Global History* (New York: Random House, 2014) and Sven Beckert and Seth Rothman, eds., *Slavery's Capitalism: A New History of American Economic Development* (Philadelphia: University of Pennsylvania Press, 2016); Stephen Aron, *American Confluence: The Missouri Frontier from Borderland to Border State* (Bloomington: Indiana University Press, 2005); Adam Rothman, *Slave Country: American Expansionism and the Origins of the Deep South* (Cambridge, MA: Harvard University Press, 2007); Carl Bridenbaugh, *Myths and Realities: Societies of the Colonial South* (New York: Atheneum, 1963); Richard Follett, *The Sugar Masters: Planters and Slaves in Louisiana's Cane World, 1820–1860* (Baton Rouge: Louisiana State University Press, 2005); Ralph H. Brown, *Historical Geography of the United States* (New York: Harcourt, Brace, 1948); John Hope Franklin, *From Slavery to Freedom: A History of Negro Americans* (New York: Vintage Books, 1947); Andrea Zimmermann, "Nineteenth Century Wheat Production in Four New York State Regions: A Comparative Examination," *Hudson Valley Regional Review*, No. 5 (September 1988); Frederick Jackson Turner, *The United States 1830–1850* (New York: W. W. Norton, 1965); Robert V. Remini, *Andrew Jackson and His Indian Wars* (New York: Penguin, 2002); William G. Thomas and Edward L. Ayers, "An Overview: The Differences Slavery Made: A Close Analysis of Two American Communities," *American Historical Review*, Vol. 108, No. 5 (December 2003); Jeff Forret, *Slave Against Slave: Plantation Violence in the Old South* (Baton Rouge: Louisiana State University Press, 2015); Claire Hope Cummins, *Uncertain Peril: Genetic Engineering and the Future of Seeds* (Boston: Beacon Press, 2008); Alan L. Olmstead and Paul W. Rhode, *Creating Abundance: Biological Innovation and American Agricultural Development* (United Kingdom: Cambridge University Press, 2008); Jennifer Jensen Wallach, *How America Eats: A Social History of U.S. Food and Culture* (Lanham, MD: Rowman & Littlefield, 2013); Carville Earle, "A Staple Interpretation of Slavery and Free Labor," *Geographical Review*, Vol. 68, No. 1 (January 1978); Sam Bowers Hilliard, *Hog Meat and Hoe Cake: Food Supply in the Old South, 1840–1860* (Carbondale: Southern Illinois University Press, 1972); Stephanie McCurry, *Masters of Small Worlds: Yeomen Households, Gender Relations, and the Political Culture of the Antebellum South Carolina Low*

Country (New York: Oxford University Press, 1995); Ray Allen Billington, *Westward Expansion: A History of the American Frontier* (New York: MacMillan Publishing, 1974); James F. Hopkins, *A History of the Hemp Industry in Kentucky,* (Lexington: University Press of Kentucky, 1998); W. F. Axton, *Tobacco and Kentucky* (Lexington: University Press of Kentucky, 1975); Nadra O. Hashim, *Hemp and the Global Economy: The Rise of Labor, Innovation, and Trade* (Lanham, MD: Lexington Books, 2017); Stanley W. Trimble, *Man-Induced Soil Erosion on the Southern Piedmont: 1700–1970* (Ankeny, IA: Soil and Water Conservation Society, 2008); Henry Hobhouse, *Seeds of Change: Five Plants that Transformed Mankind* (New York: Harper and Row, 1987); Numan V. Bartley, *The Creation of Modern Georgia* (Athens: University of Georgia Press, 1983); Mark V. Wetherington, *The New South Comes to Wiregrass Georgia, 1860–1910* (Knoxville: University of Tennessee Press, 1994); Steven Hahn, *The Roots of Southern Populism: Yeomen Farmers and the Transformation of the Georgia Upcountry, 1850–1890* (New York: Oxford University Press, 1983); David R. Montgomery, *Dirt: The Erosion of Civilizations* (Berkeley: University of California Press, 2012); G. E. Fussell, *Farming Techniques From Prehistory to Modern Times* (Oxford: Pergamon Press, 1966); John F. Kvach, *DeBow's Review: The Antebellum Vision of a New South* (Lexington: University Press of Kentucky, 2013); Avery Odelle Craven, *Soil Exhaustion as a Factor in the Agricultural History of Virginia and Maryland, 1606–1860* (Columbia: University of South Carolina Press, 2006, reprint of 1925 edition); S. Max Edelson, *Plantation Enterprise in Colonial South Carolina* (Cambridge, MA: Harvard University Press, 2006) on origins of rice cultivation; Monte Hartman, *America's 100th Meridian: A Plains Journey* (Lubbock: Texas Tech University Press, 2005); Dylan C. Penningroth, *The Claims of Kinfolk: African American Property and Community in the Nineteenth-Century South* (Chapel Hill: University of North Carolina Press, 2003); Ann K. Ferrell, *Burley: Kentucky Tobacco in a New Century* (Lexington: University Press of Kentucky, 2013); Ellen Eslinger, ed., *Running Mad for Kentucky: Frontier Travel Accounts* (Lexington: University Press of Kentucky, 2004); Howard Zinn, *A People's History of the United States* (New York: HarperCollins, 1980); Richard A. Bartlett, *The New Century: A Social History of the American Frontier, 1776–1890* (New York: Oxford University Press, 1974).

Chapter Three: Market Revolutions

Ross M. Robertson, *History of the American Economy* (New York: Harcourt, 1964); David Ward, *Cities and Immigrants: A Geography of Change in Nineteenth Century America* (New York: Oxford University Press, 1971); Ralph H. Brown, *Historical Geography of the United States* (New York: Harcourt, 1946); William Lewis, "Building Commerce: Ohio Valley Shipbuilding during the Era of the Early American Republic," *Ohio Valley History*, Vol. 16, No. 1 (Spring 2016); Richard C. Wade, *The Urban Frontier* (Cambridge, MA: Harvard University Press, 1959); David R. Meyer, *The Roots of American Industrialization* (Baltimore: Johns Hopkins University Press, 2003); Jennifer Jensen Wallach, *How America Eats: A Social History of U.S. Food and Culture* (Lanham, MD: Rowman & Littlefield, 2013); Kim M. Gruenwald, "The Invention of the Steamboat Was Intended for US: Steamboats and Western Identity in the Early Republic," *Ohio Valley History*, Vol. 12, No. 3 (Fall 2012); Harry P. Owens, "Sail and Steam Vessels Serving the Appalachacola-Chattahoochee Valley," *Alabama Review*, Vol. 21, No. 3 (July 1968) as source for Albany river trade; Jerry Green, "Wheeling and the Development of the Inland Riverboat Trade," *Ohio Valley History,* Vol. 10, No. 2 (Summer 2010); William J. Brown, *American Colossus: The Grain Elevator, 1843 to 1943* (Brooklyn, NY: Colossal Books, 2015); Geoff Cunfer, *On the Great Plains: Agriculture and Environment* (College Station: Texas A&M University Press, 2005); Neil Dahlstrom and Jeremy Dahlstrom, *The John Deere Story: A Biography on the Plowmakers John and Charles Deere* (Dekalb: Northern Illinois University Press, 2005); Daryl D. Smith, "America's Lost Landscape: The Tallgrass Prairie Settlement, Proceedings of the 17th N. A. Prairie Conference," North Iowa Area Community College, Mason City, Iowa, 2001; Ray Allen Billington, *Westward Expansion: A History of the American Experience*, Fourth Edition (New York: Macmillan, 1974); Eric Van Haute, Richard Paping, and Cormac O. Grada, "The European Subsistence Crises of 1845–1850: A Comparative Perspective," International Economic History Conference 2006 Helsinki; Michael Pearson, *Free Hearts, Free Homes* (Chapel Hill: University of North Carolina Press, 2003); Wendy Gamber, *The Boardinghouse in Nineteenth Century America* (Baltimore: Johns Hopkins University Press, 2007); John Mack Faragher, *Sugar Creek: Life on the Illinois Prairie* (New Haven, CT: Yale University Press, 1986); Nancy F. Cott, *The Bonds of Womanhood: "Woman's*

Sphere" in New England, 1780–1835 (New Haven, CT: Yale University Press, 1977); Charles Sellers, *The Market Revolution, Jacksonian America, 1815–1846* (New York: Oxford University Press, 1991); Daniel Walker Howe, *What Hath God Wrought: The Transformation of America, 1815–1848* (New York: Oxford University Press, 2009); Richard Holcombe Kilbourne Jr., *Debt, Investment, Slaves: Credit Relations in East Feliciana Parish, Louisiana, 1825–1885* (Tuscaloosa: University of Alabama Press, 1995) and *Slave Agriculture and Financial Markets in Antebellum America: The Bank of the United States in Mississippi, 1831–1852* (London: Pickering & Chatto, 2006); John R. Stilgoe, *Landscape and Images* (Charlottesville: University of Virginia Press, 2005); Robert H. Gudmestad, *Steamboats and the Rise of the Cotton Kingdom* (Baton Rouge: Louisiana State University Press, 2011) and "A History of the Steamboat Eclipse," *Ohio Valley History*, Vol. 12, No. 3 (Fall 2012); Victor M. Bogle, "New Albany's Attachment to the Ohio River," *Indiana Magazine of History*, Vol. 49, No. 3 (September 1953); Martha Kreipke, "The Falls of the Ohio and the Development of the Ohio River Trade, 1810–1860," *Filson Club History Quarterly*, Vol. 54 (April 1980); Arthur E. Hopkins, "Steamboats at Louisville and on the Ohio and Mississippi Rivers," *Filson Club History Quarterly*, Vol. 17 (July 1973); John Lauritz Larson, *The Market Revolution in America: Liberty, Ambition, and the Eclipse of the Common Good* (New York: Cambridge University Press, 2009); Andrew R. L. Cayton and Susan E. Gray, eds., *The American Midwest: Essays on Regional History* (Bloomington: Indiana University Press, 2001); Harry L. Purdy, "An Historical Analysis of the Economic Growth of St. Louis, 1840–1945" (Federal Reserve Bank of St. Louis, 1946); Henry Hobhouse, *Seeds of Change: Five Plants that Transformed Mankind* (New York: Harper and Row, 1987).

Chapter Four: Civil War and Reconstructions
R. Douglas Hurt, *Food and Agriculture during the Civil War* (Santa Barbara, CA: Praeger, 2016) and *Agriculture and the Confederacy: Policy, Productivity, and Power in the Civil War South* (Chapel Hill: University of North Carolina Press, 2015); Stephanie McCurry, *Women's War: Fighting and Surviving the American Civil War* (Cambridge, MA: Harvard University Press, 2019) and *Confederate Reckoning: Power and Politics in the Civil War South* (Cambridge, MA: Harvard University Press, 2010); John L.

204 SOURCES

Heatwole, *The Burning: Sheridan's Devastation of the Shenandoah Valley* (Charlottesville, VA: Rockbridge Publishing, 1998); Robert Tracy McKenzie, *One South or Many? Plantation Belt and Upcountry in Civil War-Era Tennessee* (Cambridge, UK: Cambridge University Press, 1994); John F. Kvach, *DeBow's Review: The Antebellum Vision of a New South* (Lexington: University Press of Kentucky, 2013); Hinton Rowan Helper, "The Impending Crisis of the South: How to Meet It," in *Ante-Bellum: Writings of George Fitzhugh and Hinton Rowan Helper on Slavery*ed. Harvey Wish (New York: Capricorn Books, 1960); Frederick Jackson Turner, *The United States 1830–1850* (New York: W. W. Norton, 1963); Jonathan H. Earle, *Jacksonian Antislavery and the Politics of Free Soil, 1824–1854* (Chapel Hill: University of North Carolina Press, 2004); Megan Kate Nelson, *Ruin Nation: Destruction and the American Civil War* (Athens: University of Georgia Press, 2012); Peter Kolchin, "Comparative Perspectives on Emancipation in the U.S. South: Reconstruction, Radicalism, and Russia," *Journal of the Civil War Era*, Vol. 2, No. 2 (June 2012); Stephen A. Vincent, *Southern Seed, Northern Soil: African American Farm Communities in the Midwest, 1765–1900* (Bloomington: Indiana University Press, 1999); Steven Hahn, *A Nation Under Our Feet: Black Political Struggles from Slavery to the Great Migration* (Cambridge, MA: Harvard University Press, 2003); James Stewart, "The Economics of American Farm Unrest, 1865–1900," EH.Net Encyclopedia, edited by Robert Whaples, February 10, 2008, http://eh.net/encyclopedia/the-economics-of-american-farm-unrest-1865-1900/; Ross M. Robertson, *History of the American Economy* (New York: Harcourt, 1964); Ronald D. Eller, *Miners, Millhands, and Mountaineers: Industrialization of the Appalachian South, 1880–1930* (Knoxville: University of Tennessee Press, 1982); Mark V. Wetherington, *The New South Comes to Wiregrass Georgia, 1860–1910* (Knoxville: University of Tennessee Press, 1994) and *Plain Folks Fight: The Civil War and Reconstruction in Piney Woods Georgia* (Chapel Hill: University of North Carolina Press, 2005); Donald Wooster, *Dustbowl: The Southern Plains in the 1930s* (Oxford: Oxford University Press, 2004); John Solomon Otto, *The Final Frontiers, 1880–1930: Settling the Southern Bottomlands* (Westport, CT: Greenwood Press, 1999); Nollie W. Hickman, *Mississippi Harvest: Lumbering in the Longleaf Pine Belt, 1840–1915* (Jackson: University Press of Mississippi, 1962); Karl Jacoby, *Crimes Against Nature: Squatters, Poachers, Thieves, and the Hidden History of*

American Conservation (Berkeley: University of California Press, 2001); D. W. Meinig, *The Shaping of America: Transcontinental America 1850–1915* (New Haven, CT: Yale University Press, 2000); Stephanie Miller, "Mystery Unresolve" (Dublin (OH) *Courier-Herald*, August 28, 2004); Pete Daniel, *The Shadow of Slavery: Peonage in the South, 1901–1969* (Urbana: University of Illinois Press, 1972); Cathal Smith, "Second Slavery, Second Landlordism, and Modernity: A Comparison of Antebellum Mississippi and Nineteenth-Century Ireland," *Journal of the Civil War Era*, Vol. 5, No. 2 (June 2015); Mary Elizabeth Hines, "Death at the Hands of Persons Unknown. The Geography of Lynching in the Deep South, 1892–1910" (PhD dissertation, Louisiana State University 1992); Lawrence S. Earley, *Looking For Longleaf: The Fall and Rise of an American Forest* (Chapel Hill: University of North Carolina Press, 2004); Harry Crews, *A Childhood: The Biography of a Place,* in *Classic Crews: A Harry Crews Reader* (New York: Touchstone Books, 1993); Margaret Ripley Wolfe, *Daughters of Canaan: A Saga of Southern Women* (Lexington: University Press of Kentucky, 1995); Gavin Wright, *Old South, New South: Revolutions in the Southern Economy Since the Civil War* (New York: Basic Books, 1986); John Wesley Powell, *The Arid Lands* (Lincoln: University of Nebraska Press, 2004); Jeremy Neely, *The Border Between Them: Violence and Reconciliation on the Kansas-Missouri Line* (Columbia: University of Missouri Press, 2007); Mark Shultz, *The Rural Face of White Supremacy: Beyond Jim Crow* (Champaign: University of Illinois Press, 2005); Jane Turner Censer, *The Reconstruction of White Southern Womanhood, 1865–1895* (Baton Rouge: Louisiana State University Press, 2003); Claire Strom, *Profiting from the Plains: The Great Northern Railway and Corporate Development of the American West* (Seattle: University of Washington Press, 2003); Thad Sitton and James H. Conrad, *Freedom Colonies: Independent Black Texans in the Time of Jim Crow* (Austin: University of Texas Press, 2005); Geoff Cunfer, *On The Great Plains: Agriculture and Environment* (College Station: Texas A&M University Press, 2005); Janisse Ray, *Ecology of a Cracker Childhood* (Minneapolis, MN: Milkweed, 1999); Steven R. Kinsella, *900 Miles from Nowhere: Voices from the Homestead Frontier* (St. Paul: Minnesota Historical Society, 2007); Matthew E. Stanley, *The Loyal West: Civil War and Reunion in Middle America* (Urbana: University of Illinois Press, 2017); Stephen V. Ash, *When the Yankees Came: Conflict and Chaos in the Occupied South, 1861–1865* (Chapel Hill: University of

North Carolina Press, 1995); Mark V. Wetherington, "A Found 'Desert' and an Imagined 'Garden': Modernity, Landscapes, and Architecture in Southern Georgia's Longleaf Pine Forest, 1865–1920" in *Across Space and Time: Architecture and the Politics of Modernity*, ed. Patrick Haughey (New Brunswick, NJ: Transaction Publishers, 2017); Tad Evans, Dodge County Newspaper Clippings, Vol. 3, 1908-1919 (Savannah: Tad Evans, 1992) 1262, 1266-67. John D. Fair, *The Tifts of Georgia: Connecticut Yankees in King Cotton's Court* (Macon, GA: Mercer University Press, 2010); Albert G. Way, *Conservative Southern Longleaf: Herbert Stoddard and the Rise of Ecological Land Management* (Athens: University of Georgia Press, 2011); Ray Allen Billington, *Westward Expansion: A History of the American Experience*, Fourth Edition (New York: Macmillan, 1974); Paul W. Gates, *Agriculture and the Civil War* (New York: Knopf, 1965); Eric Foner, *The Second Founding: How the Civil War and Reconstruction Remade the Constitution* (New York: W. W. Norton, 2019).

Chapter Five: Home on the Range?
Stephen W. Silliman, *Lost Laborers in Colonial California: Native Americans and the Archaeology of Rancho Petaluma* (Tucson: University of Arizona Press, 2004); D. W. Meinig, *Southwest: Three Peoples in Geographical Change, 1600–1970* (New York: Oxford University Press, 1971); Jimmy M. Scaggs, *Prime Cut: Livestock Raising and Meatpacking in the United States, 1607–1983* (College Station: Texas A&M University Press, 1986); Hannah Velten, *Cow* (London: Reaktion Books, 2007); Rudolph Alexander Clemen, *The American Livestock and Meat Industry* (Johnson Reprint Co., 1966, reprint of 1923 edition); Maureen Ogle, *In Meat We Trust: An Unexpected History of Carnivore America* (Houghton Mifflin Harcourt, 2013); Joanne S. Liu, *The Fence that Changed the West* (Missoula, MT: Mountain Press, 2009); Roger Horowitz, *Putting Meat on the Table: Taste, Technology, Transformation* (Baltimore: Johns Hopkins University Press, 2006); Andrew C. Isenberg, *The Destruction of the Bison: An Environmental History, 1750–1820* (Oxford, UK: Cambridge University Press, 2000); Walter Prescott Webb, *The Great Plains* (New York: Grosset and Dunlap, 1931); John Mack Faragher, *Sugar Creek: Life on the Illinois Prairie* (New Haven, CT: Yale University Press, 1986); Ray Allen Billington, *Westward Expansion: A History of the American Experience*, Fourth Edition (New York: Macmillan, 1974); Terry G. Jordan, *Trails to Texas: Southern*

Roots of Western Cattle Ranching (Albuquerque: University of New Mexico Press, 1993); Mark V. Wetherington, *New South Comes to Wiregrass Georgia, 1860–1910* (Knoxville: University of Tennessee Press, 1994); G. A. Bowling, "The Introduction of Cattle into Colonial North America," *Journal of Dairy Science*, Vol 25, No. 2 (February 1942); Mark Van Doren, ed., *Travels of William Bartram* (New York: Dover, 1955); Samuel Cole Williams, ed., *Adair's History of the American Indians* (Johnson City, TN: Wautauga Press, 1930); Ralph H. Brown, *Historical Geography of the U.S.* (New York: Harcourt, 1946); Thomas L. Purvis, *Colonial America to 1763* (New York: Facts on File, 1999) for estimates of cattle in the seventeenth century; T. H. Breen, *Colonial America in an Atlantic World* (Harlow, UK: Pearson Longman, 2004); Grady McWhiney, *Cracker Culture: Celtic Ways in the Old South* (Tuscaloosa: University of Alabama Press, 1988); John Solomon Otto, *The Final Frontiers, 1880–1930: Settling the Southern Bottomlands* (Westport, CT: Greenwood Press, 1999); R. Douglas Hurt, *Agriculture and Slavery in Missouri's "Little Dixie"* (Columbia, MO: University of Missouri Press, 1992); Monica Richmond Gisolfi, "From Crop Lien to Contract Farming: The Roots of Agribusiness in the American South, 1929–1939," *Agricultural History*, Vol. 80, No. 2 (Spring 2006); Donald J. Pisani, "The Squatter and Natural Law in Nineteenth-Century America," *Agricultural History*, Vol. 81, No. 4 (Fall 2007); Warren M. Elofson, *Frontier Cattle Ranching in the Land and Times of Charlie Russell* (Seattle: University of Washington Press, 2004); Sam Bowers Hilliard, *Hog Meat and Hoecake: Food Supply in the Old South, 1840–1860* (Carbondale and Edwardsville: Southern Illinois University Press, 1972), especially chapters five and six; Steve Striffler, *Chicken: The Dangerous Transformation of America's Favorite Food* (New Haven, CT: Yale University Press, 2005); Rachel Herbert, *Ranching Women in Southern Alberta* (Calgary: University of Calgary Press, 2017); David D. Vail, *Chemical Lands: Pesticides, Aerial Spraying, and Health in North America's Grasslands since 1945* (Tuscaloosa: University of Alabama Press, 2018); Laura Alice Watt, *The Paradoxes of Preservation: Wilderness and Working Landscapes at Point Reyes National Seashore* (Oakland: University of California Press, 2017); L. T. Burcham, "Cattle and Range Forage in California: 1770–1880," *Agricultural History*, Vol. 35 No. 3 (July 1961); Carl Abraham Zimring, *Clean and White: A History of Environmental Racism in the United States* (New York: New York University Press, 2017); J. L.

Anderson, *Capitalist Pigs: Pigs, Pork, and Power in America* (Morgantown: West Virginia University Press, 2019); Larry Hasse, *Industry and Subsistency: E. F. Cartier Van Dissel and Sawmill Phoenix: The Logging of Old Growth Timber and the Making of a Small Farm Community, 1897–1943*, Second Edition (Vancover: Friesen Press, 2019); Handbook of Texas Online, Bruce S. Cheeseman, "King, Richard," accessed July 30, 2019; Alan L. Olmstead and Paul W. Rhode, *Creating Abundance: Biological Innovation and American Agricultural Development* (Cambridge: Cambridge University Press, 2008); Peter H. Wood, *Black Majority: Negroes in Colonial South Carolina from 1670 through the Stono Rebellion* (New York: W. W. Norton, 1975); Lily Kuo, "The World Eats Cheap Bacon at the Expense of North Carolina's Rural Poor," Quartz, July 14, 2015; Paul K. Conkin, *Revolution Down on the Farm: The Transformation of American Agriculture Since 1929* (Lexington: University Press of Kentucky, 2009); USDA, "Farm Labor," National Agricultural Statistics Service (NASS), Released May 30, 2019; Thomas L. Fleischner, "Ecological Costs of Livestock Grazing in Western North America," *Conservation Biology*, Vol. 8, No. 3 (September 1994); Jason Margolis, "Two South Dakota Cattle Ranchers, Two Opinions about NAFTA," *The World*, June 19, 2018 (PRI.org); John Van Willigen and Anne Van Willigen, *Food and Everyday Life on Kentucky Family Farms, 1920–1950* (Lexington: University Press of Kentucky, 2006); Leslie C. Frank, "A State-Wide Milk Sanitation Program," *Public Health Reports*, Vol 39, No. 45 (November 7, 1924); Gary S. Dunbar, "Colonial South Carolina Cow Pens," *Agricultural History*, Vol. 35, No 3 (July 1961).

Chapter Six: Two World Wars and the Great Depression

Harry Crews, *A Childhood: The Biography of a Place,* in *Classic Crews: A Harry Crews Reader* (New York: Touchstone Books, 1993); David M. Kennedy, *Freedom From Fear: The American People in Depression and War, 1929–1945* (New York: Oxford University Press, 1999); Paul K. Conkin, *Revolution Down on the Farm: The Transformation of American Agriculture Since 1929* (Lexington: University Press of Kentucky, 2009); Richard Lowitt, *American Outback: The Oklahoma Panhandle in the Twentieth Century* (Lubbock: Texas Tech University Press, 2006); Barbara Handy-Marchello, *Women of the Northern Plains: Gender and Settlement on the Homestead Frontier, 1870–1930* (St. Paul: Minnesota Historical Society

Press, 2005); Jeanette Keith, *Rich Man's War, Poor Man's Fight: Race, Class, and Power in the Rural South during the First World War* (Chapel Hill: University of North Carolina Press, 2004); Craig Miller, *Next Year Country: Dust to Dust in Western Kansas, 1890–1940* (Lawrence: University Press of Kansas, 2006); Dennis S. Nordin and Roy V. Scott, *From Prairie Farmer to Entrepreneur: The Transformation of Midwestern Agriculture* (Bloomington: Indiana University Press, 2005); Jeffrey A. Duvall, "Knowing About the Tobacco: Women, Burley, and Farming in the Central Ohio River Valley," *Register of the Kentucky Historical Society*, Vol. 108, No. 4 (Fall 2010); Robert Wuthnow, *The Left Behind: Decline and Rage in Rural America* (Princeton, NJ: Princeton University Press, 2018); Claire Strom, *Making Catfish Bait out of Government Boys: The Fight Against Cattle Ticks and the Transformation of the Yeoman South* (Athens: University of Georgia Press, 2009); Mark V. Wetherington, "Buried in Original Records, Government Reports, Statistical Tables, and Obscure Essays? Kentucky's Twentieth Century Agricultural History," *The Register of the Kentucky Historical Society*, Vol. 113, No. 2/3, (Spring/Summer 2015); Larry Hasse, *Industry and Subsistency: E. F. Cartier Van Dissel and Sawmill Phoenix: The Logging of Old Growth Timber and the Making of a Small Farm Community, 1897–1943,* Second Edition (Vancover, BC: FriesenPress, 2019); Wallace Scott McFarlane, "Oil Boom on the Farm: The East Texas Oil Boom and the Origins of an Energy Economy," *Journal of Southern History*, Vol. 83, No. 4 (November 2017); Alice Kessler-Harris, *A Woman's Wage: Historical Meanings and Social Consequences* (Lexington: University Press of Kentucky, 1990); Ray Allen Billington, *Westward Expansion: A History of the American Frontier* (New York: MacMillan Publishing, 1974); Lawrence S. Earley, *Looking For Longleaf: The Fall and Rise of an American Forest* (Chapel Hill: University of North Carolina Press, 2004); Theodore Rosengarten, *All God's Dangers: The Life of Nate Shaw* (New York: Avon Books, 1974); Milton N. Hopkins Jr., *In One Place: The Natural History of a Georgia Farmer* (St. Simons Island, GA: The Saltmarsh Press. Inc., 2001); Paul K. Conkin, *A Revolution Down on the Farm: The Transformation of American Agriculture Since 1929* (Lexington: University Press of Kentucky, 2009); Vandana Shiva, *The Violence of the Green Revolution* (Lexington: University Press of Kentucky, 2016); USDA, "Farm Bill Spending," Economic Research Service, May 6, 2020; Chris Edwards, "Reforming Federal Farm Policies" (Cato Institute, Tax and Budget Bulletin No. 82, 2018); William White and Robert Whapler, eds., "Economic History of Tractors in the United States," EH.net Encyclopedia, http://eh.net/encyclopedia/economic-history-of-tractors-in-the-united-states/; George T. Blakey, *Hard Times & New Deal in Kentucky: 1929–1939* (Lexington: University Press of Kentucky, 1986); Melissa Walker, *Southern Farmers and their Stories: Memory and Meaning in Oral History* (Lexington: University Press of Kentucky, 2009); Elizabeth Ann Ramey, "Agriculture and Class: Contradictions of Midwestern Family Farms Across the Twentieth Century" (PhD dissertation, University of Massachusetts-Amherst, 2012).

Chapter Seven: Get Big or Get Out
Vandana Shiva, *The Violence of the Green Revolution* (Lexington: University Press of Kentucky, 2016); Matthew Roth, *Magic Bean: The Rise of Soy in America* (Lawrence: University Press of Kansas, 2018); Vandana Shiva, *Stolen Harvest: The Hijacking of the Global Food Supply* (Lexington: University Press of Kentucky, 2016); Rachel Carson, *Silent Spring* (New York: Houghton Mifflin, 1962, Anniversary Edition, 2002) touched off a national debate on science, chemical pesticides, and the impact of technology on nature and human health; Pete Daniel, *Toxic Drift: Pesticides and Health in the Post World War II South* (Baton Rouge: Louisiana State University Press, 2005); Paul K. Conkin, *A Revolution Down on the Farm: The Transformation of American Agriculture Since 1929* (Lexington: University Press of Kentucky, 2009); Jane Adams and D. Gorton, "This Land Ain't My Land: The Eviction of Sharecroppers by the Farm Security Administration," *Agricultural History*, Vol. 83, No. 3 (Summer 2009); David Carey Jr., "Guatemala's Green Revolution: Synthetic Fertilizer, Public Health, and Economic Autonomy in the Mayan Highland," *Agricultural History*, Vol. 83, No. 3 (Summer 2009); Anne B. W. Effland, "Agrarianism and Child Labor Policy for Agriculture," *Agricultural History*, Vol. 79, No. 3 (Summer 2005); Anne Blythe, "Hog Farmers Win New Protections as Lawmakers Override Roy Cooper's Veto," *The Raleigh News & Observer*, June 27, 2018, retrieved July 4, 2018; Milton N. Hopkins Jr., *In One Place: The Natural History of a Georgia Farmer* (St. Simons Island, GA: The Saltmarsh Press. Inc., 2001); Don Paarlberg and Philip Paarlberg, *The Agricultural Revolution in the 20th Century* (Ames: Iowa State University Press, 2000); Ingolf Vogeler, *The Myth of the Family Farm: Agribusiness*

Dominance of U.S. Agriculture (Boulder, CO: Westview Press, 1981); The Groundwater Foundation, *Rainmakers: A Photographic Story of Center Pivots* (Lincoln, NB: The Groundwater Foundation, 2005); Angus Wright, *The Death of Ramon Gonzalez: The Modern Agricultural Dilemma* (Austin: University of Texas Press, 2005); Michael Mayerfeld Bell, *Farming for Us All: Practical Agriculture & the Cultivation of Sustainability* (University Park: Penn State University Press, 2004); Albert Howard, *The Soil and Health: A Study of Organic Agriculture* (Lexington: University Press of Kentucky, 2007); Tim Stroshane, *Drought, Water Law, and the Origins of California's Central Valley Project* (Reno: University of Nevada Press, 2016); Benjamin J. Shultz, "Inside the Gilded Cage: The Lives of Latino Immigrant Males in Rural Central Kentucky," *Southeastern Geographer*, Vol. 48, No. 2 (August 2008); Bartow J. Elmore, "Roundup from the Ground Up: A Supply-Side Story of the World's Mostly Widely Used Herbicide," *Agricultural History*, Vol. 93, No. 1 (Winter 2019); Isabel Wilkerson, *The Warmth of Other Suns: The Epic Story of America's Great Migration* (New York: Random House, 2010); Melissa Walker, *Southern Farmers and Their Stories: Memory and Meaning in Oral History* (Lexington: University Press of Kentucky, 2009); Ross M. Robertson, *History of the American Economy* (New York: Harcourt, 1964); J. L. Anderson, *Industrializing the Corn Belt: Agriculture, Technology, and Environment, 1945–1972* (Dekalb, IL: Northern Illinois University Press, 2009); Albert E. Cowdrey, *This Land, This South, An Environmental History*, Revised Edition (Lexington: University Press of Kentucky, 1996); Heather Schoonover and Mark Muller, *Food Without Thought: How U.S. Farm Policy Contributed to Obesity* (Minneapolis: The Institute for Agriculture and Trade Policy, 2006); Elizabeth Ann Ramey, "Agriculture and Class: Contradictions of Midwestern Family Farms Across the Twentieth Century" (PhD dissertation, University of Massachusetts-Amherst, 2012); Vincent Smith, "Milking Taxpayers," *The Economist*, February 12, 2015; Walter James, Lord Northbourne, *Look to the Land* (Darlington, UK: J. M. Dent & Sons, 1942); "Earl L. Butz, Secretary Felled by Racial Remark, Is Dead at 98," *New York Times*, February 4, 2008; Federal Deposit Insurance Corporation, *History of the Eighties Lessons for the Future: An Examination of the Banking Crises of the 1980s and Early 1990s* (Federal Deposit Insurance Corporation, 1997); "$250,000 a Year Is Not Middle Class," *New York Times,* December 28, 2015.

Chapter Eight: The Future: What Kind of Agriculture Do You Want?
Paul K. Conkin, *A Revolution Down on the Farm: The Transformation of American Agriculture Since 1929* (Lexington: University Press of Kentucky, 2009); Ingolf Vogeler, *The Myth of the Family Farm: Agribusiness Dominance of U.S. Agriculture* (Boulder, CO: Westview Press, 1981); Isabel Wilkerson, *The Warmth of Other Suns: The Epic Story of America's Great Migration* (New York: Random House, 2010); Theodore Rosengarten, *All God's Dangers: The Life of Nate Shaw* (New York: Avon Books, 1974); "The Coming Demographic Challenges in Agriculture," geointelligence.com, September 8, 2016, retrieved April 2, 2018; USDA 2012 census of Agriculture; on the value of forests to farming families, see Vandana Shiva, *Stolen Harvest: The Hijacking of the Global Food Supply* (Lexington: University Press of Kentucky, 2016) and *The Violence of the Green Revolution* (Lexington: University Press of Kentucky, 2016); Tom Vilsack, "What the 2018 Farm Bill Means for Urban, Suburban, and Rural America," *The Conversation*, January 16, 2018; "Perdue Announces USDA's Farm Bill and Legislative Principles for 2018," USDA Press Release, January 24, 2018; Letter to US Secretary of Commerce Wilbur Ross, October 2017, by sixty-eight organizations protesting Trump's NAFTA proposed changes; Trump's January 8, 2018, speech before AFBF; *Organic Farming*, February/March 2015 on Rodale's Pennsylvania farm experiment, *Organic Gardening*, page 70; Jason Peters, ed., *Wendell Berry: Life and Work* (Lexington: University Press of Kentucky, 2007); Joel James Shuman and L. Roger Owens, *Wendell Berry and Religion* (Lexington: University Press of Kentucky, 2009); Fred Dallmayr, *Return to Nature? An Ecological Counterhistory* (Lexington: University Press of Kentucky, 2011); Joel Salatin, *Your Successful Farm Business: Production, Profit, Pleasure* (Swoope, VA: Polyface Books, 2017) and Folks, *This Ain't Normal: A Farmer's Advice for Happier Hens, Healthier People, and a Better World* (New York: Center Street, 2011); Karen Lanier, *The Woman Hobby Farmer* (Mount Joy, PA: Fox Chapel Publishing, 2017); Anastasia Cole Plakias, *The Farm on the Roof: What Brooklyn Grange Taught Us About Entrepreneurship, Community, and Growing a Sustainable Business* (New York: Random House, 2016); David L. Brown and Louis E. Swanson, eds., *Challenges for Rural America in the Twenty-First Century* (University Park: Pennsylvania State University Press, 2002); Sherry L. Smith, ed., *The Future of the Southern Plains* (Norman: University of

Oklahoma Press, 2003); Julie Guthman, *Agrarian Dreams: The Paradox of Organic Farming in California* (Berkeley: University of California Press, 2004); Pamela C. Ronald and Raoul W. Adamchak, *Tomorrow's Table: Organic Farming, Genetics, and the Future of Food* (New York: Oxford University Press, 2008); Lindsay King, "Five of the 'Big 6' Agricultural Corporations Looking to Merge," *Summit Daily*, April 25, 2017 and July 20, 2019; John Vidal, "Who Should Feed the World: Real People or Faceless Multinationals?" *The Guardian*, June 5, 2018; "Farm Population Lowest since 1850s," *New York Times*, July 20, 1988; Dan Paarlberg and Philip Paarlberg, *The Agricultural Revolution of the 20th Century* (Ames: Iowa State University Press, 2000); "Obama's Secretary of Agriculture Weighs in on the 2018 farm Bill," *In These Times*, January 30, 2018, https://inthesetimes.com/article/tom-vilsack-2018-farm-bill-snap-nutrition-crop-insurance-subsidies; USDA, "Perdue Announces USA's Farm Bill and Legislation Principles for 2018," USDA Press Release No. 0015.18; Wendell Berry, *Bringing It to the Table: On Farming and Food* (Berkeley, CA: Counterpoint, 2009); *The Delineator,* 1929; Walter Goldschmidt, *As You Sow: Three Studies in Social Consequences of Agribusiness* (Montclair, NJ: Allanheld, Oscar and Co., 1978); Brother David Andrews and Timothy J. Kautza, "Impact of Industrial Farm Animal Production on Rural Communities, A Report of the Pew Commission on Industrial Farm Animal Production" (nd, np); Gavin Wright, *Slavery and American Economic Development* (Baton Rouge: Louisiana State University Press, 2006); CropLife Foundation, "2005–2006 Annual Report Synopsis" (Washington DC: Crop Protection Research Institute, June 15, 2006); USDA, "Saving Money, Time, and Soil: The Economics of No-Till Farming" November 30, 2017; Robert A. Hoppe and James M. MacDonald "America's Diverse Family Farms, 2016 Edition," December 2016 USDA (EIB 164); Twelve Southerners, *I'll Take My Stand: The South and the Agrarian Tradition* (Baton Rouge: Louisiana State University Press, 1977 paperback ed.).

Index

AAA. *See* Agricultural Adjustment Act

Adair, James, 9, 10, 13–14

AFBF. *See* American Farm Bureau Federation

African Americans: Black Code laws restricting freedom of, 86; constitutional amendments legally freeing, 86; Great Depression era migration of, 129–30, 131–32, 186–87; lynchings of, 89–90; Reconstruction era violence against, 89–91; as sharecroppers, 89–90, 92; Shaw as, 129–30, 165, 169, 186–87, 193; USDA lawsuit filed by, 156–57

Africans, enslaved: in Caribbean, 22; Civil War fighting of, 82; Civil War freeing, 85–86; fear of, 31; population increase of, 51, 52; population percentage of, 25; profit from, 37; reflection on, 174

Agricultural Adjustment Act (AAA): changes to, 136–37; creation of, 134–35; farm bill origins starting with, 157–58

Agricultural Improvement Act (2018), 180

agricultural-industrial complex, 159, 161

Agricultural Marketing Act (1929), 133, 134

agricultural revolution: in Europe, 24–25; in World War II postwar era, 152–53

An Agricultural Testament (Howard), 170

Agricultural Trade Development and Assistance Act (1954), 150

allotment system: changes to, 136–37; creation of, 134–35

American Farm Bureau Federation (AFBF): family farm speech to, 175–76; founding of, 179; Trump speaking to, 192–93

American Indian agriculture: corn in, importance of, 13; Euro-American agriculture similarities to, 18–19; increase in current, 186; land clearing techniques in, 9, 12, 15; medicinal herbs used in, 10; origins of, 7–16; plant breeding system in, 14; reflection on endings to, 174; remnants of, 12; replacement of, 33; riverine practices in, 15–16; Spanish labor system destroying, 16–17; tools for, 9–10; traveling to sustain, 14–15; women managing, 10, *11*, 14

American Indians: Black Hawk War involving, 39, 74; colonial farmers allying with, 21; as cowboys, 106–7; Early National Period removal of, 38–40, 54–55; Euro-American cash crops at expense of, 20; Five Civilized Tribes of, 38–39; of Guale province, 16–17; hunter-farmers, becoming, 9; hunter-gatherer culture of, 7–8; as livestock herders, 104–5, 114, 122; migration influencing early plant domestication by, 8–9; population decline of, 20; Spanish soldiers fighting against, 19–20; woods ranching by, 106–7; Zapotec, 7

American Revolution, 32
animal power: age of, *126*, 137–38;
   industrial farming ending age of,
   146; tractors replacing, 139–40
Appalachian South, 92–96
artistry, 4, 5, 175

backcountry settlements, 27–30
Baker, Oliver E., 37
Balfour, Eve, 167
Bartram, William, 10, 13, 105–6
beef. *See* cattle/beef industry
Berry, Wendell, 177; on artistry
   of farmers, 4, 5, 175; on
   conservationist farmers, 187; on
   Latino migrant workers, 178; on
   love of farming, 4, 5, 174–75
Big Farm: critics of, 3; Great
   Depression era beginning of,
   140–43; mergers, 173–74. *See
   also* chemical farming; industrial
   farming
Big Four meatpacking corporations,
   115–16
biodiversity, 72
Bio-Dynamic Farming and Gardening
   (Pfeiffer), 167
Black Codes, 86
Black Hawk War, 39, 74
black seed cotton, 49
Borlaug, Norman, 153–54
Bradley, David, 139
Brooklyn Grange, 187
Brown, Ralph H., 106, 108
Brunswick-Altamaha Canal, 64
Bush, George H. W., 162–63, 164–65,
   192
Bush, George W., 123, 158, 179
Butz, Earl, 181; get big agricultural
   model of, 153, 154–55, 164; on
   organic farming, 123, 166

CAFOs. *See* Concentrated Animal
   Feeding Operations
California, 114
Caribbean, 21–22
Carter administration, 122–23
cash crops: Euro-American, 20;
   GMOs for, 3; overproduction
   of, encouraging, 1; in traditional
   farming, 153
cattle/beef industry: CAFOs in,
   117; California origins of, 114;
   climate causing losses to, 113–14;
   meatpacking corporations taking
   over, 115–16; PSA impacting,
   116; small farmer concerns about,
   116–17; Texas expanding, 112–13;
   urbanization increasing need for,
   113; USDA on, 117
CCC. *See* Commodity Credit
   Corporation
Charleston, South Carolina, 83
chemical farming: Big Farm mergers
   for, 173–74; considerations on,
   1; environmental degradation
   from, 194–95; extent of, 189–90;
   farmers embracing, 161; Green
   Revolution from, 152–53; local food
   movement for addressing, 196;
   microorganisms destroyed by, 136;
   NPK fertilizers for, 2, 153–54, 191;
   organic farmers against, 166–67;
   organic farming as alternative to,
   170; stage set for, 155–56; USDA
   on harm of, 190; violence and
   exploitation from, 2
Cheney, Dick, 123
Cherokee Indians, 38–39
Civil War: agricultural systems
   during, 84; casualties of, 84–85,
   100; enslaved African freedom
   following, 85–86; enslaved Africans
   fighting in, 82; environmental
   degradation prior to, 56–57;

family farm repercussions of, 81; as farmers war, 81–86; First Battle of Manassas in, 81; goals of fighting, 83–84; market revolution influencing, 82–83; migration following, 100–101; open range in post, 111–23; plantation division following, 86; Reconstruction era following, 86–87; slave labor as liability in, 81–82, 83

Clark, George Rogers, 65

Clean Water Act (1972), 118

climate: cattle industry losses from, 113–14; crop region growth determined by, 35–36

Coastal Plains South: livestock herders in, 108–10; in Reconstruction era, 87–88, 89, 93, 94

codependency, 9

Cold War, 150

colonial farmers: ambition of, 20–21; American Indians allying with, 21; American Revolution victory for, 32; farming society of, 27–30; livestock importation by, 107–8; origins of, 25–26; politics of, 30–33; voter restrictions for, 30–31; westward migration of, 35–37

Commodity Credit Corporation (CCC), 136–37

commodity crops. See cash crops

compost, 167, 170

Concentrated Animal Feeding Operations (CAFOs), 117

Conkin, Paul K., 159, 162, 179, 183; on agricultural revolution, 152; on family farms, 176–77, 178; on livestock industry changes, 121

conservationists, 187

consolidation: Big Farm mergers for, 173–74; considerations on, 1; Great Depression era land, 132; local food movement for addressing, 196; pace

of, 177; violence and exploitation from, 2; of wealth, 159–62

constitutional amendments, 86

control: Big Farm mergers for, 173–74; considerations on, 1; local food movement for addressing, 196; violence and exploitation from, 1–2

Cooper, Eli, 90–91

corn: American Indian importance of, 13; hybrid, 143; origin of, 7

Corn Belt/production: Civil War survival of, 85; Early National Period establishing, 43–46; for ethanol, 179, 190; railroad construction impacting, 62–63; slave labor for, 45; steamboats improving, 70

Cotton Belt/production: Early National Period establishing, 49–52; environmental degradation from, 55, 68–69; expansion of, 75; fertilizer for, 94; NAFTA impacting, 165–66; poultry raising replacing, 118–19; railroads improving, 71; Reconstruction era increase in, 87–88; slave labor for, 50, 51–52, 55–56; steamboats improving, 68–69; varieties in, 49–50; women impacted by, 69–70

cotton gin, 40, 49, 50, 51–52

Country Life Commission, 152

cowboys: American Indians as first, 106–7; hiring of, 108

Creek Indians, 38–39

crisis: farm, 154–57; 2008 global food, 179

crop lien system, 87–92

crop region establishment: American Indian removal for, 38–40, 54–55; Corn Belt, 43–46; Cotton Belt, 49–52; Hemp Belt, 48, 48–49; sugar production, 53; technological

change impacting, 40–41; Tobacco
Belt, 46–48; Wheat Belt, 41–43
crop regions: climate determining
growth of, 35–36; competition
over, 39–40; geographic division of,
37; market revolution impacting,
61; mixed farming and, 53–54;
railroads importance to, 71–72;
reform, 56–57; as social constructs,
36
crop rotation, 24

Dairy Belt: Civil War survival of,
85; expansion of, 119–20; market
revolution establishing, 70–71; milk
production in, 114–15, 119–20
daughters, 78–79
Dean-Doston, Ella, 90
De Bow, James Dunwoody Brownson,
56–57
Deere, John, 73, 139
deforestation: American Indian
agriculture and, 12; from lumber
companies, 92–93, 94–95; migration
from, 95–96; open range impacted
by, 111; of Pine Belt, 94–95, 126
Desoto, Hernando, 12, 104, 106
*The Discovery, Settlement, and Present
State of Kentucke* (Filson), 72
Dodge v. Williams, 95
drought, 99, 135–40
Drought Relief Service, 136
Dust Bowl, 99, 135–40

Early National Period: American
Indian removal in, 38–40, 54–55;
corn production in, 43–46;
cotton production in, 49–52; crop
regions reform in, 56–57; hemp
production in, 48, 48–49; migration
within isothermal zones during,
35–36; sugar production in, 53;
technological change in, 40–41;

tobacco production in, 46–48;
violence of agriculture in, 54–56;
wheat production in, 41–43
Eisenhower, Dwight, 159, 161, 168
electricity availability, 141–42
Eller, Ronald, 92, 93
Emancipation Proclamation, 83–84
Embargo Act (1807), 66
Enlarged Homestead Act (1909), 97
environmental degradation: from
chemical farming, 194–95; from
cotton production, 55, 68–69;
from fracking, 123–24; in Great
American Desert, 72; from
livestock industry, 117–18, 120;
from NPK fertilizers, 2, 153–54;
from pre-Civil War agriculture,
56–57; reflection on, 175. *See also*
deforestation; soil depletion/erosion
EPA: Clean Water Act of 1972 passed
by, 118; on fracking, 123–24;
Trump disregard of, 192–93
Erie Canal, 61–62, 64, 70, 78
ethanol production, 179, 190
ethnic trade, 50
Euro-American agriculture:
American Indian agriculture
similarities to, 18–19; Caribbean
experiment with, 21–22; cash
crops established by early, 20;
indentured servants for, 21–22,
23; in Jamestown Virginia, 22–23;
New England environment of,
23–24; origins of, 16–19; reflection
on beginning of, 174; repercussions
of, 35. *See also* colonial farmers;
Spanish settlers
Europe: agricultural revolution in,
24–25; livestock herders in, 110
exploitation, 1–2

family farms: Civil War repercussions
for, 81; criteria of, important, 176;

ideology of, 142; land disputes against, 95; migration from, 146–47; poultry raising on, 118; Reconstruction era migration of, *88*; reflection on state of, 175–78; safety-first farming on, 4; yeomen on self-working, 54

farm bills: agricultural-industrial complex boosted by, 159, 161; global food crisis of 2008 correlation to, 179; organic farming funding from, 191; origins of, 157–58; public ignorance of, 180; reflection on state of, 178–91; small farms destroyed by, *158*, 158–59; SNAP from, 180–81, 182; stranglehold from, 187–88; tax increases from, 137; of 2018, 182–83, 188. *See also specific legislation*

Farm Bloc, 144, 145

Farm Credit System, 134, 155

farm crisis, 154–57

farmer suicides, 4, 163, 166

Faulkner, Edward H., 193

Federal Agricultural Improvement and Reform Act (1996), 158, 162

Federal Aid Highway Act (1925), 141

Federal Aid Road Act (1916), 140

Federal Farm Loan Act (1916), 134

Federal Highway Act (1921), 140–41

Federal Organic Foods Production Act (1990), 182

Federal Reserve Board, 155

Federal Water Pollution Control Act (1948), 117

fertilizers: for cotton production, 94; experimentation with, 141–42; NPK, 2, 153–54, 191

Filson, John, 72

Finicum, Robert LaVoy, 117

First Battle of Manassas, 81

Five Civilized Tribes, 38–39

Food and Fuel Control Act (1917), 128

food-insecure households, 3

food production: crop rotation increasing, 24; tractors increasing, 139–40

Ford, Henry, 138

"The Forgotten Man" speech, 134

fracking, 123–24

Freedom to Farm Act. *See* Federal Agricultural Improvement and Reform Act

Froelich, John, 139

Garst, Roswell, 143

genetically modified organisms (GMOs): for cash crops, 3; local food movement as alternative to, 196

get big agricultural model, 153, 154–55, 164

Gilbert, Humphrey, 21

Gilded Age, 98

Glickman, Dan, 156

global food crisis (2008), 179

GMOs. *See* genetically modified organisms

grain elevators, 70

Grange and Farmers Alliances, 132

Granger Laws, 98

Great American Desert, 72–75

Great Depression era: African American migration in, 129–30, 131–32, 186–87; age of animal power in, *126*, 137–38; allotment system established in, 134–35, 136–37; Big Farm infrastructure beginning in, 140–43; challenges awaiting, 125; Dust Bowl in, 99, 135–40; hope prior to, 125; industrial farms taking over in, 132–33; land consolidation in, 132; land distribution policies impacting, 131; plea for congressional support in, 133–34; stock market crash of 1929, 127; tenant farming and sharecropping in, 125, 126; tractor development beginning in, 137–40

Great Plains, 96–101

Green Revolution: Borlaug as father of, 153–54; from chemical farming, 152–53; Midwestern plantations benefiting from, 161; overproduction from, 155

green seed cotton, 50

Guale Indians, 16–17

Gum Swamp, 88–90

Halliburton, 123

Hatch Act (1887), 133

Hay Belt, 70–71

Helper, Hinton Rowan, 82–83

Hemp Belt, *48*, 48–49

Hemp Farming Act (2018), 182

highways. *See* roads/highways

Hill, Pat, 91

hog and hominy plan, 54

hog industry, 120

Homestead Act (1862), 97, 111–12, 131

Hoover, Herbert, 129

Howard, Albert, 136, 154, 167, 170

Hudson, Charles, 14, 15

hunter-farmers, 9

hunter-gatherers, 7–8

hybrid corn, 143

hybrid seeds: farmers embracing, 161; popularity of, 168–69

I'll Take My Stand, 195–96

immigrants, 79–80

The Impending Crisis of the South (Helper), 82

indentured servants: for Euro-American agriculture, 21–22, 23; freedom for, 29, 30

Indian Removal Act (1830), 38–39

industrial farming: age of animal power ended by, 146; expansion of,

3; Great Depression era take over by, 132–33; health repercussions of dependence on, 181–82; *I'll Take My Stand* on, 195–96; land disputes won by, 95; small farms protesting against, 98–99

inflation, 155

interdisciplinary approach, 1

interstate commerce regulation, 98

Iowa, 73–74, 155–56

Iowa Beef Processors, Inc. (IPB), 116

Irish Potato Famine, 76

iron plow, 40

isothermal zones, 35–36

Jackson, Andrew, 38–39

James, Walter, 167

Jamestown, Virginia, 22–23

Jefferson, Thomas, 75

Joutel, Henry, 9–10

Keats, George, 67–68

King, Richard, 112

Kingsbury, Noel, 9, 13, 14, 24

Kinkaid Act (1904), 97

land disputes, 95

land distribution policies, 131

land lotteries, 52

land offices, 73–74

Latino migrant workers, 178

lawsuits: against IPB, 116; against USDA, 156–57

Lincoln administration, 83–84, 111–12

livestock herders: American Indians as, 104–5, 114, 122; consequences to, 122; in Europe, 110; land disputes against, 95; migration of, 103, 108–9; on Southern range, 108–10; Spanish settlers as, 104, 105–6, 114; woods ranching by, 106–8

livestock industry: central theme of, 121; colonial farmer imports in,

107–8; environmental degradation from, 117–18, 120; hired hands in, 121; hogs in, 120; organic, 122–23; origins of, 103–6; in post-Civil War, 111–23; poultry in, 118–19; sheep in, 121–22; USDA on World War II, 145. *See also* cattle/beef industry

The Living Soil (Balfour), 167

local food movement, 196

Look to the Land (James), 167

Louisiana sugarcane corridor, 53

Louisville and Portland Canal, 64, 66

love of farming, 4, 5, 174–75

lumber companies, 92–93, 94–95

lynchings, 89–90

market houses, 59

market revolution: agricultural exports during, 75–76; Civil War influenced by, 82–83; competition as unforeseen consequence of, 61; definition of agricultural, 59–60; Erie Canal role in, 61–62, 64, 70, 78; farmers place in society during, 76–80; Great American Desert and, 72–75; immigrants arriving during, 79–80; Keats as reflection of, 67–68; Louisville and Portland Canal and, 64, 66; Ohio River importance in, 64–66; overview of, 60; railroads role in, 62–63, 71–72; slave labor during, 63–64; steamboats role in, 66–72, 67; urban frontier in, 67; through western New York to Upper Mississippi Valley, 61–66; women's work impacted by, 78–79

Maya civilization, 13

meatpacking corporations, 115–16

mechanization: labor benefits of, 152; small farm abandonment from, *158*

mergers, 173–74

Mexican cotton, 50

Mexico, southern, 7

microorganisms, 136

Midwestern plantations, 159–62

migration: of African Americans in Great Depression era, 129–30, 131–32, 186–87; American Indian plant domestication influenced by, 8–9; after Civil War, 100–101; colonial farmer westward, 35–37; of Corn Belt, 43–46; of Cotton Belt, 51–52; from deforestation, 95–96; from family farms, 146–47; of family farms in Reconstruction era, *88*; to Great Plains, 97–98; of Hemp Belt, *48*, 48–49; within isothermal zones, 35–36; of livestock herders, 103, 108–9; market revolution and immigrant, 79–80; from New England, 61; patterns over time, 159; of soybean crops, 160–61; of Tobacco Belt, 46–47; of Wheat Belt, 41–43; in World War II postwar era, 147

military-industrial complex, 159, 161, 168

milk production: demand for, 119–20; importance of, 114–15

mining companies, 93

mixed farming, 53–54

Morrill Act (1862), 97, 133

NAFTA. *See* North American Free Trade Agreement

Newbold, Charles, 40

New Deal: allotment system of, 134–35, 136–37; electricity availability from, 141–42

New England: Euro-American agricultural environment in, 23–24; migration from, 61

New York, western, 61–66

nitrogen, phosphorous, and potassium fertilizers (NPK fertilizers): environmental degradation from,

2, 153–54; soil fertility decline from, 191
Nixon administration, 153
North American Free Trade Agreement (NAFTA): tariff protection removed by, 163–64; Trump on, 192–93; into twenty-first century, 164–66; USMCA and, 162–64, 191–93
NPK fertilizers. *See* nitrogen, phosphorous, and potassium fertilizers

Ohio River, 64–66
Olmsted, Frederick Law, 57
open range: destruction of, 111; fracking the, 123–24; origins of, 103–6; post-Civil War, 111–23; sharecropping as threat to, 89; Southern, 108–10; in West, 110; women impacted by end of, 95, 111; woods ranching for, 106–8
optimism, 149–50
organic farming: by Brooklyn Grange, 187; as chemical farming alternative, 170; chemical farming opposition from, 166–67; compost for, 167, 170; criticism of, 123, 166; difficulties to starting, 189; Howard as leader in, 136, 154, 167, 170; need for increased, 188; opportunities from, 191; sales from, 170–71; small farmer experimenting with, 170; threats to, 167–69; in traditional farming, 177; USDA certification of, 170–71, 182
organic livestock, 122–23
overproduction: of cash crops, encouraging, 1; from Green Revolution, 155

Packers and Stockyards Act (PSA), 116

Perdue, Sonny, 175–76, 182
Pfeiffer, Ehrenfried, 167
Pickett, Henry Lee, 116
Pigford, Timothy, 156
Pigford v Glickman, 156–57
Piggly Wiggly supermarket, 151–52
Pinckney, Charles Cotesworth, 59
Pine Belt: deforestation of, 94–95, 126; yeomen working along, 54
plantations: Civil War dividing, 86; definition of, 25; rise of Midwestern, 159–62; types and locations of, 25–26
plant breeding system, 14
Plowman's Folly (Faulkner), 193
plows: improvements in, 40–41; self-cleaning, 73
politics, colonial farmer, 30–33
pollution. *See* environmental degradation
Potato Famine, Irish, 76
poultry industry, 118–19
protests: industrial farming, 98–99; Whiskey Rebellion tax, 76–77
PSA. *See* Packers and Stockyards Act

radios, 142–43
railroads: cattle industry expansion from, 113; across Great Plains, 97–100; market revolution role of, 62–63, 71–72; monopoly of, 99; in Reconstruction era, 87, 93–94
Reagan, Ronald, 123, 162
Reconstruction era: Appalachian South in, 92–96; after Civil War, 86–87; Coastal Plains South in, 87–88, 89, 93, 94; continuation of, 101; cotton production increase in, 87–88; crop lien system developed in, 87–92; family farm migration in, 88; farmer protests rising in, 98–99; Great Plains in, 96–101; railroad construction in, 87, 93–94; violence

against African Americans in,
89–91
regenerative farming, 168
research: summary, 2–3; themes, 1–2
riverine agricultural practices, 15–16
roads/highways, 140–42
Rodale, J. I., 170
Rolfe, John, 46
Roosevelt, Franklin: on critical
outputs, 144; fireside chats with,
142; "The Forgotten Man" speech
by, 134
Roosevelt, Theodore: on cattle
industry losses, 114; Country Life
Commission of, 152

Safe Drinking Water Act (1974), 123
safety-first farming: on family farms,
4; for self-sufficiency, 53–54
Salatin, Joel, 177, 187–88
scientific-technological elite, 168
Sears Roebuck & Company, 139, 142
Selective Service Act (1917), 127–28
self-cleaning plow, 73
self-sufficiency, 53–54
sharecroppers. See tenant farming/
sharecroppers
Shaw, Nate, 129–30, 165, 169, 186–87,
193
sheep industry, 121–22
Sherman Anti-Trust Act (1890), 98–99
Shiva, Vandana, 126, 191, 195
slave labor: Charleston South
Carolina as Ellis Island of, 83;
Civil War liability of, 81–82,
83; for corn production, 45;
for cotton production, 50,
51–52, 55–56; Emancipation
Proclamation for abolishing,
83–84; indentured servant,
21–22, 23, 29, 30; during market
revolution, 63–64; smuggling of,
56; for sugar production, 53; for

tobacco production, 47–48, 56; for
wheat production, 42–43. See also
Africans, enslaved
small farming/farmers: allotment
system opt out by, 135; cattle
industry concerns of, 116–17;
farm bills destroying, 158, 158–59;
government assistance needed in,
190–91; guidance for future, 188–
89; hope from, 176–77; industrial
farming protests by, 98–99; organic
farming experiment of, 170; symbol
of disappearing, 184; in trouble
spots, 169–70; USDA on trends
in, 183–85. See also family farms;
yeomen
Smith Lever Act (1914), 134
SNAP. See Supplemental Nutrition
Assistance Program
social constructs, 36
soil: microorganisms importance
to, 136; regenerative farming for
healthy, 168
The Soil and Health (Howard), 167
Soil Conservation and Domestic Act
(1936), 136
Soil Conservation Service, 136
soil depletion/erosion: American
Indian agriculture causing, 14–15;
from cotton industry, 55; measures
taken to heal, 193–94; as national
menace, 136; from NPK fertilizers,
191
sons, 78–79
Southern range, 108–10
Southern Sharecroppers Union, 132
soybeans: migration of, 160–61; trade
war negatively impacting, 4
Spanish settlers: American Indian
labor system established by, 16–17;
American Indians fighting against,
19–20; as livestock herders, 104,
105–6, 114; spread of, 17–18

squatters, 45
steamboats, 66–72, 67
Stephens, Alexander, 83
stewards of Creation, 4, 175
stock market crash (1929), 127
stress, farmer, 3–4
sugar production, 53
suicides, farmer, 4, 163, 166
supermarket origin, 151–52
Supplemental Nutrition Assistance
    Program (SNAP), 180–81, 182

tallgrass prairies, 71–74
tariffs: NAFTA removing protective,
    163–64; soybean price drop from, 4
taxes: farm bills increasing, 137;
    Whiskey Rebellion protesting,
    76–77
technology: Early National Period
    crop region changes in, 40–41;
    meaningfulness of human
    involvement impacted by, 4–5
tenant farming/sharecroppers: African
    Americans as, 89–90, 92; in Great
    Depression era, 125, 126; open
    range threat from, 89; race and
    population regarding, 91–92; Shaw
    involved in, 129–30, 165, 169, 186–
    87, 193; violence against, 89–90
Tennessee Valley Authority (TVA),
    141
Texas, 112–13
Timber Culture Act (1873), 97
Tobacco Belt/production: Early
    National Period establishing, 46–
    48; Latino migrant worker trend in,
    178; slave labor for, 47–48, 56
Tocqueville, Alexis de, 57, 64–65
Tompkins, Steve, 90
tractors, 137–40
Trade and Tariff Act (1984), 162
trade war, 4

traditional farming: cash crops in, 153;
    organic farming in, 177
Truman, Harry, 150
Trump administration: AFBF annual
    meeting and, 192–93; trade war
    tariffs of, 4
TVA. See Tennessee Valley Authority
twenty-first century landscape, 164–66

United States Department of
    Agriculture (USDA): on cattle
    industry, 117; on chemical farming,
    190; on food-insecure households,
    3; on hired hands in livestock
    industry, 121; lawsuits against,
    156–57; organic farm certification
    from, 170–71, 182; on organic
    livestock methods, 123; on small
    farming trends, 183–85; on women
    involvement in farming, 185–86; on
    World War II livestock industry,
    145
United States-Mexico-Canada
    Agreement (USMCA): NAFTA
    and, 162–64, 191–93; reflection on,
    191–96
Upper Mississippi Valley, 61–66
urban frontier, 67
urbanization, 113
USDA. See United States Department
    of Agriculture
USMCA. See United States-Mexico-
    Canada Agreement

Vilsack, Tom, 180
violence: against African Americans
    in Reconstruction era, 89–91;
    of agriculture, 19–24, 54–56;
    from chemical farming, 2; from
    consolidation, 2; from control, 1–2;
    against nature, 20
voting: African Americans right to,

86; colonial farmer restrictions on, 30–31

Wallace, Henry, 149–50
War of 1812, 38
Washington, George: on environmental degradation, 57; land investments of, 30; whiskey tax protesters disbanded by, 77
wealth consolidation, 159–62
western New York, 61–66
Wheat Belt/production: Civil War survival of, 85; Early National Period establishing, 41–43; railroad construction impacting, 62–63; slave labor for, 42–43; steamboats improving, 70; during World War I, 127, 128–29
Whiskey Rebellion, 76–77
Whitney, Eli, 49, 51
Wilson administration, 129
WLAA. *See* Women's Land Army of America
women: American Indian agriculture managed by, 10, *11*, 14; cotton industry impacts to, 69–70; market revolution impacting work of, 78–79; open range impacting, end of, 95, 111; supermarkets empowering, 151–52; USDA on farming involvement of, 185–86; World War II work of, 144–45; World War I mobilization of, 128
Women's Land Army of America (WLAA), 144
woods ranching, 106–8
World War I: Food Administration control during, 129; Selective Service Act of 1917, 127–28; wheat production during, 127, 128–29; women mobilization in, 128
World War II: critical output production in, 144; Farm Bloc influence during, 144, 145; livestock industry in, 145; opportunities from service in, 147; Roosevelt, F., fireside chats in, 142; WLAA established in, 144; women working during, 144–45
World War II postwar era: agricultural revolution in, 152–53; changes apparent in, 145–46; downturn in, 151; migration in, 147; optimism in, 149–50; trends apparent in, 150–51

yeomen: in backcountry settlements, 28–29; family farms of, self-working, 54; identification with, 82; Jefferson on role of, 75; utopian dream of, 31–32

Zapotec Indians, 7

CPSIA information can be obtained
at www.ICGtesting.com
Printed in the USA
BVHW030508130421
604785BV00001B/1